Riccarton and the Deans Family

HISTORY AND HERITAGE

Riccarton and the Deans Family

HISTORY AND HERITAGE

JOANNA ORWIN

Text © Joanna Orwin, 2015
Design and typesetting © David Bateman Ltd, 2015

Published in 2015 by David Bateman Ltd
30 Tarndale Grove, Albany, Auckland, New Zealand

www.batemanpublishing.co.nz

A catalogue record for this book is available from the National
Library of New Zealand.

ISBN 978-1-86953-903-0

Publisher: Bill Honeybone
Book design: Carolyn Lewis
All picture credits on page 272
Printed in China through Asia Pacific Offset Ltd

Contents

Preface

Last year — 2014 — was the 100th anniversary of the Riccarton Bush Trust, set up to safeguard the future of the last remnant of floodplain forest on the Canterbury plains, gifted by the Deans family in 1914. Last year also marked the completion of the Trust's restoration of Riccarton House after it was badly damaged by the Canterbury earthquakes in 2010–11. When I was asked to write this book for David Bateman Ltd, it seemed an appropriate time to re-examine the rich early history of the Deans family on this site and update the story of Riccarton Bush and its two historic houses that comprise a major part of the family's legacy to Canterbury. I thank Bill Honeybone for giving me the opportunity and his team at David Bateman Ltd for the book's handsome production.

This book builds on some notable predecessors: Gordon Ogilvie's history of the Deans family, *Pioneers of the Plains*, published in 1996; John Deans's two earlier books — his collection of William and John Deans's pioneer letters (1937) and his account of the family history up to the early 1900s (1964); Jane Deans's *Letters to My Grandchildren*, published in 1923; and Brian Molloy's edited compilation of natural history, *Riccarton Bush: Putaringamotu* (1995). I acknowledge my considerable debt to these authors, but take full responsibility for the stories and interpretation presented here. Because my brief was the Riccarton site, this book does not include the wider and continued contribution of the Deans family to life in Canterbury. My account of the family history ends with Catherine Edith Deans, the last person to live permanently at Riccarton House. My final chapters focus on the 100 years of the Riccarton Bush Trust and its restoration of both the forest and the two historic houses at Riccarton.

Writers of history today have access to a valuable array of online resources: National Library's Papers Past, Tapuhi and DigitalNZ (the latter in partnership with numerous other public and private organisations); Victoria University's New Zealand Electronic Text Collection; Te Ara Encyclopedia of New Zealand and Te Ara Dictionary of Zealand Biography; and the online information provided by many other libraries and museums. That said, Sarah Murray and Joanna Szczepanski, heritage curators at Canterbury Museum, went to extra lengths to track down and ensure the availability of digital copies of relevant artwork amid the chaos of post-earthquake storage issues.

A book of this type is enriched by the living people whose stories it also tells. I am deeply grateful to those who shared their involvement and enthusiasm with me, either in person or by phone interviews.

First and foremost, I acknowledge the support of the Deans family, in particular Charles, Neil, Ruth, Alister and Sarah Deans, Anne Mace and Heather Murchison, who contributed family memories and information.

I thank the Riccarton Bush Trust for endorsing the project, providing frequent access to Riccarton House and the digital copies of the family papers and photographs held there, giving me permission to use its photographic record of the bush restoration, and for its generous provision of scanned copies of artwork. Jon Ward, current manager at Riccarton House, kindly shared his office space during my visits. Charles Deans in his capacity as chairman of the Trust gave me his time on numerous occasions to talk about the Trust and the earthquake repairs. Botanist Brian Molloy and ranger John Moore shared their knowledge and enthusiasm for the natural history of the bush and its management gained over the many years of their involvement.

Heritage experts Jenny May, Stephen Cashmore and Tony Ussher not only led me through the historic architectural and decorative significance of Riccarton House and its two major restorations, they also went to considerable lengths to locate suitable images for me despite much of the archival material being inaccessible since the earthquakes. My son-in-law Dave Sanders filled some of those gaps and provided images for the endpapers used in the book. Project manager for all of Christchurch's city-owned heritage repairs, John Radburn talked to me about the many complexities involved in such an extensive undertaking. Rob Dally, recently retired manager of Riccarton House, shared his personal experiences of the earthquakes and the restoration of the house. Seeing this book as complementary to his own project, a photographic record of the restoration of the house (a work in progress), Rob was generous with his permission to use many of his photographs in my last two chapters. Darryl McIntosh told me about his experience of being Simon Construction's site manager for the duration of the project, and paperhanger Lawrence Ford gave me a personal insight into the role of the many skilled craftsmen involved.

It has been a privilege and a pleasure to write this latest contribution to the story of the Deans family and their legacy to Canterbury.

Joanna Orwin, Christchurch, June 2015

Introduction

Nestled among specimen trees in suburban Christchurch is a large timber-built house dating from colonial times. That in itself is not unusual in a city characterised by grand old houses and well-established grounds. What makes Riccarton House different is its association with an unbroken span of natural and cultural history that stretches from pre-human times to the present. That this association has persisted can be attributed to the enterprise, foresight and perseverance of the pioneer Deans family and their descendants.

The story of the first two generations of this family at Riccarton is the vital link that connects both natural and cultural history to the present day. This history revolves around the last remnant of kahikatea floodplain forest surviving on the Canterbury plains. It includes the story of southern Maori for whom the forest was an integral part of a lifestyle based on the region's wide-ranging natural resources. It includes the adventures of the pioneer Deans brothers, who were equally drawn to that forest and the surrounding plains. It includes their establishment of the first successful farm in Canterbury, flourishing in the shelter of the forest. It includes the poignant story of a young woman whose sense of duty and perseverance ensured both the forest and the brothers' legacy would endure.

William and John Deans died young, both in tragic circumstances. John's death left a wife and baby son alone after a long-awaited marriage cut dramatically short. Jane Deans, barely 30 and not physically robust, spent the next 20 years managing her son's inheritance. A remarkable woman, her competent oversight ensured that he inherited a substantial estate. Her son's own marriage produced a large number of offspring, ensuring the continued presence and standing of the Deans family in Canterbury.

But the story of this family is not merely a personal and poignant one of battling pioneers. Their story encapsulates the wider story of early Canterbury. The fortunes and fates of this one family first influenced the direction of European settlement in mid-19th century Canterbury, then reflected its progress into the 20th century.

The Deans brothers migrated to New Zealand in the early 1840s in response to the New Zealand Company's recruitment of suitable landowners for organised settlements. Dissatisfied by their dealings with the Company in Wellington and Nelson, the brothers opted to squat on the Canterbury plains. The success of the farm they developed would cement the selection of the plains for the Canterbury Association's settlement scheme and the site for its accompanying city of Christchurch.

The houses built at Riccarton by the Deans family have given them a place in New Zealand's architectural history. The second dwelling built for the Deans brothers in 1843 is now the oldest surviving building on the Canterbury plains. The three architectural stages of its successor, Riccarton House, serve as a tangible reminder of the family's progressive contribution to the social history and heritage of Canterbury. In addition, the many heritage trees planted by Jane Deans are survivors of one of New Zealand's earliest colonial landscape plantings. The two houses, their landscaped grounds, and the remnant of kahikatea forest that frames them have national historic and cultural significance.

The preservation of the remnant of kahikatea forest that constitutes Riccarton Bush was one of the first conservation efforts in New Zealand. After Jane Deans had ensured the bush was conserved in accordance with her dying husband's wishes, the cause was taken up by several notable botanists and conservationists at the beginning of the 1900s. The Deans family gifted Riccarton Bush to the city in 1914, but members of the family have continued to be involved with its preservation and management under the auspices of the Riccarton Bush Trust.

Initially focused on restoring the bush, the Trust extended its attentions to Riccarton House in the 1990s, returning the house to a condition that better reflected its significant status in the social history of Canterbury. When the city was changed for ever by the series of earthquakes in 2010 and 2011, Riccarton House suffered considerable interior damage. The Trust again embarked on an extensive restoration of the house. Celebrating its first 100 years in December 2014, the Riccarton Bush Trust can take pride in having cemented the future for both the natural and the heritage elements of the Deans family's legacy at Riccarton.

• 1 •
Pioneer Adventurers

The refuge of whalers and ruffians from convict settlements across the Tasman, New Zealand held little appeal to more refined settlers in the early 1830s. Stories of bloodthirsty native inhabitants who indulged in cannibalism were added disincentives. But Britain's expanding population, industrialisation, and agricultural innovations that deprived rural workers of their livelihoods would lead to concerted efforts to encourage emigration to the other side of the world. Promises of paradise and offers of free passages by the speculative New Zealand Company were early examples of successful spin-doctoring. Amongst those who would take the bait were two young Scots brothers from Riccarton in Ayrshire — William and John Deans.

Wakefield's orderly society

The New Zealand Company's approach to its planned settlements was based on Edward Gibbon Wakefield's theory on how to achieve a tiered and orderly society. Civilised and cultured landowners would be supported by the efforts of hardworking, honest labourers. The Company would buy up large tracts of land from New Zealand's native inhabitants, who were perceived to neither cultivate it nor be aware of its true value. Bought cheap, this land would then be offered to suitable settlers in small parcels at increased 'sufficient' prices. The profit made by the Company would then be used to provide free passage to labourers of good character to work the land and build the new towns. In time, worthy labourers could earn sufficient to buy land for themselves.

This structured ideal was in complete contrast to Wakefield's own ramshackle and undisciplined life. He had been a charming and wilful playboy with an eccentric family background. At the age of 20, he eloped with a 16-year-old heiress and Chancery ward, successfully talking his way into being granted a handsome settlement as her husband. When she died four years later after the birth of their second child, Edward Jerningham, Wakefield spent the next few years trying to win an entrée into political life. His efforts ended with the bizarre tactic of conning, then abducting and marrying a 15-year-old schoolgirl in the hope her influential father would feel obliged to support his political aspirations. The tactic backfired spectacularly — the runaways were caught in Calais, the girl was rescued, and the Gretna Green marriage was annulled. Disgraced and vilified, Wakefield was put on trial, then sent to prison for three years.

It was while he was in Newgate prison that Wakefield developed his theories on social reform and controlled colonisation, based on his prison reading of social and economic classics. Historians still debate whether he was showing genuine remorse or merely embarking on yet another attempt to win friends and influence people. Whatever the reality, and despite the mixed success of the New Zealand Company's settlements, Wakefield's ideas greatly influenced the way in which New Zealand was colonised.

William and John Deans fitted the mould of the ideal landowner colonist being sought by the New Zealand Company. Educated, well bred, enthusiastic and entrepreneurial, the young Scots were attracted by the opportunity to take up parcels of land in the new settlements. Like a third brother, James, they had trained as lawyers, but the family law firm in Kilmarnock could hardly support all three

Edward Gibbon Wakefield, 1823, social idealist and founder of the New Zealand Company, from a drawing by Abraham Wivell.

Seller of Port Nicholson land to the New Zealand Company, Te Ati Awa chief Honiana Te Puni-kokopu at Petone Pa, 1845, painted by Charles Heaphy.

as well as their father, John senior. They had both expressed a desire to become farmers despite the family farm having long been sold. Their chances of finding land in Scotland were slim, so migration was their best option. As a result, their father organised agricultural cadetships for them on good farms in Scotland in preparation for their eventual departure to New Zealand.

Looking for land

Aged 22, William Deans was the first brother to leave Scotland. In September 1839, he sailed on the *Aurora*, a New Zealand Company ship bound for Port Nicholson. Like the other colonists on board, he had bought several land orders, each for 100 acres (roughly 40 hectares) of farmland and one town acre (0.4 ha) at the head of the harbour. This was where the Company had bought land from local Maori chiefs for the new settlement of Wellington (initially named Britannia). But when the *Aurora* anchored off Petone on 22 January 1840, the colonists' expectations of taking up their land orders were to be thwarted.

None of the Company's principal agents had previously visited New Zealand. The orderly grid pattern envisaged for the settlement

was ill-suited to the reality of the flood-prone flats at the head of the harbour and the surrounding hilly and forested landscape. Captain William Mein Smith's survey party had scarcely had time to begin their survey, having arrived only weeks before the *Aurora*. Worse still, it soon became clear that the Company's belief it now owned all the land surrounding the harbour was overly optimistic.

William Wakefield, brother of Edward Gibbon and a principal agent of the Company, had negotiated the sale of land with Te Ati Awa chiefs Te Puni and Te Wharepouri at Petone in September 1839. Both these chiefs supported the idea of a New Zealand Company settlement in Port Nicholson, having developed strong connections with whalers Dicky Barrett and Jacky Love a decade earlier. The presence of more Europeans could bolster their recent and precarious hold on the area amid ongoing conflict with neighbouring and competing tribes.

Although not all the local chiefs were as enthusiastic as Te Puni and Te Wharepouri, they signed a deed of sale on board the *Tory* after hasty and somewhat cursory discussion, with Barrett acting as interpreter. The Company was equally precipitate in completing the negotiations. They were anxious to purchase land cheaply before the looming formal annexation of New Zealand cramped their style and an already uncooperative Colonial Office intervened to regulate land sales.

First settler huts behind the beach at Petone in 1840, the forested Heretaunga (Hutt) Valley and the head of Port Nicholson seen from the western hills, painted by Charles Heaphy.

But not all the land included in this deed belonged to those chiefs who signed it. Indeed, the following year, after the signing of the Treaty of Waitangi, Te Puni himself admitted this, claiming he could not resist the blankets and guns offered. When efforts were made to relocate the fledgling settlement across the harbour at Te Aro and Thorndon after a disastrous flood in March 1840, the surveyors ran into problems with the chiefs living there. They were adamant they had not sold their land.

An appetite for exploring

William Deans was disinclined to sit around waiting for the Company agents to sort out which land was actually theirs to parcel out. By February, he had already dug and sown his temporarily allocated acre of land behind the beach at Petone. He had also arranged for local Maori to build him a three-roomed, fern-thatched 'New Zealand house', which he informed his father by letter was 'a more comfortable place I never saw'. This house cost him six blankets. He then negotiated a contract with Captain Mein Smith as a survey contractor. Employing his farm worker John Gebbie (who had migrated with him on the *Aurora* with his wife Mary and their small child) and four other men, he began cutting survey lines for the New Zealand Company. In another letter to his father, he explained:

> *I expect it will pay very well and afford constant employment, although it is very heavy work.*

By May 1840, with companion contractor George White, William was cutting survey lines for roads up the Heretaunga (Hutt) Valley. Later that winter, he was encountered there by Ernst Dieffenbach, the German doctor-turned-naturalist employed by the New Zealand Company to explore and report on its presumed land acquisitions.

Dieffenbach was following the survey lines William Deans and his men had cut along the western flanks of the Hutt Valley. He became stranded in William's camp for three days in early August by bad weather. When the naturalist was once again able to proceed, the young Scot and two of his labourers accompanied him. A short stint of exploration with the energetic and interesting Dieffenbach was no doubt an appealing distraction from pressing on with the road lines. Those three days crammed together in a tent saw the beginning of friendship between William and Dieffenbach. The

MOUNT EGMONT, from the North Shore of Cooke's Strait, NEW ZEALAND.
Natives burning off Wood for Potato Grounds

naturalist's humane views and interest in learning Maori language may have influenced William, who soon revealed similar attitudes.

Despite continuing rain and snow flurries, over the next four days Dieffenbach's party pushed 50 miles (80 km) up the valley from Petone, crisscrossing the swollen Heretaunga River. With William Deans and another companion, Dieffenbach bush-bashed laboriously up to the summit of the Tararua Range, from where they had a first glimpse of the Wairarapa plains.

This excursion whetted William's appetite for exploring further afield. Before the end of August 1840, he joined an ambitious survey expedition overland from Port Nicholson to Taranaki as a volunteer. A newspaper report of the time referred to him as 'one of our most enterprizing agricultural colonists' — scarcely seven months after his arrival in New Zealand. He was in good company — surveyors Robert Stokes, who was in his late twenties, and similar-aged Robert Park, who became a lifelong friend of the Deans family; Edward Jerningham Wakefield (the lively 18-year-old son of Edward Gibbon), who already had useful contacts amongst Whanganui chiefs from an earlier expedition; and, Charles Heaphy (aged 19), then the New Zealand Company's draughtsman. The

A newly cleared road through the bush in 1842, probably the road from Petone to Taita Gorge in the Heretaunga Valley, where William Deans cut survey lines for surveyor-artist, William Mein Smith.

Maori burning forest to create potato grounds in 1840, with Mt Taranaki in the background, seen from the north shore of Cook Strait, painted by Charles Heaphy.

party was completed by assistant surveyors and six men to carry their baggage and provisions.

The expedition's brief was to identify land suitable for farming and survey a land route along the coast between Port Nicholson and the Company's proposed settlement of New Plymouth. Although Stokes's detailed expedition report (published over three issues of the colonial newspaper) makes no mention of the undoubtedly present Maori guides, the expedition followed faint and narrow Maori paths through dense bush, swamps and scrubby fernland, along beaches and up precarious cliff ladders, crossing major rivers by canoe and wading others. In a letter to his father, William reported that:

> *All of us had to carry loads averaging from 30 to 60 lbs apiece* [13.5 to 27 kg], *and we accomplished over very bad tracks about 20 miles* [32 km] *a day.*

They stayed at mission stations and friendly pa along the way, sometimes spending several days surveying the length of the rivers and potential agricultural land. Many of the Maori chiefs they met already had contact with whalers, traders and missionaries. The Reverends Hadfield at Waikanae and Matthews and Mason on either side of the Whanganui River were at the time travelling extensively throughout the area. Their presence undoubtedly eased the way for the surveyors, although Stokes reported that they were the subject of much curiosity whenever they stayed at pa. William estimated the whole return journey covered some 650 miles (1040 km), though Stokes himself claimed a more modest — and more realistic — 550 miles (880 km).

The occupants of pa at Whanganui and Nga Motu (Taranaki) were already building large whare and clearing land for more extensive potato plantings than usual to supply the settlers they expected, having sold land to the New Zealand Company agents who visited from the *Tory* in 1839. Unfortunately for Stokes's expedition, the people at Nga Motu were unable to feed them. Their current season's supplies had already been depleted 'owing to the influx of immigrants'.

Prevented from travelling further into fertile Taranaki territory because of this lack of provisions, the expedition reluctantly retraced its path to Whanganui. From there, William Deans and Robert Park opted to complete the leg to Port Nicholson by sea. That journey

*Head of the Wairarapa Lake
New Zealand*

Ideal country for pastoralism, the Wairarapa plains and lake painted by Wiliam Fox in 1843.

itself proved adventurous. Their small boat was driven far out to sea in a gale for three days and nights before they made it to shelter on Kapiti Island. There they were picked up by Captain James Bruce on the barque *Magnet*, on his way to Port Nicholson from Sydney. All members of the expedition reached Petone safely in mid-October.

Discouraged by the effort it would take to acquire and then clear any holdings in the hinterland they had traversed, and by the absence of decent harbours, William then took a closer look at the Wairarapa he had glimpsed earlier from the summit of the Tararua Range. Before the end of October, he walked the south coast from Wellington 40 miles (64 km) around to Palliser Bay with an unnamed Maori guide. According to several sources, this was Te Puni himself. But it seems unlikely that William would not have named the chief in the letter in which he told his father he had heard 'great things from the natives' about the Wairarapa, since he was proud of his good relationship with Te Puni. The inference may be the result of confusion with a pig-hunting expedition to the Wairarapa planned soon afterwards, on which he accompanied Te Puni and a 'great host of minor chiefs'.

William Deans thought the Wairarapa would be ideal for pastoralism, and Te Puni apparently called him 'tangata "widerup" [wairarapa]' in anticipation that he would be the first colonist to take up land there. Presumably its Maori ownership proved to be just as problematic as Port Nicholson because, in January the following year, the colonial newspaper noted that William had instead leased a 'preliminary section' of about 10 acres (four hectares) at Okiwi (now Eastbourne) on the east side of the harbour.

For the first half of 1841, William concentrated on developing his Okiwi farmlet, clearing land for cultivation and putting up a 'most comfortable, substantial, and commodious dwelling-house' with the help of John Gebbie. Brother John Deans later wrote to their father that William had 'a very pretty little place ... and a good house erected on it. ... He has about 200 fowls besides ducks and turkeys'.

A poultry run was not quite what any aspiring sheep and cattle farmer would have in mind. So in June, when the New Zealand Company asked another frustrated Wellington gentleman farmer, George Duppa, to sail south with Captain Daniell on the *Bailey*, it is believed that William Deans went with them. Certainly, John was under the impression that his brother visited Port Cooper twice before 1843.

Tasked with assessing the potential of land and harbours in the vicinity of 'Cook's Mistake' (Banks Peninsula) for the Company's planned next settlement of Nelson, Duppa returned with a glowing report. He had seen from the Port Hills:

> *... an immense plain containing millions of acres of the richest soil ... watered by several small rivers and sprinkled with numerous groves of pine timber.*

But Governor Hobson chose to ignore this report. Mindful of existing French claims to Banks Peninsula, he opted instead to site Nelson in Blind Bay, close at hand to Port Nicholson across the strait.

By the end of 1841, 2500 European settlers were living around Port Nicholson. Their land orders were no further ahead, now being stymied by the Colonial Government's investigation of the New Zealand Company's somewhat dubious purchases. Local Maori chiefs were increasingly alarmed by the accelerating influx of settlers and the activities of surveyors on land subject to disputed sales. The chiefs were also becoming aware of the discrepancies between the payments offered them by either the Colonial Government or the New Zealand Company and what the settlers were then having to pay. Despite Te Puni's continued support and friendship with the Wellington settlers, the ongoing disputes suggested final agreements about land at Port Nicholson were unlikely any time soon.

As a result, in July 1842, a thoroughly disillusioned William Deans seized the opportunity to go south again. He took a passage on the *Brothers* with Captain Bruce, who was now supplying whaling stations the length of the South Island. During that voyage, they anchored for a second time in Port Levy. Whaler Phillip Ryan later recalled taking William and Captain Bruce in a whaleboat around into the estuary, then some way up the Otakaro (Avon River) onto the Port Cooper plains. They then traversed flax swampland on foot further inland. It was on this excursion that William, clambering onto Ryan's shoulders, caught his first glimpse of Putaringamotu in the distance — a tract of dark bush rising out of a great expanse of golden tussock. Ryan says he exclaimed, 'That will do for me! I will make it my home.'

A 'notorious deception'

William Deans had written to his brother John in April 1842, advising him to wait until he arrived and could select land for himself rather than buying a land order for Nelson from the New Zealand Company: 'The site chosen is not a good one.'

His advice was received too late. John had already bought land orders for the settlement at Nelson and was soon on his way. He reached Nelson on board the *Thomas Harrison* on 25 October 1842. Accompanying him were his contracted workers, carpenter Samuel Manson, wife Jean, and their three small children — one a baby born on the voyage. His first impression of the new settlement and the sections already allotted to him and friends he was representing as agent was far from positive. He complained in a letter to his father that:

> *The New Zealand Company have been guilty of the most notorious deception. The place is not at all like what it is represented to be.*

The allotted suburban sections were distant from the planned township, surrounded by marshy land, and 'scarcely in sight of wood'. The amount of yet unsurveyed rural land was clearly insufficient to cover the already-issued land orders, and likely to 'be very bad indeed'.

John's own town acre was located on what was later named Haulashore Island. This was the bulbous end of the bar across the harbour, within sight of the wreck of the *Fifeshire*, which in February that year had run aground on Arrow Rock in the narrow passage between the bar and the mainland shore. Although John acknowledged the potential of this section: 'It is thought to be worth a good deal for the purpose of erecting a patent slip and dock', realising its value would depend on the success of a settlement

about which he had grave doubts. It was certainly worth nothing to him right then. He wasted no time in renting out his suburban section for 14 years (with a right of purchase at any time) and started looking for someone to buy his town acre. He then set about trying to extricate himself from having any further involvement in the Nelson settlement.

Adding to John's chagrin and his already unfavourable opinion of the New Zealand Company's dubious dealings, his land orders had been reissued, changing the wording so that he was liable to repay the £75 for his passage if he did not stay 12 months in Nelson. The Deans brothers, both the two in New Zealand and James in Scotland, put their legal training to good use. After long and rancorous correspondence with Captain Arthur Wakefield (Edward Gibbon's brother and the Company's principal agent in Nelson) and the directors in England, the Company eventually admitted defeat and sent John replacement copies of his original and non-binding land orders.

Southern squatters

When William Deans returned to Wellington after his trip around the southern whaling stations, the colonial newspaper cited his report as giving favourable information about the South Island east coast, but he kept his own plans for the Port Cooper plains to himself. When William revealed those plans to his brother, John agreed wholeheartedly. They would go to Port Cooper — at that stage nicely beyond the influence of the New Zealand Company — and squat there to graze sheep and cattle.

John left Nelson to join William in Port Nicholson in December 1842, accompanied by the Manson family. Later that month, William advertised the lease of his Okiwi farmlet for sale, and the brothers made arrangements to move south. Embarking on correspondence with the Colonial Government authorities, the Deans brothers sought permission to squat on the Port Cooper plains. This was eventually granted on 20 February 1843 by Lieutenant Willoughby Shortland, with some reluctance, as long as they avoided being in the vicinity of any Maori settlement or cultivations.

Not patient enough to wait for this final approval, William was already on his way to Port Cooper. He sailed on a new trading schooner, *Richmond*, built and owned by Captain Francis Sinclair, another Scot fed up with Wellington, who later settled at Pigeon Bay on Banks Peninsula. With William were the Gebbie and

Early days of settlement on the beach in Nelson Haven, 1841. A ship negotiates the narrow passage between Arrow Rock and Haulashore Island, with others anchored inside the Boulder Bank, painted by Charles Heaphy.

Manson families, weatherboards, chimney bricks and joinery for the house they would share at Putaringamotu, provisions, personal belongings, and some dogs already well trained by William for managing stock. At the same time, John headed for New South Wales to buy cattle, sheep, horses, poultry and sundry other farm animals for their new venture.

Well aware that the Port Cooper plains would eventually attract other settlers, and likely yet another planned Company settlement, the astute Deans brothers intended taking full advantage of being the first arrivals. After a few years of hard work, their farm should be in an excellent position to supply any new settlers. In the meantime, what meat, dairy products or grain they raised could be either sold to whalers around Banks Peninsula or sent to Wellington.

Once the *Richmond* arrived in Port Levy, where William already had contacts among the whalers from his previous visits, he left John Gebbie there to look after the women and children. Accompanied by Samuel Manson and James Robinson Clough (from Akaroa), he set off for Putaringamotu.

The small party travelled up the Otakaro by whaleboat as far as they could (a point near the present corner of Barbadoes Street and Oxford Terrace). There they off-loaded the bricks brought for their chimneys, then transferred themselves and the rest of the building

The Port Cooper plains, seen from the Port Hills in 1852, showing the dark smudges of forest at Putaringamotu (left) and Papanui (centre), with larger patches beyond the Waimakariri at Rangiora and Kaiapoi, drawn by Edmund Norman.

materials to a canoe. This got them a few miles further (as far as the bend in the river between the Botanic Gardens and the United Lawn Tennis Club in Hagley Park). From there, they trundled everything by barrow in several trips overland through fern and scrub to the patch of bush they could see beckoning in the distance.

Over the next couple of months, with Samuel Manson supervising them, the three men put together a long weatherboard structure like a barn, with a storage loft in its steep roof space. Although Manson had constructed the added nicety of doors and windows while in Wellington, they had inadvertently left the essential keg of nails behind. Every joint and weatherboard had to be fastened with hand-made wooden pegs whittled each evening in the tent. The finished building was divided internally into three rooms by the judicious hanging of blankets — one room for the Deans brothers, with a room on either side of them for the Gebbie and Manson families. In May, leaving William in possession, the other two men went back to Port Levy to collect the families.

In mid-June 1843, John Deans arrived back in Port Cooper with the stock he had purchased in Australia. With a house to live in, reliable and staunch Scots workers to assist them, ground to plough and stock to look after, the two Deans brothers were at last ready to establish the mixed cropping and stock farm they had dreamt of and trained for in Scotland.

This modest foothold beside the bush at Putaringamotu signalled the beginning of the presence of the Deans family in Canterbury — a presence that would influence the later siting of the settlement of Christchurch; a presence that would continue both uninterrupted and influential to the present day.

Built in February 1843 with materials brought from Wellington, this first house at Putaringamotu was home to William and John Deans, the Manson family and the Gebbie family, from a sketch by Jesse Hollobon.

• 2 •
Putaringamotu

What did William Deans see during his trip(s) to Port Levy that persuaded him to settle at Putaringamotu? The open tussock and fern plains surrounding the patch of tall forest nestled beside a spring-fed river were a far cry from the damp, bush-clad and hilly hinterland of Wellington. Even more inviting was the apparent lack of occupation by troublesome local Maori. Both these attributes were the consequence of complex natural and human histories.

A layered landscape

If Captain Cook had arrived thousands of years earlier, he would have been correct in thinking Banks Peninsula was an island. Its cluster of volcanic peaks had been separated from the mainland until a link was formed by accumulating sands and gravels eroded from the Southern Alps during the Ice Age.

Over many thousands of years, these eroded materials were carried towards the coast by three powerful braided rivers: the Waimakariri, Rangitata and Rakaia. Their numerous river channels constantly branched and shifted, depositing their loads to build fans and deltas. Over time, these deposits coalesced to create extensive low-lying floodplains between the mountains and the sea. Eventually, some 20,000 years ago, the increasingly shallow sea passage that separated the expanding plains and the volcanic peaks of the offshore island disappeared. Although sea level continued to fluctuate, and the coast was only tens of metres from the site of Putaringamotu as recently as 6500 years ago, the once-island remained firmly linked to the mainland.

Once post-glacial climates began to change, the plains stretching between the foothills and the new peninsula eventually supported forests that reflected the underlying soils. Across much of the

Looking across the Canterbury plains to where the braided channels of the gravel-laden Waimakariri River emerge from the mountains.

plains, free-draining, infertile stony soils were occupied by low kanuka forests. On fertile soils near the rivers, totara/matai forests favoured well-drained sites. Where the floodplain of the Waimakariri butted against the barrier of the hilly peninsula, a 50,000-hectare tract of low-lying wetlands developed; a maze of wandering waterways, sand dunes, waterlogged swamps and shallow pools. The water trapped in these wetlands counteracted the drying effects of the Canterbury climate. Peaty sites between the mouth of the Waimakariri and the peninsula favoured swamp forests dominated by kahikatea. Where the soils were slow-draining but peat-free, floodplain forest flourished, also dominated by kahikatea.

This was not a static landscape. For at least the past 300,000 years, periodic flooding and shifting river channels on the Waimakariri floodplain created a cyclic mosaic of kahikatea forests. Although kahikatea tolerates flooding, it does not survive being inundated by deep, poorly aerated silt, so generations of floodplain forest were intermittently destroyed. At the same time, freshly deposited surfaces favoured the establishment of new forests nearby. As a result, sequential layers of inundated then renewed floodplain forests lie beneath the area now covered by greater Christchurch. Described by botanist Brian Molloy as a 'giant club sandwich', the accumulated layers of buried wood, soil and peat separated by gravel aquifers are 400 metres thick in some places.

The final flood to destroy forest at Putaringamotu itself is dated at about 3000 years ago. Floodplain forest has persisted on this site ever since. The kahikatea trees present when the Deans brothers settled here in 1843 were the last representatives of successive generations of kahikatea spanning the 3000 years since that flood. Some of those trees are still alive today. They range in age from 300 to 600 years old.

Even more significantly, the patch of tall forest that first attracted William Deans to Putaringamotu was and is the only remnant of kahikatea floodplain forest left in Canterbury. The story of its survival is one of remarkable continuity that encompasses the 3000-year forest cycle on this site just described, the arrival of ancestral Maori on the plains 700–800 years ago, their development of a southern lifestyle that persisted until settlement by Europeans, and the continued human transformation of the natural landscape of Canterbury during the last 170 years.

Ancient kahikatea trees at Putaringamotu tower above the canopy of the last floodplain forest remnant in Canterbury.

Climate change and charcoal

Forests had been widespread on the plains for thousands of years, but by the time William Deans first stepped out of a canoe in the vicinity of what would become Hagley Park, these forests had mostly retreated. In 1842, all that was left between the southern side of the Waimakariri River and Banks Peninsula were two small patches, one at Papanui and another at Putaringamotu. What caused this dramatic disappearance?

The floodplain forest that established on the Putaringamotu site about 3000 years ago coincided with the post-glacial climate that was optimal for forest growth — both warmer and wetter than Canterbury's present climate. Since then, summers have been much drier and winters cooler. As the climate became drier, floods were not the only natural disturbances that destroyed forest on the plains; fires also played a significant role. Charcoal and fossil pollens in the layers of soil show that major fires triggered by lightning strikes destroyed forest in various places across the plains and in coastal areas. Throughout the post-glacial period, such fires

Fires, both natural and human-induced, had reduced once-extensive forest cover on the Canterbury plains to a few scattered remnants by the time the Deans brothers arrived in 1843.

occurred at intervals of 500 to 1500 years, each time resulting in the temporary replacement of forest by grass and fern. Since 3000 years ago, re-establishment of forest on the increasingly drought-prone, stony soils of the plains became more difficult.

Throughout the now dry eastern areas of New Zealand, the frequency of fires increased catastrophically after human settlement. Over the centuries of Maori occupation, charcoal in the soils shows that forest cover on the Canterbury plains declined rapidly as the result of both accidental and deliberate human-induced fires. Ngai Tahu tradition refers to the fire of Tamatea that swept across vast areas of Nga Pakihi Whakatekateka o Waitaha (Canterbury plains) in the earliest period of settlement, destroying the forests. One interpretation of the name Putaringamotu is 'the severed ear', referring to this patch of forest becoming isolated from the rest after that fire.

Fires continued to alter the vegetation on the plains. Surface logs and stumps were still scattered across the landscape when the Deans brothers arrived in 1843. New Zealand Company surveyor Frederick Tuckett, visiting in 1844, noted:

It is evident that there was formerly an extensive pine forest, which has been from time to time diminished and destroyed by fire, and since then successive and frequent fires on the grass completely exhausted and impoverished a once fertile district.

On the Putaringamotu site itself, charcoal and buried kahikatea roots in the grounds of Riccarton House have been radiocarbon-dated at 235 years old, showing that part of the forest was destroyed at that time. Charlotte Godley, staying at the Deans's farm in 1852,

Once-forested foothills and terraces now support a mosaic of open vegetation.

commented in her *Letters From Early New Zealand* that the ground opposite the cottage was covered in tall fern, and:

> *... having once been forest had also a great many stumps, and the trunks of trees lying about it, which make excellent firewood ...*

As a result of the ongoing loss of forest on the plains, patches like Putaringamotu became all the more precious to local Ngai Tahu, both as village sites and as part of their wide-ranging network of mahinga kai (food-gathering sites).

People of the land

When William and John Deans arrived at Putaringamotu, Ngai Tuahuriri — a sub-tribe of Ngai Tahu — were tangata whenua (people of the land) of North Canterbury. This gave them occupation and food-gathering rights to an area that extended from the Hurunui River, which bounded the coastal hill country north of the plains, south to the Hakatere (Ashburton) River. Its eastern boundary was the coastline and its western boundary the Main Divide. Although kumara and other Polynesian food crops may have been cultivated as far south as Taumutu on the shores of Te Waihora (Lake Ellesmere), Canterbury's cold winters and droughty summers meant harvests were never reliable. Instead, the Canterbury Maori economy focused on fish, eels, birds and natural plant foods gathered from all the habitats found from the coast to the inland mountains.

Coastal lagoons and estuaries provided a variety of fish and eels and many water birds; the rivers and creeks were a source of eels, lamprey and native trout. The swamplands provided the main fibres used by Canterbury Maori — harakeke (flax), raupo and ti (cabbage tree). Even on the forest-depleted plains, the pickings were rich. Weka and native quail (now extinct) roamed grass and fernlands. Groves of ti scattered across the landscape were regularly harvested for kauru, the sweet molasses-like sugar that could be extracted from their fibrous trunks. Supplies of aruhe (bracken fernroot), a staple food, could be renewed by burning the land. The forests of the foothills and inland mountains were visited seasonally for berry-fattened birds and kiore (native rats). The readily accessible patches of forest left on the plains — Putaringamotu and Papanui south of the Waimakariri and the larger patches near Kaiapoi and Rangiora north of the river — each had their own suite of sought-after natural foods. Putaringamotu was

Trish Bowles's representation of Ngai Tahu food-gathering activities in the forest at Putaringamotu.

particularly known for its eels and native trout; kereru (wood pigeon), kaka, tui and weka; and berries from hinau, kahikatea and matai.

Over many generations, Ngai Tahu developed complex systems for managing such a wide range of resources. Within each sub-tribe and region, families inherited rights to individual food-gathering sites — often defined areas (wakawaka) within larger resource sites like the coastal wetlands. In total, such rights gave people access to all their region's resources. Some resources, like titi (muttonbirds) from the islets in Foveaux Strait, were found far beyond the borders of the region in which the holders of inherited harvesting rights lived. More typically, each region had its own specialities, which were harvested in bulk at the appropriate time by communal effort, then preserved in a variety of ways to provide food for times of scarcity, trade goods for bartering, and gift exchange throughout the South Island.

Exploitation of resources spread over large geographic areas required a high degree of seasonal mobility. An extensive system of trails linked food-gathering sites from the coast to the mountains, each with its named markers, camping sites and readily available food sources for travellers. The traditional knowledge, customs and stories associated with each resource, each site and the network of trails provided the foundation of a southern lifestyle that revolved around seasonal journeys to food-gathering sites and travel to trade or to strengthen alliances and relationships.

Ngai Tuahuriri trapping eels in the Horotueka Stream, near Kaiapoi in 1855, drawn by Charles Haubroe.

Most permanent settlements were coastal, often at the mouths of rivers that provided easy access to the hinterland, and many other Ngai Tahu settlements were temporary or occupied only seasonally. From late spring to autumn, people were often away from the coast, harvesting their inland mahinga kai. As it seems likely that Ngai Tahu numbers were never greater than a few thousand, it is perhaps no surprise that the first Europeans to arrive in the South Island saw what they thought was an empty, largely uninhabited landscape and came to the conclusion that the land was theirs for the taking.

In Canterbury, this perception was reinforced by local Ngai Tahu numbers being at a low ebb as the result of a tumultuous period of warfare, displacement and disease that had beset them since the late 18th century.

Conflict and catastrophe

Ngai Tahu had been the last wave of Maori incomers to settle the Canterbury area, arriving from the North Island in the mid-1700s. They were preceded by Ngati Mamoe, who in turn had migrated from the North Island in the 1500s. Before them, the first Maori settlers in Canterbury were Waitaha. Both later waves of migration from the north in turn won authority over the land and its resources from the previous inhabitants by a combination of intermarriage, warfare and negotiated peace. Putaringamotu itself had been the site of one skirmish between Ngai Tahu and Ngati Mamoe.

Ngai Tahu's authority spread throughout the South Island, with battles to assert their dominance continuing into the early years of the 19th century. In Canterbury, one of Ngai Tahu's main settlements was Kaiapoi, Ngai Tuahuriri's fortified pa on the edge of coastal swampland on the northern side of the Waimakariri River. Strategically placed as a major trading centre, Kaiapoi was at the hub of the network of trails across the plains that led to the coastal and inland food-gathering places. This network also linked the outlying Ngai Tahu settlements of North Canterbury and those of Banks Peninsula. Putaringamotu was the site of one of these outlying settlements, and included a fortified pa at one stage. But by the time the Deans brothers arrived in 1843, neither Kaiapoi nor Putaringamotu was occupied.

Fighting between rival but closely related families had erupted on Banks Peninsula in the mid-1820s. Known as the Kaihuanga feud, it escalated to engulf both northern and southern Ngai Tahu

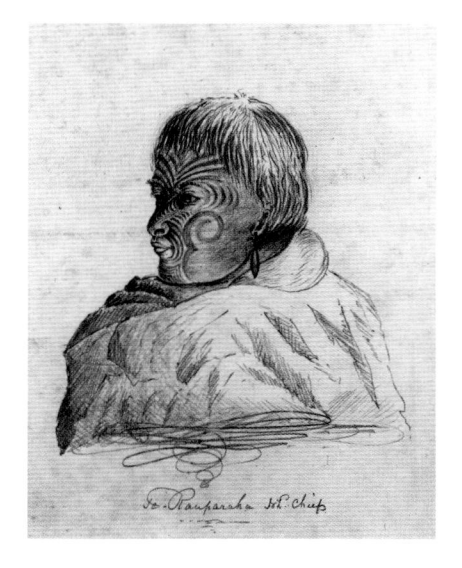

Ngati Toa warrior chief Te Rauparaha in 1839, drawn by Charles Heaphy.

sub-tribes. By its conclusion in 1830, many people had been killed and Ngai Tahu's cohesion in the face of a growing external threat was severely weakened. That threat came from incursions into Ngai Tahu territory by the northern chief Te Rauparaha.

Although Ngai Tuahuriri successfully thwarted Te Rauparaha's first attempt on Kaiapoi, the pa eventually fell to him after a lengthy siege in 1832. The pa was burnt to the ground and many of its inhabitants were killed or taken back to Te Rauparaha's stronghold on Kapiti Island as prisoners. His war party went on to attack Onawe in Akaroa harbour. The survivors of both attacks fled elsewhere on Banks Peninsula and, later, many migrated further south. Te Rauparaha's war parties continued their raids south and

west until the mid-1830s. But by late 1839, counter raids by reunited Ngai Tahu chiefs, operating from Ruapuke in Foveaux Strait and Banks Peninsula, succeeded in driving him back to Kapiti.

Adding to the woes of Ngai Tahu were epidemics of measles, influenza and tuberculosis — the inadvertent contribution of the European sealers, flax traders and whalers present in the South Island from 1810 onwards. These diseases had further reduced Ngai Tahu numbers. Despite a negotiated truce with Te Rauparaha and the return of their prisoners, a weakened and wary Ngai Tahu remained defensively grouped at Ruapuke and at Koukourarata (Port Levy) on Banks Peninsula throughout the 1840s. Ngai Tuahuriri only gradually returned to the Canterbury plains, and the site of Kaiapoi itself was never re-occupied. The landscape of the plains was indeed one emptied of most human presence when the Deans brothers settled at Putaringamotu in 1843.

Obtaining rights to land

If Europeans saw empty landscapes and resources ripe for exploiting, Maori throughout New Zealand saw arriving traders and settlers as richly endowed people with desirable trade items. Always entrepreneurial, Maori adopted any element of European culture that suited their own purposes. In the South Island, contact with Europeans had already brought both economic and social change by the early 1840s.

By the time the Deans brothers arrived on the plains, Ngai Tahu had been dealing with Europeans for at least 30 years. Potatoes and pigs introduced early by sealers had soon become an integral part of the southern economy. With flax fibre, they became the basis of a lucrative trading venture with Europeans. Ngai Tahu people even moved their settlements closer to sealing and whaling stations so they could take advantage of trading opportunities and participate in these new industries. Some of the European incomers settled in Maori communities and married Ngai Tahu women, their access to local resources endorsed by oral agreement. Contact with missionaries meant many Ngai Tahu converts both spoke more than adequate English and were now literate.

When tribal warfare escalated in the early decades of the 19th century, Te Rauparaha's success was to some extent enabled by the acquisition of muskets. If Ngai Tahu were to have any chance of defeating him, they also needed muskets to replace stone mere

Ngai Tuahuriri were slow to return to live on the Canterbury plains after the loss of Kaiapoi pa in 1832. This small village painted by Charles Haubroe is on the banks of the Horotueka Stream, near Kaiapoi.

and whaleboats to replace war canoes. The sea-borne expedition that eventually repelled Te Rauparaha in 1839 travelled the length of the eastern coast in a flotilla of whaleboats bought from whaling stations at Waikouaiti on the Otago coast and at Peraki on Banks Peninsula.

Many incoming Europeans wanted to buy land once the British Government indicated its intention to annex New Zealand as its next colony. In return for muskets and ammunition as well as other trade goods, all the chiefs had to do was sign the proffered pieces of paper — often blank land deeds printed in Sydney. But what was seen by European speculators as payment that transferred ownership of large tracts of land to them was to Maori merely payment for the temporary right to share in the resources of that land. Land itself was not a commodity that could be owned, sold or bought.

By 1840, various southern chiefs had 'sold' parts of Banks Peninsula several times over, each time gaining valuable trade goods. It could be claimed, perhaps, that on both sides of such transactions the participants were taking advantage of the perceived gullibility of the other party. Many of these land deals were overthrown or invalidated after Ngai Tahu chiefs signed the Treaty of Waitangi in mid-1840.

In theory, the Treaty meant that only the Crown's agents could now buy land from Maori, and only from those willing to sell. In practice, it was not until 1846 that direct purchases or leases from Maori were made illegal. It was also clear that it would be some time before Crown agents embroiled in growing land disputes in Wellington could embark on land acquisition in the South Island. This provided a window of opportunity for those who wished to stake a claim to land that might stand them in good stead when either the Crown or the New Zealand Company turned their attention to the south. The Deans brothers were among those who seized that opportunity.

William Deans's experience in Wellington had made him well aware that it would be wise to negotiate with the chiefs who held rights to any land on the Port Cooper plains before he squatted there. Before leaving Port Levy after his excursion onto the plains in 1842, he had held 'conversations ... with the Natives resident in Port Couper and Port Levie, the proprietors of the land in question', as noted in the brothers' 1843 request to the Colonial authorities for permission to squat at Putaringamotu. William

The 21-year lease signed by 14 Ngai Tahu chiefs at Putaringamotu in 1846 that gave William and John Deans sole grazing rights to land 'extending six miles in every direction' for an annual rental of £8.

We the Undersigned Native Owners of the Land under mentioned
have Leased to William and John Deans the sole liberty of grazing
cattle and Sheep and to cultivate what ground they may chuse
at Potaringa motu and to the Heads of the Rivers Kaimaura
and Wairarapa and following them down to where they join
the Otagaro at their present cultivation and upwards
and across the plain Six Miles in every direction, and they
acknowledge the receipt of Eight pounds as the first
years rent — the Lease to Continue for Twenty one years at
the said yearly rent of Eight pounds and We the said
William and John Deans agree to pay the said Eight pounds
yearly or so long as we they may retain possession. — Signed at
Potaringamotu this 3d day of December 1846

William Tod Kitson

Cuki Core
Saaky   his   Link,
    mark
his
Paika
  mark
his
No Knotu
  mark
his
Gonwa
  mark
his
Kuwhanu
  mark
his
Koukmanou
  mark
his
Fakaha
  mark

Kaih Roa

Matiu
his
Kaikruika
  Mark

Tu   ea   Kirou
his
Faika
  mark
his
Wihia
  mark

Will Deans

John Deans

also reported that the said proprietors were 'very anxious for respectable white settlers'. In the same document, he noted that the brothers intended giving the proprietors some cattle and sheep annually (by way of rent), to satisfy Maori eagerness to undertake 'pastoral pursuits'.

Although William was justifiably proud of the good relationship he had developed with Maori in Wellington, there was nothing particularly altruistic about the arrangement he made with the Ngai Tuahuriri chiefs living at Port Levy. A pragmatic and legally trained entrepreneur, his intention was to be well-established at Putaringamotu, with the blessing of its Maori owners, in anticipation of the Crown eventually 'having the power to grant Squatting licences'.

Indeed, at the end of 1844, on learning that the new Governor, Fitzroy, had briefly waived the Crown's Treaty right of pre-emption over Maori land for an area near Auckland, the brothers promptly wrote to him requesting the same concession for two square miles of land at Putaringamotu. They pointed out they had been settled there since early 1843 and were on 'the most friendly terms' with the Maori owners, who 'had an abundance of land and a desire to sell the surplus'. The Deans brothers would be happy to accept the Governor's advice on what would be 'sufficient payment' to the owners.

Their request was denied. In 1845, having been unsuccessful in gaining either a Crown squatting licence or consent to buy the land outright, and aware that their existing agreement with Ngai Tahu lacked any real status in the eyes of the Crown, the Deans brothers negotiated a new and more formal lease with Ngai Tuahuriri chief Te One Te Uki acting on behalf of all the Maori owners.

It is not entirely clear who initiated this new lease — the brothers or Te Uki. In 1844, Edward Shortland (Assistant Protector of Aborigines) had investigated Ngai Tahu complaints about European squatters on Banks Peninsula refusing to pay rents and allowing their cattle to damage Maori crops. He observed that the Deans brothers were not only paying rent, but there were also no complaints about them or their cattle. The Canterbury chiefs would therefore perhaps have been keen to accommodate or even encourage squatters like William and John Deans, who both acknowledged Ngai Tahu ownership of the land and were causing no problems.

At some stage in 1845, Te Uki approached the Government superintendent responsible for the Middle (South) Island about leasing the Deans brothers 'a tract of land for a cattle run at Putaringamotu'. Superintendent Richmond wrote to William and John Deans in August, offering '... no objection to such an arrangement, provided that you enter into equitable terms with the native possessors ...' William responded, writing:

I have no objection to this procedure provided we can have the land for a term of years and that Major Richmond will specify the amount of the rent and who is to receive it.

He went on to point out that they had 'already given £20'.

Receipt for advance rent paid to Ngai Tahu by the Deans brothers for December 1847 to December 1848, the last payment made to the Maori owners of Putaringamotu.

It was to be another year before the negotiations were complete. The lease was signed at Putaringamotu in December 1846 by 14 Ngai Tahu chiefs (sub-tribes other than Ngai Tuahuriri also held rights to Putaringamotu), William and John Deans, and William Tod (their farm worker) as witness. The lease gave the Deans brothers sole grazing rights over land extending 'six miles in every direction' from Putaringamotu — in effect, a handsome 29,000 hectares. The term of the lease was 21 years, and the rental was £8 per year. There was no intention that this amount reflected the value of the land; in Maori terms it was sufficient and formal acknowledgment that the Deans brothers were under an obligation to Ngai Tahu as the true owners of the land.

The Deans's housekeeper at the time, William Tod's wife Mary writes of the Maori 'landlords' coming once a year to get their money:

Some from Rapaki, Pigeon Bay, and Port Levy and in fact from all over the Plains. The money was divided among them, a rangatira, that is a maori gentleman, would get £1, another 10 shillings and some 5 shillings and as low as half a crown.

As well as monetary payment, feast goods were provided: a bag of flour, a pig, potatoes and sugar. 'Rent day' was accompanied by due ceremony and feasting that could spread over an entire week, accompanied by speech-making that Mary Tod terms 'spouting all night'. The visitors had the use of a whare they built on the river bank in the vicinity of the farm buildings.

For the feast, the pork was cut up into a pot 'with sugar, potatoes and doughboys all together'. One chief was 'too proud to eat off the Maori kit'. Addressing her as 'Mary, the queen of Putaringamotu', he asked for a plate and utensils, which she provided. When he returned them several days later, the plate was broken in two. Annoyed, Mary 'picked it up and threw it after him'. It was not uncommon for chiefs to break European dishes after use to prevent any unintended transgression against the tapu attached to anything handled by someone of high rank, but she would not have known this.

In the event, the Deans brothers paid rent for two years only. The last recorded payment was in December 1847 — advance payment for 1848. By the time their next payment was due, the Crown had bought a large parcel of Canterbury land from Ngai Tahu, including the Port Cooper plains (Kemp's Purchase, signed in 1848). This was the moment the Deans brothers had been waiting

Settlers often built their houses close to the Maori they relied on in the early months after their arrival. This thatched cottage sketched by William Swainson about 1845 is behind the beach at Petone, with Te Puni's pa not far away.

for. They promptly began negotiations, firstly with the New Zealand Company, then with its successor, the Canterbury Association, to freehold the land at Putaringamotu.

That the Deans brothers immediately stopped paying rent to Ngai Tahu is confirmed in their April 1851 letter to Godley (principal agent of the Canterbury Association) offering to make good:

> *… the arrears of rent unpaid since the district was purchased from the natives.*

On the most friendly terms

As a man of his times, William Deans's opinion of the Maori with whom he had dealings was inevitably coloured by his assumption of European superiority. His admiration of the Maori he met was expressed in an early letter to his father with a degree of paternalistic condescension:

The New Zealanders are certainly a very extraordinary people, and may one day by means of education and the example shewn them by Englishmen become the best mechanics, the best sailors, and altogether the most ingenious people on the face of the earth.

By the end of the expedition to Taranaki in 1840, William had gained some knowledge of Maori language. Although he claimed as a result to 'now speak [it] well', it is unlikely that in a short two months he had more than useful day-to-day vocabulary and understanding. His level of language would not have matched the acquisition of English by many Maori, some of whom had had several years of contact with English speakers by 1840. Nevertheless, William's ability to communicate in their own tongue undoubtedly helped him develop the 'great favour with the natives' he claimed.

By the time John joined him at Okiwi, Port Nicholson, William's claim had some justification. Te Puni's people living nearby were willingly helping with anything he required, whether it was canoe transport across the harbour to Wellington, help with unloading gear, or excursions into the country. John reported to a friend back in Scotland:

William is a great favourite with them … They will do anything for him. He has been kind to them, and they know as well as possible who is good to them.

John, a recent arrival in New Zealand with little experience of Maori, was not as enthusiastic as his brother about their neighbours at Okiwi:

The natives are a queer lot. You would laugh to see some of them with their tattooed faces, wrapt up in a blanket, and occasionally a swell coming along with a shirt, coat and trousers on … fancying himself as a man of some consequence.

His good Scots work ethic made John consider Maori 'generally lazy … not fond of working at any one thing for any length of time …' He was even more disparaging in a letter to his father. After noting that Maori were becoming 'cunning' about the value of things, he wrote:

All the old ones are rather lazy, but some of the young ones are pretty serviceable … If they do any harm, the best way is to give them a good thrashing, and they are very civil afterwards …

Europeans trading with the occupants of Rakawakaputa village, near Kaiapoi, in 1848, painted by William Fox.

Nevertheless John was soon also learning Maori, from a lad who spoke a great deal of English and who slept on the floor of John's bedroom at Okiwi whenever he visited the brothers. So by the time the Deans brothers shifted to the Port Cooper plains, both could communicate adequately and amicably with the Ngai Tahu owners of the land on which they wished to squat. But it is unlikely that they understood enough to be aware that Ngai Tahu's willingness for them to have grazing and living rights at Putaringamotu did not extend to losing their own rights to the resources they had harvested there for generations. That Ngai Tahu and the Deans family continued to have cordial relationships at Putaringamotu, with Maori workers employed for the annual harvests until 1880, should be seen as a tribute to both sides.

•3•
Farming on the Plains

The Deans brothers were not the first Scots to attempt farming on the Port Cooper plains, but they would become the first to be successful. In the seven years from 1843 to the arrival of the first Canterbury settlers in 1850, they would work tirelessly with the help of a succession of loyal Scottish couples to establish a model stock and cropping farm at Putaringamotu.

A first failure

The Weller brothers of Otago whaling fame became land speculators on a large scale in the rush to secure land before the Crown annexed New Zealand. By 1840, Sydney-based George Weller had 'bought' millions of acres of land from visiting Ngai Tahu chiefs — amongst the payments was one of their desired whaleboats (see Chapter 2). He then made a handsome profit selling the land on to unsuspecting buyers. Among them were two Scots, James Herriot and William Purves, who paid five shillings an acre for 7560 acres (3060 hectares) of land on the Port Cooper plains.

Herriot and McGillivray (first name unknown; employed as a manager for Purves) landed at the Goashore whaling station on Banks Peninsula in April 1840, accompanied by two married couples, one small child, a single man, seed grain, implements, bullocks and a dray. Together with surveyors employed by the Weller brothers, the small group of intending settlers made their way along the Kaitorete spit to Taumutu, then laboriously across the swampy plains to Putaringamotu.

While the surveyors laid out the land bought by Herriot and Purves, the settlers built huts beside the patch of bush and began breaking up the rough grass and fernland with their bullock-drawn ploughs. They successfully sowed about 12 hectares of ploughed land in wheat and potatoes, and made progress on ploughing a further 20.

The entrance to Akaroa Harbour, painted by Joseph Welch.

Despite this enterprise and hard work, they abandoned the emerging farm sometime in mid-1841.

Accumulating difficulties and disasters precipitated their departure. They were alone on the plains, with other early European arrivals staying near Maori villages and whaling stations on Banks Peninsula. As a result, someone had to walk once a fortnight to Akaroa for provisions, either to Price's whaling station at Ikoraki or to William Rhodes's store at Red House Bay, where they built up substantial debt. A ship bringing much-needed supplies and more settlers was wrecked. Native rats (kiore) wreaked havoc among their ripening crops. The final straw was receiving word that George Weller's claim to any land north of Banks Peninsula had been disallowed by the Crown agents. With uncertain title to the land and little return on the large expenses already incurred, both Herriot and Purves lost any enthusiasm for throwing good money after bad.

Malcolm McKinnon and his family stayed a little longer than the rest of the dispirited settlers. But he then faced trouble with local Maori, who disputed he had any right to be on the land at Putaringamotu. Abandoning all that these first settlers had achieved, he too left for Akaroa. According to James Hay's reminiscences published in 1915, he drove 'four bullocks before him, while Mary McKinnon carried their child on her back'.

When Captain Mein Smith visited the Port Cooper plains in late 1842, he reported that valuable property abandoned at Putaringamotu — houses, farming equipment and stacks of wheat — had been destroyed by fire. Lit by Maori eeling on the shores of Te Waihora (Lake Ellesmere), this fire had swept out of control across the plains. By the time William Deans, the Gebbies and the Mansons arrived in early 1843, all that was left was the ploughed land and a few stacks of unthreshed wheat straw.

Captain James Bruce, with whom William Deans sailed to Port Cooper in 1842, ended up owning this hotel in Akaroa, sketched by Walter Mantell in 1849.

Nouvelle-Zélande. — Village de Port-Cooper.

A Maori village on the shore of Port Cooper 1840s to early 1850s, probably Rapaki, where the Deans brothers had a temporary stockyard nearby, unknown French artist.

Settling in

Although some of the animals bought by John Deans died during a rough passage from New South Wales, or soon after landing, 61 head of cattle, three mares and 43 sheep arrived safely at Port Cooper in June 1843. The newspapers of the time, aroused by the recent Wairau massacre, reported that some Maori then 'molested' the Deans brothers and demolished their stockyard at the port. William refuted this in a letter to his father, saying that they had erected a temporary stockyard to ensure the cattle were calm before they drove them over the hill to Putaringamotu. Although 'a sort of under chief' did threaten to pull it down, in the hope of getting some payment, nothing actually happened:

> *We are on very good terms with them all, and never had an angry word with any of them.*

At the same time, William had reason to write an indignant letter to brother James, telling him the rumour reported to the family in Scotland that he had married or co-habited with a Maori woman in Wellington was malicious and false, and its perpetrator 'a coward and a blackguard'. William got his friend, surveyor Robert Park and his wife, Maryanne (still in Wellington), to sign an affidavit to that effect. Being on good terms with Maori could only go so far, it seems.

It is ironic that it was Robert Park who went on to marry a Maori woman after the death of his first wife. Terenui was the well-connected daughter of a Ngati Ruanui chief, a relative of Te Puni and a niece of Titokowaru. Their descendants have continued to be among Wellington's leading Maori families. Perhaps even more ironic in the face of William's strongly expressed scruples was the later (albeit indirect) connection of those families to the Deans family — John's son would marry one of Robert Park's daughters from yet another marriage (his third, see pages 149–50).

But in mid-1843, settling in and breeding good dairy stock was what was preoccupying the Deans brothers, not prospects of marriage (disputed or otherwise) or potential offspring. John's first selections were driven over the hills from their temporary yard at Rapaki in Port Cooper, then across the plains to become the nucleus of the stock that would continue to be raised at Putaringamotu. William reported to his father that John had made 'a very judicious selection ... much better than those generally brought here'.

By spring, the squatters had survived a cold winter in the draughty dwelling they had erected, all three mares were close to foaling, and three cows had already produced healthy calves. As well as working as stockman, John Deans was being taught how to milk by experienced stockman John Gebbie, with the intention of producing butter and cheese for sale. Mary Gebbie and Jean Manson managed the dairy as well as being busy with domestic duties, making soap and candles, and looking after their children. William Deans was hard at work establishing about a hectare of sheltered vegetable garden in the lee of the bush — cabbages, peas, potatoes, onions, leeks and parsnips were doing well, but carrots, turnips, melons and cucumbers were being eaten by some sort of small fly as soon as they germinated. He was also trying his hand at grafting fruit trees (see Chapter 8).

Taking advantage of the ground already broken in by their short-lived predecessors at Putaringamotu, John Deans and John Gebbie had re-ploughed enough land to sow a hectare or so each of wheat, barley and oats by the end of October. They were able to reap the barley on Christmas Day, threshing the grain with flails. Lucerne was sown for horse feed, and new ground was broken for potatoes. John reported that their yields were light as they were late getting the seed in (not being able to work the mares too hard since they were in foal). Surveyor Frederick Tuckett, visiting in April 1844, noted:

The Messrs. Deans have a few acres of land in tillage (previously grass land without manure); it has produced a moderate crop of wheat and potatoes; it appeared to work easily. Mr. Deans states that he can break it up with two horses …

To deal with their newly harvested grain, William had bought a hand-held, steel flour mill in Wellington, on which a man could grind 40 pounds (18 kg) of flour an hour — a useful evening occupation.

Samuel Manson continued to put his carpentry skills to good use. Late in 1843, he had built a more substantial house for the Deans brothers, weatherboard and timber-lined throughout, with two small bedrooms, a sitting room with a fireplace and an upstairs storeroom, using pit-sawn timber from trees felled in the neighbouring bush. Kahikatea was used for roof shingles, framing and weatherboards, and matai for trusses, flooring and wall linings. This house (now known as Deans Cottage) was lived in by the Deans family until 1856. Although it has been moved several times from its original site (near Kahu Road), this modest cottage is now the oldest surviving building on the Canterbury plains.

In the meantime, the two farm couples kept living in the original building, which also served as the kitchen. By 1845, Manson had built another cottage (for the Gebbies), as well as farm buildings (a large shed with milking stalls, a stable and a calf house) and stockyards. The new two-roomed cottage was larger than that built for the Deans brothers, but was rougher and unlined. The farm buildings and stockyards were conveniently separated from all three dwellings by the stream, which was now bridged in two places. William noted with some satisfaction:

… the cattle, etc., [also are separated] *from the land in crop, which will save us the expense of fencing for some time to come.*

Several other spring-fed streams near the bush proved useful for separating the stock into three components: non-breeding heifers in one, milk cows and those near calving in another, then the bull, steers and rest of the cows in the third 'without any danger of intermixing'.

John Deans later made an undated note of the Maori names of these streams (found by Jane Deans among his papers): 'Orangipowa' (the branch in front of the house); 'Waimairou'

The earliest known illustration of the Deans brothers' establishment at Putaringamotu, sketched in 1844 by John Barnicoat. The new 1843 cottage is nearest the stream, with the framework for the 'ploughman's cottage' between it and the first dwelling built beside the bush on their arrival. The milking shed is across the bridge on the left.

(mid branch); 'Wairerapa' (north branch); and 'Otakarow' (the united stream). He also noted that 'Autautahi was the first native who claimed the country'. This was probably a slight misinterpretation of what he was told — Tautahi was an important Ngai Tuahuriri chief in the Christchurch area, which became known as Otautahi (Tautahi's place), and the city now uses this as its formal Maori name. However, the note gives some insight into John's knowledge and understanding of Maori language, and is an indication that the Deans brothers were continuing to interact with the Maori owners of the land at Putaringamotu.

The Deans's second summer (1844–45) proved profitable, with good rains producing excellent wheat and potato crops; more than they could comfortably dispose of. The fruit trees were beginning to produce — 20 apples on one tree and a plum that proved to be a greengage.

With so much going on, it is no surprise that both James and their father wrote from Scotland in February 1845 complaining that they had not heard from the brothers for well over a year. John, in an apologetic reply (though not until September), blamed the rapid passage of time and not knowing soon enough when ships were calling at Akaroa for mail.

Faithful servants and loyal friends

In May 1845, the Gebbies and the Mansons left Putaringamotu to take up land they leased from Maori at the head of Port Cooper. Gebbie's place was on the east side of the stream draining the valley that led to what would later be named Gebbies Pass. The Mansons were on the west side of the stream. John Gebbie's employment term had been completed four months earlier, the five years with William earning him almost enough to buy a 'steading' (farmstead), a year's provisions, a mare and two good cows. Also keen to set up on his own, Samuel Manson asked to leave at the same time, although his five-year term with John was only halfway through so he could not afford to buy stock. The Deans brothers were willing to let him go with their blessing as most of the carpentry work was complete. A year later, William told his father that brother John had been:

> ... trying his hand at carpentering since Samuel left and makes a capital hand at it, being able to do anything we require in that way.

By the time they left, both families had expanded to four children each — Jeannie Manson being born at Putaringamotu in January 1844. With William escorting them, the two families made their way down the river by canoes, intending to negotiate the estuary bar, then sail around into Port Cooper by whaleboat. But by the time they reached the estuary, the wind had risen and the sea was rough. Off-loading the women and the eight children, the men tried to take the whaleboat across the bar. The boat capsized — the first recorded of many such mishaps on the bar that would later beset the Canterbury settlers. William struggled ashore only by clinging to a box of tea. They all spent a cold and hungry night in a cave behind the beach.

At the time, Jean Manson was again heavily pregnant, baby John being born scarcely a week later. Mary Gebbie would have been in full sympathy, having similarly given birth to one of her children in a tent soon after their arrival at Petone in 1840. John and Mary Gebbie ended up with six children, but Samuel and Jean Manson eventually had 16 living children.

Although the Gebbies and the Mansons started out as farm servants, they were known to John Deans senior back in Scotland. He was always interested to hear of their progress, and he passed on news from their families. The brothers mentioned their workers in many of their letters home, the relationship becoming one of lifelong friendship.

Samuel Manson.

Jean Manson, wife of Samuel.

On leaving Putaringamotu, both families were set up with a 'bowen' of 14 cows each to establish dairy farms. They would raise the calves for the Deans brothers and pay 50 shillings for the annual lease of each cow, keeping for themselves any profit made from butter and cheese. The brothers also ordered cheese-making equipment for them from Sydney.

In September the following year, William reported that the two families now had their houses built (with the help of two neighbours, one a young Hay, whose family had settled at Pigeon Bay at the same time as Captain Francis Sinclair, soon after the Deans brothers settled on the plains). The families were doing well with their leased milk cows despite the winter of 1846 having been intensely cold, with frequent storms, rain and snow. Unfortunately, they lost a substantial portion of their produce when Sinclair's newly built cutter was wrecked on its way to Wellington, drowning Sinclair, his eldest son, and two other young men.

Despite this setback, John noted in December 1847 that John Gebbie and Samuel Manson continued to hold bowens of cows from Putaringamotu and were gradually increasing their own stock:

> By next spring Gebbie should have six cows of his own to milk besides some young stock, a mare, a colt, and a foal. Manson should have at least three cows and some young stock of his own.

Three years later, they were still delivering the annual complement of calves to the Deans brothers. Their dairy farms were prospering and their close relationship with the brothers continued. William had bought land orders on John Gebbie's behalf from the Canterbury Association; 50 acres (20 hectares) where his house stood and 750 acres (300 ha) of pasturage. A similar package had been bought for Samuel Manson, and James back in Scotland was arranging finances for more of the Manson family to emigrate with assisted passages from the Canterbury Association. Edward Ward, a Canterbury settler who arrived on the *Charlotte Jane* in December 1850, spent a pleasurable night with the Mansons in February the following year:

> We were entertained hospitably by Manson and his wife, who live in the lone farmhouse, Gebbie their only neighbour, surrounded by comforts and children—eleven children, twenty-nine cows and about one hundred hens.

Samuel was already 'in a fair way of reaching wealth' from his cheese operation, making a cheese every day, each selling for 24 to 25 shillings.

Like Jean Manson, by 1850 Mary Gebbie had also earned a reputation for her hospitality and 'good table'. Both families were well on the way to becoming Banks Peninsula identities.

When John Gebbie died in 1851 of a long-running chest complaint (presumably tuberculosis), the Deans brothers were executors of his will with Mary Gebbie. His burgeoning estate, by then valued at over £1000, was mostly to be divided amongst his children as they reached 21, with the financially savvy brothers arranging suitable investments in the meantime. Mary was to continue running the dairy farm, retaining one-third of the profits.

Mary Gebbie, wife of John.

Making progress

Replacing such stalwart workers were William Tod and his wife Mary, a couple from Perthshire with two small children. They proved more than equal to the task. The couple had been at Port Nicholson since 1841, where William Tod sometimes worked as a surveyor's labourer. They had also tried settling in the Manawatu, where William Deans had eventually opted to take up his New Zealand Company land orders. As a result, he may well have known the Tods beforehand. They arrived at Purau in Port Cooper in April 1845, then were brought around to the estuary to travel up the river to Putaringamotu. Their crossing of the bar was far from the alarming reverse crossing experienced by the Gebbies and Mansons a month later. Mary Tod remembered that:

> *They* [sic] *were over the bar before they knew where they were. We landed at the 'Bricks', and Mr Gebbie came down to meet us.*

The new workers overlapped with the old for more than a month. Mary Tod bided her time until the Gebbies and Mansons left, 'not liking to interfere', but the minute they had gone, she set about making proper yeast bread to replace the clearly inferior scones that had prevailed at the Deans's farm till then. She mixed up a 'nice batter' with yeast she had brought with her from Port Nicholson, adding mashed potato, flour and sugar, then let it stand overnight. Cooking facilities were primitive — an open fireplace in the workers' cottage. At her request, husband William lined half the dirt floor of the fireplace with 'some bricks lying around outside' — presumably left over from the chimney bricks the Deans brothers had brought from Wellington in 1843. Mary allowed the new brick hearth to heat while she cooked the dinner. After sweeping it clean, she placed three shaped pieces of dough on the heated bricks, then covered each with an upturned, three-legged camp oven. An enterprising Mary then bent a piece of hoop iron around the upturned legs, and filled the space with hot coals.

> *The bread turned out beautiful.*

From then on, for the next two to three years, each time Mary baked bread she used a starter made by mixing a little cold water and salt with a piece of raw dough she had put aside from the previous batch.

By the end of the Tods' first year with them (1845), the Deans brothers were already regretting that the 200 sheep ordered by John

during his first New South Wales stock-buying expedition had not arrived at the port before the ship set sail. William noted that they had shorn 130 pounds (nearly 59 kg) of wool from the 28 sheep they did have, and commented that the Port Cooper plains and the inland foothills could prove an easier option for raising sheep than Australia, with its less fertile land and greater distances to market.

At Putaringamotu, with no sizable market close by for surplus grain, when the continual bad weather in winter 1846 prevented ploughing, the Deans brothers opted not to sow wheat that year. John explained to their father:

We have as much wheat in the barn as will serve ourselves for two years, and it is of very little use raising more as boat hire, freight to Port Nicholson, etc., carry away almost all the profit.

They may have had wheat for bread that winter, but they went without tea or sugar for several months (the order having gone down with Sinclair's wrecked cutter). Mary Tod collected 'a kind of herb called kovi kovi' from the bush that she boiled up in the kettle as a substitute for tea. Life at remote Putaringamotu that year required all sorts of innovative accommodations: William Tod fashioned a pair of serviceable shoes from some old watertight boots, using a home-made last, and Mary adapted some whaler's dungarees into clothes for her little boy. Her sewing thread was obtained using a technique she must have been taught by local Maori:

We had no thread, but I managed to make some out of the flax what we called phoetow [whitau].

In mid-1847, John returned to New South Wales to buy more sheep. He arrived back at Port Cooper with his carefully selected animals on board a chartered vessel (*Comet*), losing only 46 of the 600 he shipped. Unfortunately, bad weather then reduced the new flock to 430, but he was confident that these would survive once they acclimatised to the conditions. With the sheep they already had, they were expecting close to 500 ewes to lamb. Their cattle were also doing well. Sixty to 70 cows were in calf, and, while John was away, William had taken more than 30 fattened bullocks (about half averaging 900 pounds each, over 400 kg) up to Port Nicholson, having sold them to a Government meat contractor for a good price. They would have more ready to ship to Port Nicholson early the following year.

Settler activities at Putaringamotu, as depicted by Trish Bowles.

Mary Tod, wife of William.

Although the Deans brothers continued to focus on raising stock and shipping fattened beasts to Wellington, they were aware prices were decreasing fast as cattle runs on the Wairarapa plains became established. Their surplus stock would need to be salt-cured or rendered down for tallow (the least profitable option). John was thinking of importing a good bull or two from Scotland to improve the quality of their meat for salting. They were also becoming convinced that obtaining land in the foothills would be better for running sheep than the plains, with some initial outlay needed for erecting a house and farm buildings.

By mid-1848, the brothers had fenced the short distances linking the streams to create four decent paddocks — about 800 acres (320 hectares) in total, with another 200 (80 ha) ready to be fenced. The fencing consisted of a bank and ditch with one rail along the top for the largest paddock, and the others involved posts and rails. They enclosed the sheep in the large paddock at night and in bad weather to prevent them straying across the plains. Horses were kept in one of the smaller paddocks, and milk cows, bulls and a few pigs in another. The fourth was cultivated. On the dwelling side of the stream, they had fenced the hectare of vegetable garden, their fruit trees were flourishing, and another two hectares around the house were oversown with English grasses for raising calves and rams. At the end of the following year, John wrote with some pride to his father:

> *Near to the house, which was, when we came here, entirely covered with fern or brackins, we have sown grass and lucerne seeds after burning off the fern, and the pasture will now carry as much stock per acre as the bank in front of your house.*

Beyond their farm, others were beginning to see the advantage of running sheep inland on the plains. By mid-1848, John Hay had built a hut on the banks of the Kowai River and was setting up a sheep station. One of the Rhodes brothers was doing likewise nearby. The following year, John Deans, having proved to have an excellent eye for stock, made yet another trip to New South Wales to purchase enough sheep to double their flock.

It was now becoming clear that the Port Cooper plains could become the site of the New Zealand Company's latest settlement, to be known as Canterbury. The brothers were anxious to capitalise on their foresight in settling at Putaringamotu, so sent their father

A camp oven over an open fire was the sole means of cooking at Riccarton for more than 10 years.

The Deans's farm in 1848, painted by William Fox.

copies of all the correspondence they had already had with the Crown representatives and the Company before they took up the 1846 lease with Ngai Tahu. They wanted him and brother James to pursue an agreement with the New Zealand Company principals in London to purchase the 1000 acres (400 hectares) they had improved. They expected to pay for 600 of those acres (at £1 per acre), after compensatory substitutions for William's 100 unavailable Company acres in the Manawatu and John's 300 equally unavailable Company acres in Nelson. If John senior and James were willing to advance the £600, the brothers considered:

It would be much more satisfactory to have a piece of ground we could call our own than being tenants to the Maoris or the New Zealand Company.

• 4 •
Surveyors
and Settlers

Within 18 months of the Deans brothers settling on the Port Cooper plains, their flourishing farm was to act as a magnet to a succession of surveyors searching for suitable South Island sites for the next New Zealand Company settlements. Not only did the brothers' presence demonstrate the viability of the plains for agriculture, their increasing local knowledge and legendary hospitality were to provide the catalyst for the final decision to site the new Canterbury settlement nearby.

Sept. 12

Deans

Sept 12

Selecting southern sites

Negotiating a free hand from the New Zealand Company to select
whatever South Island site he favoured for a settlement to be named
New Edinburgh, surveyor Frederick Tuckett visited Port Cooper
in April 1844. With a companion, he crossed over the head of the
harbour to the shores of Te Waihora (Lake Ellesmere), then headed
for the Deans's residence on the plains. Although they hoped to
find a guide, the one Maori they came across pointed out the right
path but could not be prevailed upon to accompany them. Perhaps
a matter of payment requested and denied, since an indignant
Tuckett wrote in his diary:

> *Nor did I care to obtain his company, for he was a most*
> *impudent and importunate beggar.*

Confident that he could find his way to the nearest of the only
two 'small pine groves visible on this great tract', Tuckett and his
companion went on their way. All was well until they were tempted to
divert across the river they were following (possibly the Halswell) on a
'native ferry', a mokihi (flax-stalk raft) tethered at a crossing. Trying to
stay dry, Tuckett knelt rather than straddled the raft and was promptly
tipped into the water. On the other side of the river and now off
course, the two men were benighted in the swamp. Soaked to the skin,

Walter Mantell's 1848 sketch of the farm
buildings at Riccarton, with the milking
shed on the left, the 1843 cottage across
the bridge on the right, and the 1844-45
ploughmans's cottage behind the cart.

without a blanket or the means to light a fire, Tuckett spent a wretched night. When they finally reached Putaringamotu the next morning, it was no help to find that others of his party had arrived comfortably the night before, having taking the direct route over the hills from Rapaki.

Despite the Deans's hospitality and the visible health of their cattle, Tuckett was unconvinced by their apparent farming success:

> *The great plain is not worth occupying in small sections. It would be absolute ruin to the occupier, however able and industrious. It should never be subdivided into sections less than a square mile ...*

Perhaps jaundiced by immersion and a miserable night, and his attention caught by the early frosting of the Deans's potato tops (it was only April after all), Tuckett turned his back on the Port Cooper plains. Choosing to ignore his own conclusion that the land on the direct route between the Deans's farm and the Port Cooper hills, bounded by the Putaringamotu (Otakaro) and Opawa (Heathcote) streams, was of good quality and suitable for subdivision into small sections, he proceeded further south to the Otago peninsula.

It would be more than four years before other Company surveyors or Government agents ventured onto the plains. Walter Mantell passed through Putaringamotu in September 1848, on his way to Kaiapoi to peg out the land to be reserved there for Ngai Tahu in accordance with Kemp's Deed — though he was secretly instructed by Governor Grey to keep the reserves to the minimum possible. Despite the immediate and ongoing protests of Ngai Tahu chiefs, whose expectations of entitlement to large areas were ignored, Mantell's meagre allocations succeeded in impoverishing South Island Maori for generations to come.

With Maori title effectively extinguished, the Port Cooper plains were again a potential site for the next Company settlement. This time, the plains were to have an unexpected supporter. Bishop Selwyn had accompanied Mantell on this leg of his own lengthy perambulations through the country, visiting his newly converted Maori flock. Although he had apparently not been in favour of Port Cooper for the intended Anglican cathedral city of a Wakefield-inspired, civilised Canterbury settlement, the Deans's flourishing farm changed his mind.

And, perhaps contributing to his now-favourable impression were the excellent dinner provided by housekeeper Mary Tod and her solicitous attentions. It seems that, like Tuckett before him, the bishop arrived at the farm soaked to the skin, having plunged fully clad into the Opawa River, not bothering to strip before crossing. A story recorded by the writer of *Canterbury Sketches* (CL Innes) claims that, after dinner, when the bishop was sitting in the parlour eating stored apples from the Deans's trees and drinking fresh milk, Mary looked at him and said:

Eh! Sir, you're unco' wet, wull ye no gae and pit on some of the Maister's claithes.

The staunch bishop thanked her but declined, then took himself off — still in his wet clothes — to walk back to Port Cooper that evening.

A few months later, Captain Joseph Thomas and his team of surveyors, with William Fox (principal agent for the New Zealand Company), arrived at Putaringamotu. They were to work on behalf of the newly formed Canterbury Association, a subsidiary of the Company. After buying provisions from the Deans brothers (60 pounds of mutton and 50 of pork; 27 and 22 kg, respectively), they set off to take a first look at the Waimakariri River.

The surveyors returned in time to enjoy Christmas 1848 at the Deans's farm. Surveyor Charles Torlesse merely notes this fact in his diary, but Mary Tod was more forthcoming. It seems that the survey party was accommodated in the original dwelling, now known as the 'old barn', which they proceeded to decorate with greenery. A table laid out from one end to the other was laden with feast goods:

They got a round of beef from Mr Deans ... they also got a goose and plenty of vegetables. My husband and myself had to go over at night. There were two broken down swells giving speeches, one Bruce and one Fox. So you may guess we had a jolly evening.

The beef had been well hung for a fortnight beforehand in a waterproof cask with a lid sunk in the river in the shade under the bridge — an innovative cooling system that was possibly of the enterprising Mary's making.

Between Christmas and early January 1849, several significant steps were taken. At Thomas's request, the Deans brothers wrote a detailed report, drawing on their extensive and probably unequalled experience in New Zealand to assess their six years of farming on the plains. The report addressed 10 questions on subjects covering a full range: climate and soils; their advice on crops and rotations,

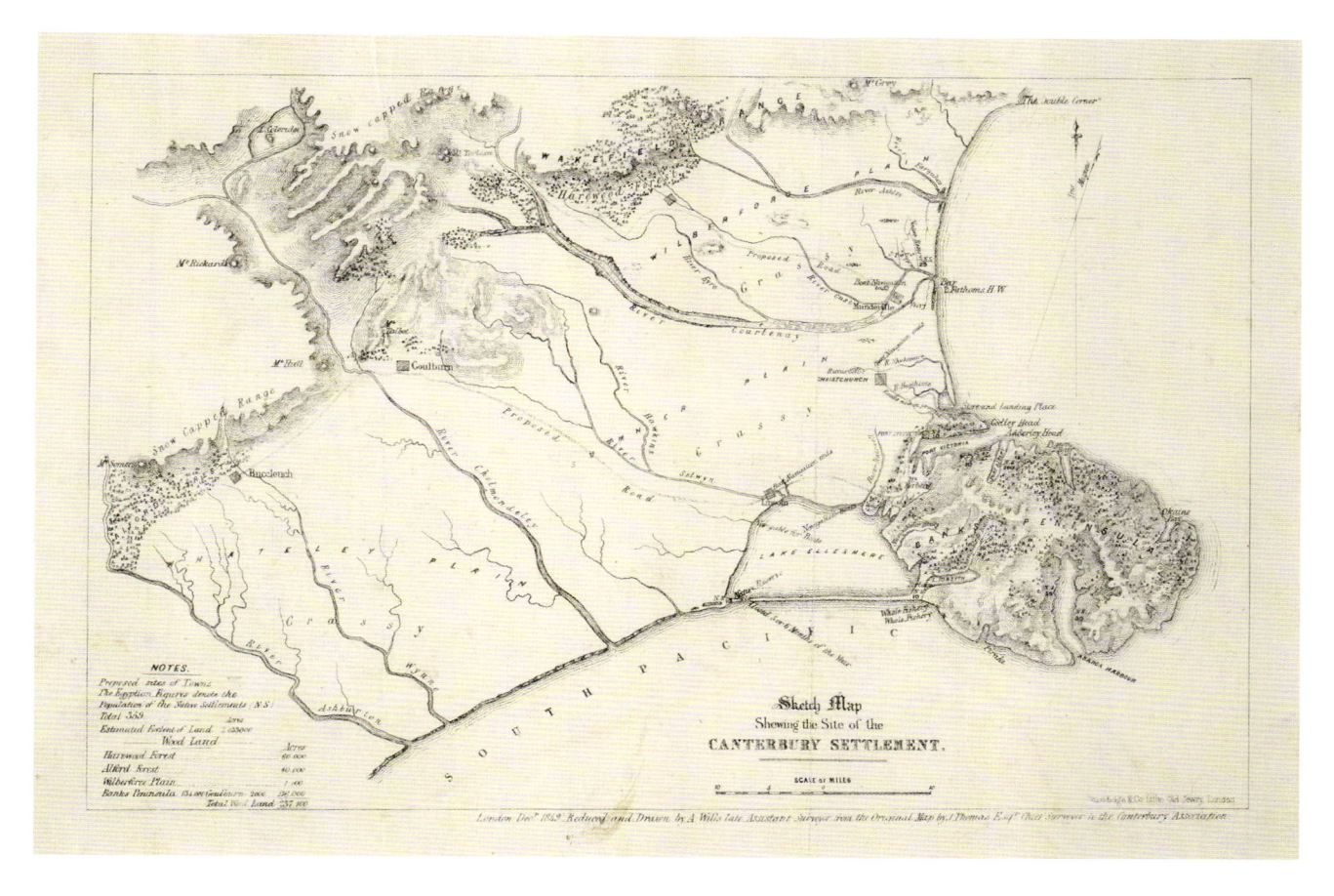

Sketch Map
Shewing the Site of the
CANTERBURY SETTLEMENT.

The site of the Canterbury settlement, 1849, based on the original sketch map drawn by Captain Thomas, chief surveyor for the Canterbury Association.

appropriate stock breeds and farming equipment; what survey supplies they could provide and at what cost; the cost of their own imported staples; the availability of local building materials (timber and bricks); and, roading potential and fencing systems. They concluded by congratulating the Company on:

> ... *being able to secure this district as the site for the Canterbury settlement; for ... we do not believe a suitable site could ever have been secured elsewhere in the Company's territory; and we are certain no equal site to this is now open for selection.*

Such congratulations were premature — the decision had not yet been made. The brothers were well aware that the Wairarapa was still in the running, so they may have been indulging in some subtle lobbying. They succeeded. There is little doubt that their informative and positive report, backed up by the physical evidence of their successful establishment on the plains, was instrumental in sealing the decision to opt for the Port Cooper plains for the new Canterbury settlement.

On their own behalf, that Christmas the brothers won signed agreement from Fox and Thomas that they would be granted 400 acres (160 hectares) in exchange for their Wellington and

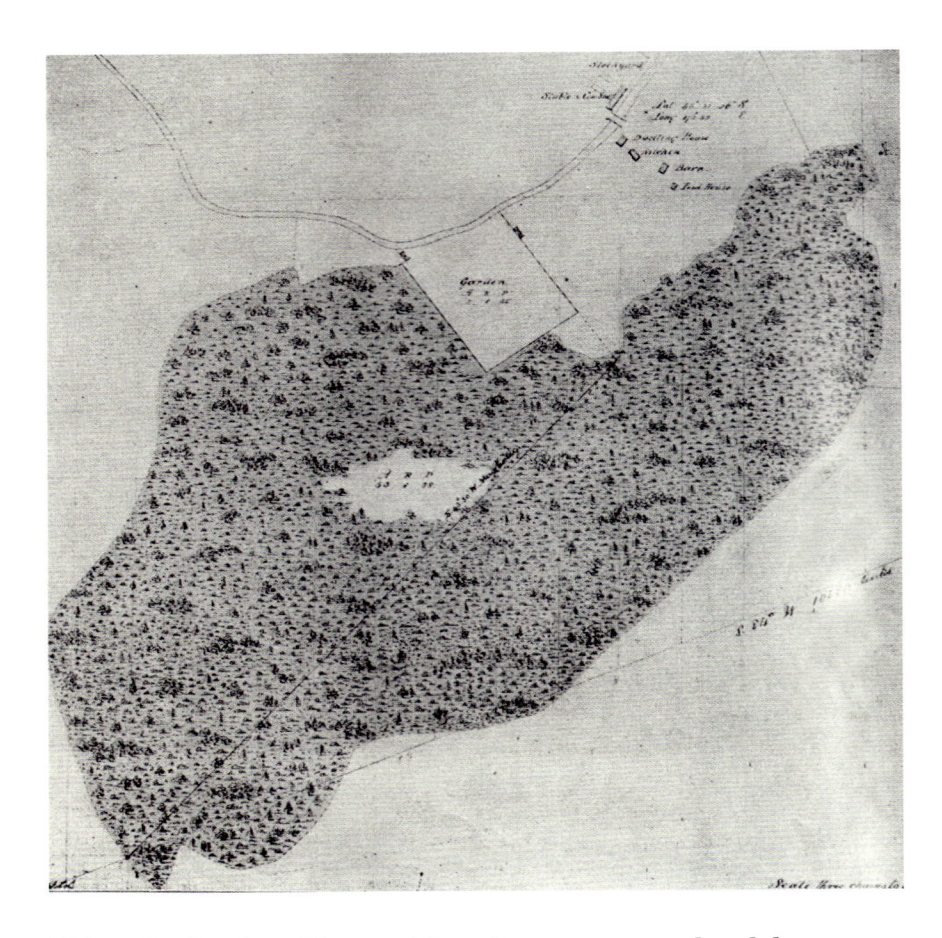

Nelson land orders. The resulting plan was surveyed and drawn up by Charles Torlesse in May 1849, but not signed off by Captain Thomas until August that year, and not without further negotiation.

The historical significance of this agreement cannot be overemphasised. The Deans's freehold block was to include half the all-important tract of the bush at Putaringamotu — part of which the Deans family was later to reserve as a gift to the city of Christchurch. The other half was to be put aside for the use of arriving settlers to offset the lack of closely accessible timber that had been the one stumbling block to the plains being selected.

And there was more. Torlesse's plan revealed that some significant names had changed; changes that reflected the inexorable passing of the land from Ngai Tahu hands to those of the incoming settlers. With great satisfaction, John Deans wrote to his father in January 1849 to confirm the official adoption of the Scottish place names they had been using only since the Christmas agreement (a letter home dated 21 December 1848 was still headed Putaringamotu):

The river up which we now bring our supplies is to be called the Avon, at our request, and our place Riccarton, which will at least remind us of these two places at home.

Charles Torlesse's 1849 part-plan of Riccarton, showing the bush with its central gap (probably fire-induced), the line dividing off the settlers' portion (to the right), the garden and the farm buildings beside the Avon.

Surveyors at Riccarton

Using the newly named Riccarton as their base, at the end of December 1848 a team of surveyors began mapping the plains with the help of Maori workers. The Deans brothers provided provisions and logistical support: William Tod with a horse and cart to first establish then later dismantle a base camp on the banks of the Waimakariri, the use of their canoe while the team surveyed the estuary of the newly named Avon, and frequent respite at Riccarton from tent camps. On his first survey trip, a somewhat careless Torlesse at various times managed to run out of food, lose his telescope, his compass and his belt, had to borrow £2 from the Deans brothers after paying his Maori workers and, to cap it all off, his horse bolted and was not found until three weeks later.

In mid-February 1849, Captain Thomas left for Auckland to confirm his choice of site for the Canterbury settlement. The surveyors continued their work, now moving to map the plains and foothills south of Banks Peninsula. Others were mapping the harbour. Charles Torlesse borrowed another £2 from the ever-obliging Deans brothers, along with a double-barrelled shotgun, powder and shot, tobacco and shoes for his newly retrieved horse. These shoes were fitted by Samuel Manson, who seems to have added blacksmith skills to his cheese-making activities at the head of Port Cooper.

While Torlesse was staying at Riccarton in May and June 1849, ostensibly to survey their all-important 400 acres, he spent many pleasurable hours with one or other Deans brother, helping move stock, fire the grass, or indulge in frequent shooting trips. A welcome change of diet was provided in the form of weka, ducks, quail, wood pigeons and kaka, among other birds, and additional good sport was provided by the occasional wild dog and pig.

Crossing the Courtenay (Waimakariri) where it emerges from the foothills, sketched by William Fox during a Canterbury Association survey expedition (published in 1851).

Charles Torlesse, surveyor and frequent stayer at Riccarton.

Numerous braces of quail often featured in their bags, and in those of the settlers who followed them, proving to be 'if properly cooked, quite equal to partridge', according to Torlesse. An easy prey, native quail were to vanish from the plains within two decades. Equally easy were the wood pigeons. John Deans reported that they visited the bush from April to June to feed on matai and kahikatea berries, and could be shot:

> *... as fast as* [a person] *can charge his gun, and if he misses one it will very often not fly away till he is ready to give it another shot.*

John's interest in the bird life extended beyond shooting and eating them. He wrote detailed descriptions of plumage for his father, and skinned and stuffed any more unusual specimens — among them a bittern and an owl (caught by one of the dogs). Some of the taxidermy still on display in Riccarton House may well be John's work. The Deans brothers and their guests also ate eel frequently and were 'very fond of them'; also a type of flounder they could spear from the canoe in the Avon. William caught over 30 pounds (13 kg) of eels one summer morning, using a hinaki (Maori eel trap).

In mid-June, with growing numbers of surveyors and labourers needing accommodation at Riccarton, two Maori and their wives arrived to help build a house for the surveyors. A description of this 'grass-built cottage beside the wood' was recorded in Edward Ward's journal when he visited Riccarton in December 1850:

> *It was composed of uprights and framework of poles of different thickness, tied together with flax. The room was hung around with saddles, bridles & 'gear' of every kind—guns, knives, a few books & beds all round the room on a sort of shelf.*

By September 1849, over 100 men were working on preparations for the new settlement, with more labourers arriving from Wellington by the day. William Deans helped assess the best route for a dray road from Riccarton to the banks of the Waimakariri to supply a new camp for surveying the land beyond there to the Ashley. But Torlesse complained in a letter to his mother that only two surveyors (himself and Thomas Cass) were engaged on the detailed trigonometrical survey of the plains needed to make parcels of land available to the expected settlers. Captain Thomas was concentrating all his effort and most of the labour on building barracks and other 'public works'

The bittern on display in Riccarton House may have been John's taxidermy work.

A typical surveyors' camp, Frederick Weld's sketch of their camp at Rangiora Bush probably shows the Godleys among others during their adventurous expedition with his survey party in December 1850 (see page 78).

at Lyttelton. He was also constructing a road from the port over the hill to the plains, a road that swallowed most of the available funds and was eventually abandoned. The increasingly contrary agent was busy alienating his surveyors, with Torlesse saying he was 'showing evident signs of unfitness for his duties'. By the following year he was also upsetting existing squatters like the Deans brothers to the extent that John Deans told his father:

> It is to be hoped that … a proper agent may be sent out, as the present one, Captain Thomas, is not at all adapted for the situation on account of his overbearing manner and hasty temper.

Despite Torlesse's concerns about Thomas's priorities, by December 1849 William Deans noted that about 130 Maori with 'white overseers' were working on the roads 'in this neighbourhood', as well as another 60 'white people'. Six surveyors were now working on the plains, and the Deans brothers were supplying them with beef and mutton at the rate of 300 pounds (135 kg) of meat per week, yielding a good price. Ever the canny businessman, William pointed out to brother James in Scotland that although the animals they butchered were still young and underweight, they could import lean cattle to replace them at less than half that price, with plenty of time to fatten them to sell to the settlers expected to arrive the following year.

They had also had an excellent lambing season (125 per cent), and had just finished shearing — yielding 4000 pounds (1800 kg) of high-quality wool that would fetch a respectable price. Added to the sums being lent by their father and brother James, they would soon be in a position to purchase more stock, should they proceed with the extensive sheep run they were busy negotiating with the New Zealand Company.

A new pastoral run

Although the Deans brothers had now successfully gained the freehold of 400 acres (160 hectares) of improved land at Riccarton, the status of the surrounding grazing land held under their 1846 lease with Ngai Tahu was in dispute. Once they realised this land would probably become part of the settlement subdivisions, the brothers had embarked on protracted negotiations about their entitlement to an equivalent tract of land beyond the boundaries of the Canterbury Settlement block. They had first to deal with the New Zealand Company (until July 1850), and then with the Canterbury Association's chief agent, John Robert Godley. The correspondence became increasingly obdurate — although on the surface the Deans brothers continued to be polite, and Fox, then Godley, conciliatory.

In the meantime, with cautious approval from Fox, by early 1850 the Deans brothers had selected a replacement run in the Malvern Hills, an area surveyed the previous year by Charles Torlesse. While John left for Sydney in April 1850 to buy stock for the new run, William took physical possession of the land (about 20,000 acres — 8000 hectares), with stock from Riccarton being moved there the same month. He set about arranging for a house and sheep pens to be built.

Much of the disagreement about the brothers' entitlement to run land centred round the validity of their lease with Ngai Tahu. Although the Deans brothers had written approval from the Government for this lease, by the time the document was actually signed, such leases had been deemed illegal. Both Fox and Godley were to insist on the lease being illegal, using this as a reason to deny the Deans brothers entitlement to a replacement run and any prior rights over the incoming settlers.

Godley found himself in a difficult situation. An admirer of the

John Robert Godley, founder of Christchurch, principal agent for the Canterbury Association and chief negotiator with the Deans brothers over their land rights at Riccarton.

Deans brothers and acknowledging their enterprise, integrity and unfailing kindness to the arriving settlers, he nevertheless felt legally bound to put the interests of the Canterbury Association before theirs. That they were Scots squatters and Presbyterian, not carefully selected English settlers and Anglican, did not help. In one of her letters home in 1851, Godley's wife Charlotte gives an interesting perspective on what she seems to have considered the Deans's dubious claim:

> *This claim, I think, is to a space of two miles, all round Riccarton, on the old story of having purchased it from the natives, which would of course annihilate Christchurch and turn all the settlers about there off their land. Deans has lately put this forward, not apparently expecting, or hoping, to get the land itself, but ... in compensation, some particular 'run' for cattle about fifty miles [80 km] off.*

Ideal country for a sheep run. 'Huts built for the commencement of a sheep station, about two miles from Mr Deans' Homebush station, 1851', a painting by James Fitzgerald showing tussock country and the Malvern Hills.

Godley eventually conceded that the Deans brothers were owed some compensation for losing the run at Riccarton. He suggested that they retain the 2000 acres (800 hectares) of the Malvern run to which they could become entitled in proportion to their 400 freehold acres at Riccarton (the Association's land order terms), but in the meantime pay rent for it while continuing to use the rest of the run informally. He was in the midst of persuading the Canterbury Association management in London that more favourable terms should be granted to pastoralists, recognising that large inland sheep runs would be essential for the settlement's economic success.

The Deans brothers found this compromise and the uncertain outcome of Godley's proposition to London unsatisfactory. In February 1851, they promptly sold their sheep and improvements on the Malvern Hills run to Canterbury settler John Watts Russell. They withdrew to Riccarton, opting to focus their efforts there until gaining a resolution. William wrote to his father:

> To enable us to take high ground with Mr. Godley, we gave up the sheep run we had taken possession of shortly before the arrival of the settlers and sold off our sheep.

With no intention of yielding their position, they pointed out that the lease land at Riccarton had recently been surveyed as more than 33,000 acres (13,300 hectares), appealed directly to Governor Grey (a recipient of their hospitality at Riccarton in 1849), and threatened legal action if they were not granted a replacement run. They had already set their sights on a new run in the Malvern Hills, and William was planning a voyage to Sydney in August to buy 2000 'maiden ewes' to stock it.

Godley now backed off; this was all becoming too difficult and he had no wish to lose the Deans's personal friendship. When Governor Grey refused to arbitrate (no friend to Godley, he saw no reason to extricate the Canterbury Association agent from his difficulties), Godley handed on any final decision to the London management committee, which had already been lobbied extensively from Scotland by John Deans senior and brother James.

The Deans brothers' persistence paid off handsomely. They were duly granted a Canterbury Association lease for the new run Thomas Cass had already surveyed for them between the Waimakariri and Selwyn Rivers. What was more, the run was to be held on the same terms as their original lease with Ngai Tahu. For a mere £8 a year for the remaining 16 years of the original 21-year term (and with no record that they ever did repay the intervening three years of rental arrears), the brothers gained the 33,000 acres that would become Homebush station.

On passing along the jetty you have the Custom House on the right, farther on is Major Hornby's Hotel, Boat house, Shed & you you next come upon Emigration Square cont.d 4 barracks for 400 persons, a Public Cook house & well of ... in the Store in port of the road, is the tempory Office of the Union Bank than follows Mr Godleys Lawn & House at the back — the Land office in front the next building at the corner of Sumner road is the post Office & above it towards Godleys is the Town Hall the Market place in the centre with the Jail & Hospital — On the left hand from the Association Store House, the Esplanade, Settlers huts — behind is the Church, parsonage & School house.

Port Lyttelton, Cavendish Bay Victoria Harbour.

Visitors at Riccarton

Added to Godley's burden during his first dealings with the Deans brothers was the uncertain status of the Canterbury Association scheme. By mid-July 1850, land orders had been sold for only 9000 of the intended 100,000 acres (40,000 hectares). Before retreating to Wellington in April 1850 (after only two days at Port Cooper), Godley had ordered Captain Thomas to stop work on the money-hungry road over the hill to Sumner. The surveyors were left out of work and owed money, languishing in Lyttelton. Their one respite was spending time at Riccarton for some shooting with the Deans brothers. Godley's friends in England had to raise money to rescue the scheme. In the end, four ships carrying settlers with a good range of skills and occupations set sail from England in September 1850, with more ships to follow. When Edward Ward arrived on the *Charlotte Jane* in mid-December 1850 and was greeted by Charles Torlesse, an old school friend, he summed up the resulting stagnation:

> *He* [Torlesse] *told me all the news, which was merely that they had lain dead and buried for the last eight or nine months in perfect inaction, without money or anything to do.*

Godley had returned to Port Cooper a few weeks before the settlers arrived. With his wife Charlotte and their three-year-old son Arthur, he stayed at Riccarton — welcome guests despite being in the thick of their difficult negotiations. Charlotte may have been the first white woman to visit Riccarton since the Tods arrived in 1845.

Looking from Governors Bay towards Lyttelton, with arriving settlers' ships anchored in the harbour in 1850-51, painted by Henry Cridland.

Riccarton. november 1850.

Like the Deans brothers, Mary Tod had been looking forward to the arrival of the settlers:

> You may think how excited I was — I had not seen a white woman for 5 years.

Although Mary does not name Mrs Godley, Charlotte notes with approval that the Tod offspring were 'doing credit to the place, quite prize children anywhere'. The Godleys were on their way to camp on the banks of the Waimakariri with surveyor Frederick Weld. The adventurous Charlotte had decided that tenting rough could be no worse than the conditions they were enduring in a makeshift Lyttelton. They were accompanied by several of the other surveyors, among them Charles Torlesse and his cousin Edward Jerningham Wakefield, who had also been languishing in Lyttelton over the winter and had no doubt enjoyed renewing acquaintance with William Deans, a friend from Wellington survey days (see Chapter 1).

That evening, the Godleys dined with John Deans (William was away at the Malvern Hills run), and Charlotte lists the plentiful fare to be had at Riccarton:

> Fresh-killed mutton, salt beef ... bread which is generally rather sour, [Mary Tod would not have been pleased if she heard this opinion of her bread] and capital scones; flour and water baked on a girdle, and made good a plaisir by the addition of milk and soda, or butter, or sugar; and there too we had damper, the regular bush fare ... Then we had plenty of butter and milk, and tea three times a day.

The next day, John Deans sent them on their way with a leg of mutton and some bottles of fresh milk to supplement their provisions. They were to be the first of many parties of arriving settlers to visit Riccarton over the next few months and experience the generosity of the Deans brothers.

Riccarton sketched by Henry Cridland just before the arrival of the Canterbury settlers.

With Christchurch itself still a swampy wasteland recognisable only by its grid of survey lines, traipsing over the hill and across the plains to visit the established Deans's farm became the accepted thing to do for disillusioned settlers arriving in rudimentary Lyttelton, perhaps for reassurance that it would indeed be possible at some time in the future to build a civilised life. The writer of *Canterbury Sketches* sums up the reception all comers received at Riccarton:

> *... the genial brothers of Riccarton did all they could to help us, both with advice and substantial kindness of every sort. It was always open house ... you just walked in and were treated with warm hospitality ...*

The Deans's 1851 summer garden was luxuriant, with apples, plums and peaches in full glory. Edward Ward commented that the fruit trees were overladen, and John Deans wrote to his father that he was 'afraid propping them [the standard peach trees] up will scarcely save them from bursting asunder'.

No matter, they had plenty of guests to help eat the fruit. Many visitors stayed overnight, rolled in blankets on the floor of the sitting room or taking advantage of William's frequent absences at the new sheep run in the Malvern Hills. Mary Tod was hard put to keep up with the catering. According to Jane Deans's later account, the housekeeper ended up asking to be allowed to give the flour and meat to the visitors so they could cook for themselves.

Early in March, while the Godleys were camping temporarily in a raupo hut on the barren site of Christchurch, William Deans had to come to Charlotte's rescue. The thatched walls of the hut caught fire, but someone at the nearby Riccarton farm saw the smoke, and William, with half a dozen of his men, was quickly there to retrieve the Godleys' possessions. Charlotte lamented that the hut itself was 'in five minutes all down, and only bare poles left standing'. When rain caught them out before the replacement hut being built for them by local Maori was finished, the stoic Godleys put their valuables and clothes under the table and themselves in bed with an umbrella over their heads. In the morning, miserably wet, they sought shelter with the Deans brothers, by whom they were 'as usual most hospitably received'.

But all was not well with the Deans brothers. Despite the continuing success of their farming enterprise at Riccarton and the gaining of the new inland run, both their fortunes and their circumstances were changing.

• 5 •
Fate and Fortunes

———————

By 1851, the Deans brothers' shared plans and predictions were coming to fruition: their future seemed secured, their isolation on the plains was ending, and their farm was in an ideal situation to profit from the arriving Canterbury settlers. But their personal goals and intentions were already diverging before the intervention of fate changed the direction of both their futures.

A proposal of marriage

As early as 1847, John Deans was talking about his 'great desire' to return, at least temporarily, to Scotland. Unlike William, John at that time was far from committed to making New Zealand his permanent home. But he knew that such a trip would involve his absence from the farm for about a year, so the longer he delayed the harder it would become since each year their growing stock numbers increased the workload. At the time he was coy about his reasons for wanting to return to Scotland, but marriage was what was on his mind.

In 1839, before William Deans left for New Zealand, a picnic was held to farewell him at Knockdolian. Among the guests were the McIlraiths from nearby Auchenflower. John had a year before set his sights on a romantic liaison with Jane McIlraith, then 16. He had been firmly rejected. She was by her own account (written in 1878 and refreshingly direct for the times) attached to Gavin Brackenridge, 'a very handsome lad' (known to her from school and also a friend to both the Deans brothers). Indeed Jane's friends expected them ultimately to 'become a pair'. So the rejected 19-year-old John switched his attentions to Jane's cousin Jeanie Gibson — 'the beauty of four counties', according to Jane. But Jeanie was equally unmoved when 'he confessed his love'. She also rejected him.

Jane was later to profess in her *Letters to My Grandchildren* that the Knockdolian picnic was her first meeting with John. It was there they:

> *… formed their first impressions of each other, he thinking 'I would do for New Zealand', I thinking 'he looked like the head of a family, so staid and quiet'.*

But this was an edited version she perhaps thought more seemly for the youngsters she was now writing for — and she herself was 10 years older and a grandmother. The reality was that she had been both dismayed and horrified when her father accepted her rejected suitor as a farm cadet for two years (1839–41). Worse, John would board with the McIlraith family for that time:

> *Could my father be in necessitous circumstances requiring him to do so, or was he losing his senses, taking a young gentleman into his family with one daughter grown up & another nearly so, he who was so particular?*

Although Jane 'resolved to *hate* the new comer ... it was no use. I had to give in and treat him as a brother'. By the time John left Auchenflower in September 1841 to gain other farming experience, their friendship had blossomed beyond that of mere siblings:

> *We were young, bright & spirited & enjoyed life to the full in all its phases. He was the life & soul of 'young parties'...*

Before John sailed for Nelson early in 1842, they 'quite understood each other's feelings that we were made for each other', although Jane records that he had made 'no further attempts to win a promise from me to wait for him'. Cautious John did not want to commit someone so young to a life in New Zealand that one or other of them might not like. Instead, as he later explained to his father, although he had intended to ask Jane to marry him before he left Scotland, he decided it was wiser to wait until he was sure about his prospects and commitment to New Zealand:

Jane Deans, painted during John's visit to Scotland in 1852 for their marriage.

John Deans, painted during his visit to Scotland in 1852.

> *... although I many a time thought how much happier I should be with a helpmate, I could not bring myself to ask her to join me in so out of the way place as this, where often for months we did not see a strange face.*

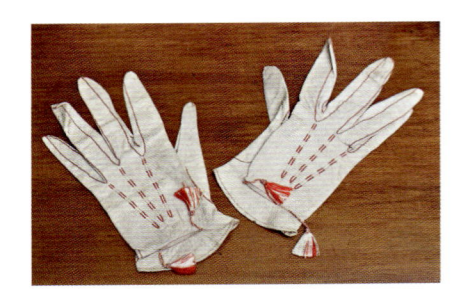

Perhaps fearing yet another rejection, he was to keep her waiting for eight years before he had the courage to broach the all-important question in mid-1850. Both Jane and her father took several long months to respond to his first overtures. During that time, he heard from his own father and brother in Scotland that she may have already married. To his great relief this proved a misconception (it was her sister who had married).

James McIlraith senior had no objections to John Deans as a son-in-law, but left it entirely to Jane to decide. Her response was cooler than John had hoped. She expressed scruples about travelling out to New Zealand (among them her proneness to seasickness); he must return to Scotland to fetch her himself. Perhaps she needed stronger evidence of his ardour than the pair of gloves he gave her when he left in 1842. Admittedly handsome, the gift would still seem inadequate to compensate for the apparent lack of any communication between them during the ensuing eight years.

John wrote to Jane several times more during 1850, and was convinced his persuasive letters should be more than enough for her to change her mind. In September, he complained to his father that it 'would be a considerable loss to be obliged to go home to fetch her out', but hastened to add that he would do so if necessary. He does seem to have become aware that perhaps he had waited overlong to ask her to marry him. That letter to his father is full of self-justification — the uncertainty, the isolation, the need for their prospects to improve, his own recent decision that he could settle at Riccarton 'for life' — and he rounded off his excuses by saying it was only now that the Canterbury settlement was imminent that the time was right.

By February 1851, a perplexed John had not had any further replies to his many letters. And he was still hoping that Jane could be prevailed upon to travel 'under the protection of some respectable married couple'. He thought of arranging for her to come out with bishop-designate Thomas Jackson:

Miss McIlraith says she is a very bad sailor, but in such a large ship as that the Bishop will return in, it will be quite different from any one she has ever been in.

He added, perhaps remembering the fun-loving Jane of their youth:

I am sure she would enjoy the voyage and laugh at the danger.

These gloves were John Deans's gift to Jane McIlraith on his departure from Scotland for New Zealand in 1842.

John was now beginning to worry that Jane 'might not start some objections to come out with me, even if I were to go home for her'. But the satisfactory letters he at last received in July from both Jane and her father made him decide to leave for Scotland as soon as brother William returned from a stock-buying trip to Sydney. He expected to be away for less than a year.

Splits and divisions

At the same time that John Deans was contemplating taking a wife, he was also considering the possibility of dividing up the land he and William were farming. He was well aware that he owned 300 of the freehold 400 acres they held at Riccarton; William only 100. As early as December 1849, a few months after the land officially became freehold, he told his father, 'It is all laid out in one block, but we can easily divide it at any time.'

A few months after John received that first, cautiously favourable response from Jane McIlraith and her father (late July 1850), he broached the subject of dividing the land with William. Rather than discuss his proposition directly, John chose to write to his brother while William was away at the sheep station in October for the start of lambing. Although William replied that he would do 'whatever I can to meet your views', he was dismayed. He wrote two letters to John, 10 days apart, the first with an undertone of betrayal, the second a more considered response on how best to divide the land and formalise their partnership if his brother was determined to have separate establishments.

But William saw no reason why John's proposed marriage should alter the way they were running Riccarton and the inland sheep station. He had assumed that 'all the speculations' they had entered into together were on the basis that their intentions were the same and the properties were to be managed together. If John insisted on separate farming establishments at Riccarton, or chose to stay in Scotland, selling his share to brother James (who at that stage was considering moving to Canterbury himself), William would need an equal share of the Riccarton land since his 100 acres would be inadequate:

> If I cannot get more than 100 acres of land there it appears to me better to remove elsewhere.

Pointing out that he felt he had some claim on purchasing a share

of John's land at Riccarton, William next proposed that John immediately sell 100 acres to him. He further proposed that they should now draw up a formal partnership, with regular accounts and division of the profits at regular intervals. If John objected to selling, William would sell his own Riccarton share to him, sell his share of the stock at the inland run and 'commence afresh as a sheep farmer alone'. What was more, if he could not find a suitable station in Canterbury at a reasonable price — and here perhaps a touch of bitterness can be detected — 'I shall be off to Taranaki and settle there, I hope, for the remainder of my days'.

Over the next four months, William was often absent from Riccarton, spending a lot of his time at the inland station until the brothers sold their stock and assets there to Watts Russell in February 1851. His bedroom in the cottage at Riccarton was occupied more by visitors than by him once the Canterbury settlers began arriving in December 1850, as noted by Charlotte Godley. There is another indication that he was now concentrating his effort as well as his time at the sheep run rather than at Riccarton. For the seven years from their arrival on the plains, it had been John who made the necessary trips to New South Wales to purchase stock, his eye for quality well acknowledged. But now their lengthy negotiations for a new run with Godley were near completion, it was William who was planning to go to Sydney to choose the sheep needed to stock the new station in the Malvern Hills. Jane Deans was to explain in an 1895 letter to her grandchildren that the switch was to allow John time to make his arrangements to go to Scotland, but this, of course, would have been John's version of events.

John later reported to his father that William had proposed that:

As only 100 acres of the land belonged to him, that we should get the grant [for the run] *in our joint names, so that he might have half during his life, and he would afterwards make his share over to me and my heirs.*

Clearly, no agreement had been reached for William to buy the 100 freehold acres that would have given him equal shares at Riccarton and entitle him to half the run grant as of right. Another clue that William may have intended living at the new run is given by Jane Deans, who comments in one of her letters to her grandchildren that John had promised William timber from Riccarton for a house on the run 'when required'.

William Deans at Riccarton, painted in imagined silhouette by Paul Deans in 2000 (no contemporaneous portrait of William exists).

Delayed by the need to settle John Gebbie's affairs after his death in March 1851, William eventually set sail on 20 July for Wellington, intending to take more legal advice on the grant for the run before carrying on to Sydney. He had originally been booked on the *Endora*, but on learning that this ship would now bypass Wellington, he switched at the last moment to the *Maria*. Others planning to be on board missed a precipitate departure from Lyttelton (after being detained for several days by contrary winds the ship set sail as soon as she could), but as Charlotte Godley points out:

> *Mr Deans, who was, I should think, never too late for anything, managed to board her just as she was about to sail.*

Both William's last-minute change of plans and his reputed punctuality were to prove fatal. Three days later, before dawn on 23 July, the *Maria* struck a rock near Cape Terawhiti while she was attempting to enter Wellington harbour in a gale. She broke up, and only two men reached shore safely. William Deans was not one of them, and his body was never found. He was only 34.

This sketch by Laurence Kennaway that accompanied his description of droving sheep from Nelson to Canterbury in 1854 would have resonated with William Deans.

Trials and tribulations

It was a month before a letter from long-standing friend William Lyon, now a merchant in Wellington, reached John Deans with the news. Mary Tod reported that in his distress, John stayed up all night, fully dressed, with Mrs Caverhill keeping him company. It was another week before he could bring himself to write to his father, and then he borrowed the wording used by William Lyon:

> *It is with a sad and heavy heart that I sit down to write you the melancholy intelligence of the death of our dear William.*

A shocked and grieving John hoped that the family in Scotland would be as much comforted as he was by the knowledge that:

> [William] *was universally beloved and esteemed by everyone that knew him ... wherever he was known he was respected. He was everything one could wish in a son, brother or friend.*

Several Canterbury settlers recorded their sadness at William's death. CL Innes in *Canterbury Sketches* noted that he was 'respected among us for his kindness, usefulness, and sterling worth, and his loss was felt by all'. An obituary in the *Lyttelton Times* emphasised the 'bountiful and yet unostentatious good cheer offered to all comers ...' Expressing similar sentiments, Charlotte Godley added 'his brother will feel his loss sadly; they were so united and so happy together ...' Any tension between the brothers over dividing the land was hidden from onlookers, and it is clear from William's letters to John that despite his opposition to any such division, above all else he wanted to avoid causing a rift between them.

Even with the solace provided by his religious belief that his brother had gone to a better place, John's grief must nevertheless have been made all the more poignant by the knowledge that he had upset and disappointed William with his determination to separate their holdings. The letter he wrote to his father a month later, outlining the arrangements he had made for the administration of his brother's estate, has some of the elements of self-justification of his earlier explanations for his delay in proposing to Jane McIlraith. He took it on himself to administer William's affairs as his next-of-kin in New Zealand 'to prevent the whole getting into the hands of the Registrar at Wellington', for his brother had not left a will.

Perhaps this is not surprising despite William's canny business sense and legal background. The correspondence quoted above implies that William did not intend to marry, he was still young, and the brothers had yet to finalise the details of their newly formal partnership. They were waiting for the Crown grant to materialise before doing so.

John claims he made a generous estimate of the value of William's assets, then briefly describes the proposal he had made to him about dividing the land, being honest enough to acknowledge that his brother had been averse to the idea. After outlining William's counter-proposal that they should share the Crown grant land equally, he could not resist pointing out to his father that:

> It was also understood between us that as I had invested a great deal more money than he had in the concern, that I should have sufficient money out of the joint funds to pay my expenses to and from Scotland and have a separate house built.

While John was in Scotland in 1852, he gained his father's consent to negotiate an agreement with his surviving brother James that divided William's estate equally between them. Before John left with his new bride to return to New Zealand, the brothers exchanged letters that formally acknowledged the division. According to Jane Deans's later detailed account of these transactions, William's 100 acres at Riccarton went to John, in return for which he bought land of equal value at Burnside for James. John then leased this property to William Boag on James's behalf, with a seven-year right of renewal or purchase (Boag eventually bought the property). The run in the Malvern Hills was to be divided equally between John and James, and James's remaining share of William's assets was lodged as New Zealand Government debentures. He gave John power of attorney to manage his New Zealand affairs in the meantime, including buying sheep to stock his half of the Malvern run.

The finest type of pioneer

Both William and John Deans were liked and respected by all the people they had dealings with in New Zealand — Maori as well as colonial settlers. Yet their personalities on the whole remain enigmatic. Apart from the extensive letters to and from Scotland (collated and edited by John Deans's grandson), which provide some insight, little is known about William. No portrait was ever made of him, although his friend and fellow surveyor Robert Park later made several sketches of John and formal portraits of John and Jane were commissioned on the occasion of their marriage.

Something of William's nature can be gleaned from the rugged exploratory expeditions he relished and the energy with which he pursued both finding a suitable site for their New Zealand venture and establishing such a flourishing enterprise at Riccarton in the seven years before the Canterbury settlers arrived. Although John worked as tirelessly, William seems to have been the driving force behind their operations. Both brothers saw the value of an inland sheep run, but John seems to have preferred the established comfort of the farm at Riccarton. It was William who drove newly acquired stock from the ships over the hills and across the plains to Riccarton or the first Malvern Hills run, and William who stayed at the run for weeks at a time, living in primitive conditions. It could also be inferred from their correspondence over dividing the land, William's frequent absences upcountry, and his taking over the sheep-buying role for the replacement run that he may have been considering moving to live there as a solution to their differences.

John Deans, painted by Robert Park, possibly during a visit to Riccarton in 1854.

Many of the men with whom William formed lasting friendships were intelligent and artistically talented, often unorthodox in their behaviour and beliefs, or with strong personalities: Ernst Dieffenbach, Edward Jerningham Wakefield and Robert Park, for example.

At the same time, William was known for his level-headedness, sound judgment and practical good sense. He was appointed senior Justice of the Peace and a magistrate in the newly established Canterbury district — despite being Scots and not a Canterbury Association settler. In 1851, Sir George Grey tried to persuade him to take a seat on the Legislative Council, not just because his name was 'first on the Commission of Peace for the settlement of Canterbury'. In the letter from the Colonial Secretary summonsing William to attend the Council in Wellington, it stated that the Governor particularly desired his advice and the advantage of his 'experience and local knowledge'. Although William was 'quite with him on the subject of colonial politics', he turned down the invitation as the meeting was 'quite out of my way'. It was also William who conducted most of the lengthy negotiation with Fox and Godley over the brothers' disputed land entitlement, adopting considerable firmness but never resorting to language that reflected the frustration he was undoubtedly feeling.

On a personal level, William seems to have intended remaining single (see the correspondence quoted above). Although his detailed advice to his younger brother on what was prudent to bring out to New Zealand in 1842 included a wife 'better imported than acquired on the spot' (and who should be 'capable of managing a dairy'), he showed no inclination to follow his own advice. His indignation at the rumour he had taken a Maori wife seems extreme considering the respect he accorded high-born Maori and the example of his friend Robert Park, who did just that (see chapters 3 and 9). On attending an afternoon tea party with him in 1851, Charles Torlesse was to remark jocularly that one of the four Misses Townsends present (and probably the most eligible young ladies in town) would make an ideal Mrs Deans. William did not rise to the bait.

John may have been the younger brother, and perhaps had a quieter and more conservative personality, but he was equally strong-willed and not easily deflected from the paths he chose. When William warned him that the Nelson settlement scheme was dubious, he nevertheless took time to assess it for himself before coming to the same conclusion. His persistent attempts to persuade

Jane McIlraith to come out to join him rather than put him to the inconvenience of having to travel to Scotland to fetch her could be interpreted as a level of selfishness or at least self-interest. And it was William who had to come up with acceptable compromises to John's upsetting desire to divide their land and have a separate house.

Yet in his dealings with the Canterbury settlers, John, like William, was generous and kind, both liked and admired. Charlotte Godley writes:

He is a very nice person, so very straight-forward and honest, and so very free from anything of a 'colonial spirit' in his dealings with everyone.

Most of the Deans brothers' employees remained loyal to them, and were looked after once they left — endorsing Charlotte Godley's assessment. On his return to Scotland to marry Jane McIlraith, John found the time to make many purchases on their behalf: harrows and plough for William Tod, clothing and cheese presses for Mary Gebbie, bedding and cheese-making equipment for Samuel Manson. Similar purchases were made for friends.

The ploughman's cottage and tents occupied by the Godleys at Riccarton from January to May 1852, painted by James Fitzgerald.

Manse of Ballantrae 13th Septem. 1852

that John Deans, Junior, of the Parish of Riccarton and Jane McIlraith of the Parish of Ballantrae were three times proclaimed in order to marriage in the Parish Church of Ballantrae on Sabbath the 12th day of September current — and that no objections were offered is hereby certified by

John McIlroy Minister
and Session Clerk Pro: tem:

The above named Parties were married by me at Auchenflower the fifteenth day of Sept. 1852   B. Laing D.D.
Minister of the Free Church Colmonell

Notification of John Deans's marriage to Jane McIlraith, September 1852.

Sojourn in Scotland

William Deans's death meant John had to delay his trip back to Scotland for some months. During that time, he sorted out his brother's affairs and bought 200 acres (80 hectares) near Riccarton on James Deans's account — the Burnside property. He arranged for friend David Theodore Williams and his wife Mary to take over the management of Riccarton during his expected year-long absence, providing them with detailed written instructions. He sent all the breeding cattle up to the new inland run, where he employed James Robinson Clough to manage them. Although the formal negotiations with Godley were not quite complete, William had reached some understanding with him; his last letter was written the day before he left Lyttelton, instructing John on what remained to be done and which documents should be forwarded to Godley to clarify their position. With what seems a considerable gesture of goodwill, John invited the Godleys to stay in the ploughman's cottage at Riccarton for four months (January to May 1852) while he was away so they could be closer to Christchurch than at their house in Lyttelton.

Once the year's crops were planted at Riccarton, John was at last free to board his ship in early January 1852. He reached Scotland in April. It was 10 long years since he and Jane McIlraith had set eyes on each other.

All was well. Their feelings for each other had not altered, and they set about preparing for a return together as newlyweds to New Zealand. The five months between John's arrival and their marriage

Notification of John Deans's marriage to Jane McIlraith, September 1852.

in September 1852 were spent in a whirl of visiting old friends and shopping. John showed none of the Scottish frugality that features in the many letters outlining his financial dealings with his father and brother James. Both he and Jane bought quantities of classy clothing and items that would increase their personal comfort and pleasure: wine decanters, a backgammon set, a gold watch, telescope and barometer, numerous books, and a pair of pistols for John; silver teaspoons and religious books for Jane. Household items included furniture, wallpaper, bedding, china, cutlery and glassware — enough goods to fill 50 large boxes for shipping to New Zealand.

On a more pragmatic level, 15 of these boxes contained mill equipment, a waterwheel 15 feet (4.5 metres) in diameter, and its buckets and gearing. Other purchases included a dog cart, ploughs, seed driller and harrows, saddles and harnesses, tools, and everything imaginable that could be needed for the farm. John had ambitious plans for improvements at Riccarton, plans that had been shared by William.

Before the wedding, John went to London to organise first-class cabin accommodation aboard the *Minerva*, a fine ship chartered by the Canterbury Association to transport more migrants to Christchurch. Two poop cabins were fitted out with every luxury for the young couple — at extra expense. John also paid for two young Scots to travel on the ship, with work offered at Riccarton. One of them was Jane's cousin, Douglas Graham.

Others on board would include two notables from the Canterbury Association. Edward Gibbon Wakefield, on a first visit to New Zealand to inspect the results of his settlement schemes, would occupy the cabin next to John and Jane. Henry Sewell was charged with the task of winding up the affairs of the Canterbury Association. Neither man was to meet with John Deans's later approval for their attempts at 'saddling the colony with the Association's debts'. He would add with some vehemence:

Wakefield is a man I detest more than any other I know.

The couple married at last at Auchenflower on 15 September, then spent two weeks at a hotel in London for their honeymoon. No expense was spared, and their luxurious stay cost almost as much as a single passage to New Zealand. The farewell dinner they held for many friends before their departure itself cost half that again. But they had surely earned such indulgence.

Jane Deans Wedding Dress, 1852

A postcard depicting Jane McIraith's wedding dress (the dress itself is housed in the Canterbury Museum).

Extra comforts were bought for the poop cabin occupied by John and Jane Deans on the *Minerva*.

Mr Deane

Dr to Joseph Brown
71 Leadenhall St

Item	£.s.d
1 Double Ship Sofa with 2 horse hair Mattrass & 2 Pillows fixed on Board	7.10.0
2 Extra Feather Pillows @ 4/6 each	.9
1 Mahogany one Flap Washstand	1.15.0
1 Reclining Easy Chair spring stuffed all hair in Morocco	4.10.0
1 Easy Chair spring stuffed all hair Morocco	3.10.0
1 British Plate Glass 10/ one & @ 2/6	0.12.6
3 Candle Lamps with Globes @ 7/6 ea	1.2.6
2 Pieces of Floor Cloth for Cabins	1.16.0
1 Water Filter @ 9/6	0.9.6
27 lbs of Sterine Candles @ 1/lb	1.7.0
18 lbs of Windsor Soap @ 1/lb	.18
1 Pair of Best Whitney Blankits	1.2.0
1 Pair of Do	0.18.0
3 Pair Do @ 7/6 each Pair	1.2.6
1 Swing Cot fixed above Sofa horse hair Mattrass & Bolster	2.10.0
1 Extra Feather Pillow @ 4/6	0.4.6
1 Ship Sofa with horse hair mattrass & Bolster	3.10.0
1 Large Lock put on a Chest	0.3.0
1 Latch for Door 1/6 1 Pad Lock for Door 1/6	0.3.0
2 Fine Canvass Cloths Bags @ 4/6 each	.9
1 Iron Handle 7/8 1 Iron Bolt 1/	.1.8
1 Swing Tray 3/6 1 Curtain for Door 2/6	0.6.0
2 Brown Holland Covers for Chairs	0.13.0
Foot Bath & Can 10/6 1 Swiss Chair 10/6	1.1.0
Shelving 7/6 Fixing 5/- 6 Hat Pegs Brass 6/	.18.6
Dock Charges 5/10 1 Corner Washstand 10/6	.16.4
1st Oct Settled by Cash 37 £ J Brown	37.18.0

• 6 •
Together at Riccarton

The return of the newly married couple to Riccarton was marred by ill health. But the farm had been well managed in John's absence and he was intent on further improvements. Jane was equally intent, determined to settle down in this new country and make the most of it. What lay ahead was to prove a far greater challenge than either of them could possibly have anticipated. Their long-awaited happiness would be short-lived.

First impressions

The *Minerva* with John and Jane Deans on board reached Lyttelton on 2 February 1853. The voyage had been uneventful and the weather mostly fair, but Jane had been terribly seasick throughout, as she had feared and predicted. That she was now in the early stages of pregnancy would not have helped. Weak and out of sorts, she was severely taxed by the trip on horseback over the Bridle Path, even with a man supporting her on either side. Once they reached the Ferrymead side of the hill, Jane was left to recuperate overnight with the Reverend Edward Puckle and his wife before she continued on to Riccarton late the next afternoon. John and the two young Scots who were to work for him had returned back over the hill to Lyttelton to organise the off-loading of their substantial luggage, so could not accompany her the rest of the way. She reached the farm a few hours before them.

Riding in John Watts Russell's spring cart, Jane had plenty of time to absorb the rawness of the new settlement on her journey from the foot of the Port Hills. She later wrote an account of her arrival for her grandchildren, mentioning boulders and potholes on a narrow road little more than a track, separated on both sides by deep ditches from 'almost impassable swamps, covered with

A view of Lyttelton from the hill behind the settlement, painted by Janetta Cookson a year before Jane Deans arrived.

tall flax'. They crossed the Heathcote on a rope-drawn punt, then traversed the extensive flax swamp that still occupied the site of Christchurch, the town's presence barely signalled by the few houses that had been built by then.

Jane's first impressions of Riccarton were bleak. The half of the bush reserved for the Canterbury settlers had already been felled, leaving dead stumps standing a metre or more in height. Two fields at the farm were also thick with stumps, both them and the ground blackened by a recent fire. Heavy cloud had spread over the sky by the time she arrived, with only a 'small clear opening to the nor'west'. And the little house that was to be her new home looked dark to her:

> *I have often thought of it since as a presentiment of my future life in loneliness ...*

That recent fire had come close to destroying the houses, the farm buildings and the bush, according to Charlotte Godley, who was living in the ploughman's cottage at the time. William Tod, now farming his own land in nearby Fendalton, had been contracted to plough the ground once the many logs and stumps had been collected and stacked for sale as firewood. Before that could happen, Tod set fire to the fern cover in preparation for ploughing, but an unexpected nor'wester drove the flames towards the buildings, setting alight the many fallen trees and stumps that lined the river bank. Charlotte gives a graphic description:

Early Christchurch 1851, much as it was when Jane Deans arrived in 1853, probably sketched from an Alfred Barker photograph.

A tall dead tree, standing just between us and the corn ricks, caught fire ... then the sparks from that flew quite into the bush, before they could cut it down.

The men rushed about with pails of water and managed to fell some of the tallest burning stumps, but it was only the wind dying away that prevented calamity. That evening, as darkness fell, a puff of wind rekindled the fire:

In a moment, every stump and every clump of fern that had escaped, seemed in a blaze; the whole of the ground before us seeming covered with little furnaces, glowing brightly through the darkness ...

Despite the men's efforts, it was two days before the stumps stopped burning. All the potential firewood from the two fields was lost.

An exhausted Jane, confronted by the blackened residue of this fire, was made welcome by Mary Williams. A resourceful woman, Mary had managed the farm with some help from surveyor Thomas Cass when her husband died barely two months after John Deans had left for Scotland. When Jane and John Deans arrived home, Cass, whom Mary later married, was building her a house on her own land. As this was not yet complete, she stayed on at Riccarton for a while longer, much to Jane's relief:

I was very weak and useless, and preferred being the guest of, rather than the hostess to, Mrs Williams.

Next morning, a little revived by a glass of new milk in place of the tea she had not been able to tolerate since early in the voyage, Jane took her first look at the garden. Able to walk only with John's assistance, she enjoyed seeing the laden fruit trees and eating ripe plums, but mourned the gooseberries she had craved on the ship, the last of them picked a mere week before they landed:

How I did wish they had saved a bush for us when they knew we were expected so soon.

Before Jane had time to recover her strength, she had 'innumerable callers', eager to meet John's new wife and accustomed to open house at Riccarton. She confessed to being irked by their lack of consideration, and sometimes escaped to rest out of sight on the river bank when she saw visitors coming, leaving Mrs Williams or the housekeeper Mrs Wraight to look after them. But with a good cheese sent by Mrs Gebbie and a diet of fresh eggs and milk delivered every morning and evening, Jane 'soon got fat and rosy'. Even so, she did not regain her strength until after the birth of her baby. For the duration of her pregnancy, she was able to walk only as far as the island in the Avon, a few hundred metres at the most (no longer in existence, this island extended north of the Riccarton scout den upstream to about the Kahu Road–Totara Street corner). Neither could she stand the jolting of driving in the new dog cart on the rough, rutted roads.

It was some time before Jane Deans got her head around the domestic arrangements at Riccarton. Until their luggage was delivered and unpacked (which took several months), the furnishings of the cottage were spartan: an armchair kindly lent by Mrs Williams, several plain chairs fashioned from black pine, a double bed with feather mattress, a stretcher similarly equipped, and a small table with a drawer. The kitchen — housed separately in the ploughman's cottage and 'more under the control of the married couple' — was also scantily equipped. An open fireplace and camp ovens were still the only means of cooking.

During the ongoing process of clearing and improving new pasture, firewood was salvaged from the numerous stumps and logs — burnt and otherwise — still scattered throughout the farm (including the section of bush cleared by the settlers). The work was mostly let out on contract as a source of revenue, kahikatea yielding 10 shillings a cord and matai 15. For Riccarton itself, waste wood from the bush (top branches, often green and often wet) was mostly used to fuel the domestic fires. Jane gained considerable expertise in the art of drying wet wood by stacking it on end around the hearth:

It was no fun getting breakfast ready with such fuel. When dry, it made splendid fires, both hot and quick ... The roots always made better fires than the branches.

Although Mrs Wraight proved to be a good cook and housekeeper, and Jane was grateful to be able to depend on her, the sturdy fare at Riccarton was unsophisticated: potatoes, beef, mutton or pork, and the occasional fowl, supplemented by vegetables and fruit from the garden. The bread was stale by the end of the week, and that year the wheat was afflicted by smut:

Dark panelling inside Deans Cottage reinforced Jane Deans's sense of doom on her arrival at Riccarton.

*Consequently the bread was both black and bitter in taste, but I
never heard of anyone being the worse for eating it. It may have
been a tonic.*

Although the berry fruit was finished by the time John and Jane
Deans arrived in early February, the stone and pip fruit were soon
ready to harvest. The settlers had to be told firmly that they could
not continue to help themselves as they had been accustomed
during the previous two years, often as a Sunday excursion. Jane
had other purposes in mind for the surplus fruit. Jam-making
became a passion that was to occupy her throughout her long life.

She was only slightly more tolerant of another practice established
in John's absence. Church of England services had been held by the
Reverend Puckle in the cottage once a fortnight, and the couple
consented to their continuance for a few months, until the baby
was due:

*We had to hurry over breakfast, get the room arranged with a
white cloth on the table ... These Sunday gatherings were not, as
a rule, enjoyable to me ... knowing that some of the worshippers
had previously been helping themselves to fruit in the garden,
and had hidden it till after the service was over.*

It rankled even more when Jane asked for the services to be held elsewhere after baby John was born, only to find 'weeks and months went
past' with no other house being made available. Suspecting an attempt
to recruit them as Anglicans, Jane and John Deans no longer attended
'any of the churches', despite liking the Reverend Puckle himself as 'a
friend and a minister'. This was to be the first of several brushes with
Canterbury's Anglicans that would result in Jane recording many a
terse remark (see Chapter 11). It would be 1857 before a Presbyterian
church was built in Christchurch — St Andrew's Scotch Church —
with which Jane was to have a close and lifelong association.

Wonders in the superintendence

At the same time that Jane was finding her feet as the new chatelaine
of Riccarton, John Deans was busy inspecting what had taken place
during his year-long absence and initiating the improvements he
desired. After the sudden and untimely death of Theodore Williams
on 5 March 1852, the indomitable Mary Williams had resolved to

carry on with the management of both Riccarton and Homebush. She sought authority to do so from William Lyon, who was both a personal friend of the Deans brothers and acted as their Wellington agent in the sale of stock and merchandise. He promptly visited Riccarton and pronounced his satisfaction with the arrangement, writing to assure John that Thomas Cass was on hand to assist:

> *I am very glad to say that Mrs Williams at once agreed with me that she was the only person that could remain in overall management until your return; your instructions fortunately are so minute that no difficulty is likely to arise ...*

Thomas Cass had also written, reporting that all was satisfactory despite a poor season for the grain crops, which had been harvested and stacked but mostly unsold. In early April, the potato harvest began, using Maori labour as had become the annual practice at Riccarton. Cass reported that 18 Maori were employed 'beside two or three white men', supervised by Mary Williams. He did not expect them to dawdle over the harvest as they had work promised on a new road, but in the event the harvest took nearly three weeks.

It is Charlotte Godley who adds a personal touch to Cass's account of the 1852 potato harvest. The Maori labourers were living in 'a small encampment' nearby, and often spent their leisure time around the cooking fire lit outside the ploughman's cottage occupied by the Godleys. On noticing washing on the line, one of them enquired of Charlotte's servant how much it would cost to have some shirts ironed. Liking the reply, he promptly brought four shirts to be so treated, and an amused John Godley said he would ask his wife what she would charge. Always up for a challenge, Charlotte took the task on board at tuppence a shirt. Once the shirts had been re-washed, dried and starched, she ironed them herself and had them ready at eight o'clock, as promised:

> *... the man came back and paid me a copper eightpence that I am not a little proud of. Indeed, though I say it, they were so well done that I begin to think I have an undeveloped talent for laundry-work. You should have seen how beautiful the fronts and collars were, and not one button 'ironed off'.*

Although the Godleys were neighbours to Mary Williams during the months they lived at Riccarton that year, they seem to have kept to themselves. Charlotte makes no mention of Mary in her letters, and Thomas Cass says the Godleys 'were friendly, but not on intimate terms'. It was Mrs Puckle, the Reverend's wife, and a Mrs Earle who took turns to stay at Riccarton and keep the newly bereaved Mary and her children company.

The only issue that gave Mary Williams any concern was the management of the stock at Homebush. Robinson Clough and his two young sons were holding the fort more than adequately, living in a whare built out of timber transported there from the bush at Riccarton in December 1851. However, Clough was often bothered by the stream of visitors from the new settlement at times when he had little enough in the way of provisions for himself, his sons and the others working on the run. When his well-known and frequent bouts of drunkenness and resultant 'on the loose' behaviour were compounded by rumours about the 'undesirable' but unspecified misdemeanours of another stock hand, William Lyon and Thomas Cass appointed a newly arrived settler to oversee Clough and the operations at Homebush.

Despite these difficulties, Mary continued to provide firm but friendly guidance, sending advice on the garden and the occasional parcel of books to Robinson Clough. He himself remained loyal to the Deans family for the rest of his life. John Deans continued to rely on Clough's expert advice about cattle until he retired to a small cottage at Alford forest at the end of December 1853.

On John's return to Riccarton, he wrote to his father that he was much relieved to find he would not lose out on the value he had agreed with brother James for the stock, since that price was still holding. Although he would be forced to sell some cattle or horses to pay for the 1853 harvest work, now under way, and to cover customs duty and the costs of transporting their luggage to Riccarton from the port, he expected to do well out of that year's crops. Perhaps he was now regretting his uncharacteristic extravagance in London. Financial concerns aside, all in all, he professed himself well-satisfied with how everything had been managed in his absence:

Mrs Williams has certainly done wonders in the superintendence.

A great deal still to be done

John Deans wasted no time in getting on with his planned improvements. At Riccarton, the mill was his highest priority since he was expecting to get good prices for flour, so the mill lead was

To Mr Dean Esquire

Sir

I will undertake to Construct a dam across the river in a workman like manner to last for years I will find all Labour and Iron work, you to find Carting of materials and sawing of timber; for the Sum of £ s d 80-0-0 — 40 to be advanced while the work is in progress and the remainder when finished

2nd Sept, 1853   Singned Wm Wright

required 700 ft of 2 planks, 200 ft of 1 Board or slabs any widths will do

If you approve of this be so kind as send me a Copy with your Signature

excavated within a month of his return. At the same time, James Johnston, Christchurch's first commercial builder, was at work on the housing for the waterwheel and a new barn, using timber pit-sawn from the bush. Although both buildings were completed by May, the dam across the Avon for the millpond proved problematic. Three attempts were made to build a viable dam, but either the earthworks or the adjacent river banks burst each time. The strength of the current had been underestimated, and numerous submerged trunks on the bottom of the river needed to be cleared out before a proper foundation could be achieved. Eventually, William Wright took on the contract to build the dam, for the princely sum of £80. It was not completed until late spring, too late for threshing that year's harvest, which had to be processed elsewhere.

As well as the anxiety caused by the difficulties and disappointments with the dam, John Deans had been juggling the harvest itself, managing two trips by dog cart to Homebush to inspect his stock, and supervising the laborious retrieval of their shipped boxes. These had to be brought by cutter from the port around to Sumner and across the treacherous bar, then up the

Heathcote River to the newly built Christchurch Quay before being off-loaded onto drays. Although all 50 boxes reached Riccarton safely within two months, unpacking furniture and machinery was time-consuming and heavy work. He admitted in a letter to his father that he was grateful for the able assistance of Jane's cousin Douglas Graham, who had come on the *Minerva* with them. He now intended employing Graham as overseer at Riccarton for the next few years as the workload was too much for him on his own. Although he tried to make light of it, John was far from well, with a racking cough that had 'occasionally troubled me when at home'.

A later story attributes this cough to his being soaked by a downpour while crossing the Panama isthmus on his way to Scotland to marry Jane, but his own shipboard account records the ease of that journey by mule, in warm weather with a 'nice cool breeze', and his own 'very good health'. Whatever its trigger, by the time John returned to New Zealand, the troubling cough had become deep-seated. He had contracted tuberculosis. The seeds of the disease may have already been in his system, for he had alluded to feeling unwell before he left for Scotland:

> *I have not been in such good health for a few months back as I usually have. I am, however, getting much better, and I think the change of scene and sea voyage will do me good.*

During the rest of 1853, any medical treatment served only to relieve his symptoms temporarily, although he continued to insist he was getting better. There was a 'great deal still to be done' to achieve all the improvements he had in mind, and he anticipated that would take at least two more years of hard work. Jane's view of her husband's state of health was more realistic:

The sluice gate and the mill pond, photographed in the 1920s.

The waterwheel imported by John Deans in 1853 and still in use in the early twentieth century, photo taken at the time of its demolition in the 1920s.

We had only been a fortnight here when one morning, looking out of the window, I caught a glance of him standing in pain, that told me unmistakeably that he could never recover.

John's preoccupation with farm matters and finances continued to dominate his letters to Scotland. That year's harvest was selling well, despite John not being able to thresh their wheat at Riccarton. All the barley had been sold unthreshed to Wellington brewers and he intended exporting the oats to Sydney or Melbourne rather than deal with the Canterbury Pilgrims, as the settlers termed themselves:

The pilgrims are the worst payers I ever had to do with, and as soon as I can get them out of my books, I will steer as clear of them as possible.

Homebush-fattened cattle were fetching good prices, but John was holding off buying any sheep for James to stock his half of the run as planned. Few sheep were available and their prices were too high because of the demands of the gold diggings now under way in Australia. John's close attention to financial matters extended to the legal arrangement he had with his brother. He took care to ensure he would not have any of the issues over property that he had experienced with William. Soon after his return, he had the inland run formally surveyed, and by October his application for the farm at Riccarton to be granted in his own name had been forwarded to the Commissioner for Crown lands.

By late spring 1853, the new season's crops had all been sown, and prices looked to remain high as long as the gold diggings continued to provide a market. Although the diggings had siphoned off a lot of labour from Canterbury, and others were struggling to find workmen,

John Deans seems to have had no trouble recruiting good workers. Since his health continued to cause alarm, he now made arrangements for the management of his two properties. Douglas Graham was contracted to take over the management of the farm at Riccarton, and John Cordy was engaged for Homebush in December 1853 to replace Robinson Clough and his settler overseer. An older man, Cordy was an experienced Suffolk farmer with a capable wife and five children.

Later still, Cordy was given a seven-year lease for John's half of Homebush. The terms of this lease, signed in April 1854, were that he should look after the cattle, have the use of about 60 milking cows, and raise their calves. John's half of the station would therefore cost him 'near to nothing and yield a very handsome return for fat cattle'. Stocking James's half with sheep would still have to wait until prices and availability improved.

With his affairs satisfactorily arranged, John could at last divert some of his flagging energy to his life with Jane and the son she had safely delivered on 6 August 1853.

Joy and sorrow

Jane recovered quickly after baby Johnnie's birth, enjoying improved strength and dry spring weather after a wet autumn and winter. She records with some satisfaction that her first employment was making up 15 pairs of new blankets from woollen strips woven in Kilmarnock and packed in rolls for shipping on the *Minerva*. 'They are blue-bordered, with the seam up the middle.' She added that great care had to be taken as anything woollen could become flyblown if it was left outside after sunset — a hot iron being the only way to destroy the maggots.

This threshing machine was first used at Riccarton before being taken to Temuka, where it was photographed in 1861.

For a while, the small family was able to embark on excursions in the dog cart, Jane seeing these as a means of diverting her husband from working in the garden 'beyond his strength'. But after a consultation with Dr Barker in October, she was told that even in the better Canterbury climate, John might be spared only 'a little longer' than the six months he could have expected to live back in Scotland. At the end of October, their baby was christened by the Reverend John Moir, who held a first Presbyterian service for pioneer Scots in James Johnston's carpentry shop while he was visiting Christchurch. By then John Deans was already so frail that Jane stood close to him in the fear that he might drop the baby.

With John himself stoically insisting that he was improving, and Jane under firm instructions from the doctors to hide her own anxiety and remain cheerful, the next few months were difficult:

I tried … to banish the thought … the terrible thought that the desire of my eyes was withering like grass before them, and that nothing known to medical skill could arrest the quick march of the disease.

There were many times when Jane could not hide her grief and despair. Babe in arms, she would run to the kitchen at the ploughman's house where Mrs Wraight would without a word let her through into the bedroom for her 'to relieve my burdened heart and compose myself before returning to the house'.

As Jane had no nurse for Johnnie, the infant was with his parents constantly, providing his ailing father with 'pleasure and amusement' while he sat on Jane's lap or lay on the sofa alongside him. But John was soon not strong enough to hold his son for more than a few minutes at a time. He continued, however, to write home to Scotland at length about the farm's affairs and finances as though nothing much was amiss. In December, he reported his satisfaction with the new mill, working well now that the problems with the dam had been resolved:

Nobody here seems to have ever seen a thrashing machine of the kind … we can thrash as much in two hours as they [the standard portable threshers driven by oxen] *do in a whole day and with fewer hands.*

Summer 1853–54 was hot and the harvest was well under way when the bush was threatened by yet another fire, discovered by John on one of his short strolls. It spread to the bush edge through the grass from the Maori encampment, where the workers had left after dinner without ensuring their cooking fires were properly out. Fortunately, with many hands available to help extinguish it, the fire was under control before the wind rose. But 'some trees on the very edge were singed'. As a precaution against any further mishaps, the Maori workers were sent to make new huts on the island in the Avon for the rest of the harvest and the following potato season. Jane says in her letters to her grandchildren that, some years later, local Maori wanted to claim the island on the basis that it had been given to them.

Another mishap that loomed large in Jane's mind that summer was the loss of a sizable pot of precious blackcurrant jam, recommended for John's cough. Made late one day, the jam was left to Mrs Wraight to spoon it into the jars after Jane had returned to the house. Next morning, to her chagrin (and no doubt the housekeeper's), she had to be told that the lamp had fallen off the table into the pot. The whale oil contaminated the jam and it had to be discarded:

> *Fortunately there were plenty more black currants nearly ripe, but the accident was a terrible disappointment, for your grandfather* [John] *and I had gathered and prepared them all ourselves. I took care of the next lot.*

Early that autumn, John was well enough to attend a traditional harvest home, with a feast prepared on trestles in the 'old barn' (the first 1843 dwelling) for the workers as thanks for their hard work. After the baby was put to bed and left in the care of Jane's young housemaid, the couple joined the workers for an hour before leaving them to dance until dawn:

> *We heard some songs from them, drank their health in good whisky toddy, wished them a pleasant evening and retired.*

At the end of March 1854, William Lyon and his wife visited from Wellington on business. They stayed at Riccarton until the beginning of May. It was the start of a friendship for Jane that lasted their lifetime, 'being more of our own style of people than any we know here'. William Lyon was to serve as co-trustee with Jane, which was no doubt arranged during this visit. After the Lyons left, John discussed his approaching death openly with Jane for the first time. He had been quietly arranging his affairs for some months, but now it was time to talk of what the future would hold for his wife and her

infant son. Although John suggested she might be happier returning to Scotland, Jane resolved to stay on in Canterbury.

For the next few months, the couple now spent as much time together as they could, John on the sofa in the little sitting room, the baby on Jane's knee or playing on the floor:

We often sat for hours together, clasping each other's hands ...

John was not allowed to talk much so Jane read to him, often from the Bible, which was of great solace to them both. Whenever he was able, John continued to arrange his affairs: the lease of Homebush to John Cordy, arranging for a new house to be built for Jane, and instructions to Douglas Graham on continued improvements at Riccarton. One of his requests — perhaps mindful of the recent fire — was that the remaining bush at Riccarton should be preserved, a request that would be formalised after Jane's own death in 1911.

John's old friends the Hays visited from Pigeon Bay for the last time in late May, then Mary Gebbie arrived in mid-June to help Jane with Johnnie, then 10 and a half months old. By then John was too ill to leave his bed on the sofa in the sitting room. Several friends, as well as Douglas Graham, took turns to sit with him to give Jane some respite from her vigil.

John Deans died on 23 June 1854 with Jane beside him. He was only 34 (dying at the same age as his brother William), and Jane 31. They had been married barely 20 months.

Robert Park's poignant 1854 sketch of Jane and John Deans in the cottage a few months before his death.

• 7 •
Alone at Riccarton

Left on her own with a baby in a colonial country that was still new to her, Jane Deans was to spend the next 20 years overseeing the farms at Riccarton and Homebush that were her son's inheritance. Although she had the help of her co-trustees and able farm managers, looking after her husband's estate until her son came of age would prove a daunting task. Determination, intelligence and a strong sense of duty would help her through a great many difficulties, despite her own physical frailty. But she would pay a high personal price.

Jane Deans in c.1865, showing the stress of a decade of trusteeship.

Left in charge

Jane wrote in her letters to her grandchildren an often-quoted, heart-felt reflection on her feeling of isolation after the death of her husband:

May you never know what it is to be left alone (a stranger in a strange land among strangers, let them be ever so kind), with the charge of an infant to train for useful work here.

A thread of seldom finding good companions of 'our sort' runs through much of Jane Deans's writing. During the years of bringing up Johnnie, she seems to have never felt totally at home in Canterbury, and it is significant that the people she was most at ease with continued to be Scots and Presbyterian like herself. On his deathbed, John had given her the option of returning to Scotland to be with her family and friends, but she instead chose to stay on at Riccarton, surrounded by English and Anglican settlers. What possessed her?

In the back of Jane's mind, no doubt, was dread at the thought of such a long sea voyage. Her memory of extreme seasickness would still have been fresh and, to add to the difficulties, she would have young Johnnie to look after. She did mention her reluctance to undertake such a voyage to an aunt in Scotland. Her father tried to persuade her that returning was still her best option, and suggested various routes that would reduce the time she would have to spend at sea. But any such fears for her own personal discomfort are unlikely to have been her prime reason for staying.

Jane Deans had a well-developed sense of duty, instilled by her strict upbringing in the austere traditions of the Presbyterian Church in Scotland. She considered her greatest personal failings were the 'strong, wayward will, and rebellious nature' she had struggled to 'conquer and subdue'. An outsider might instead interpret these 'failings' as an independence of spirit and a forthright sense of fairness. Both such attributes are revealed by her writings and were perhaps recognised by her father when he left Jane to make up her own mind about marrying John Deans and migrating to New Zealand. It was to be those very attributes and her unswerving religious faith that gave her the strength to carry out what she saw as her duty and God's will.

Jane had spent her first 18 months at Riccarton observing her ailing husband steadfastly pursuing his ambition to develop a model farm and leave a valuable inheritance for his son, often to the detriment of his health. Who was she to abandon such heroic efforts? She would have thrust her own needs aside, thinking only

that she had an obligation to ensure her husband's dreams were fulfilled. Their son would receive his inheritance in the best possible shape she could achieve.

And that meant Jane Deans had no intention of leaving the management of the estate to the three co-trustees appointed by her husband, however capable and trustworthy: brother-in-law James Deans in Scotland (who owned half the lease at Homebush), William Lyon in Wellington, and William Brittan in Christchurch (in charge of the Land Office). With only adolescent memories of her father's management of Auchenflower to draw on, but an intelligence fostered by a sound Scottish education, Jane set about reading every document she could find that was relevant to both the lengthy wrangles over rights to land and the management of Riccarton and Homebush — no small task considering the Deans brothers had kept every scrap of paper.

In the meantime, Jane's cousin Douglas Graham continued with his efficient day-to-day management of Riccarton, and part of Homebush had already been leased to John Cordy. It was now agreed that one of her half-brothers, Hugh McIlraith, would come out from Scotland to assist her. When Hugh reached New Zealand in 1856, he was accompanied by his brother George, and they were soon joined by James (who had been in Australia for some years). The plan was for Hugh to set up the inland sheep station by leasing James Deans's half of Homebush, paying an annual rental and borrowing money from him to buy the initial sheep needed to stock it. The terms of this lease later became a source of friction between the McIlraiths and James Deans, and a considerable worry to Jane, caught in the middle between her brothers and her brother-in-law.

The stackyard at Riccarton about 1860, when grain crops were still a large part of the farm's production. The dwellings in this view are the 'old barn' (far left), the ploughman's cottage or farm kitchen (centre) and Deans Cottage (right), with a low farm building between it and the stackyard.

Until her brothers arrived, Jane soldiered on alone through 1855, already experiencing some tribulations that did not make her life easy. Work had begun on building the new house at Riccarton that John Deans had planned for her, with all the difficulties this entailed (see Chapter 8). When the loyal married couple at Riccarton, the Wraights, left in early 1855 to farm on their own account, the pair chosen by Douglas Graham to replace them did not meet with Jane's liking. John McLachlan was 'an old man', although suited to the farm work, and his wife was 'anything but nice'. Jane's maidservant left after falling out with Mrs McLachlan, so Jane was having to do her own housework. The casual labourer she employed to handle the heavy winter work in the garden 'took the world easy'. He abandoned the work before it was complete, leaving Jane to prune her precious gooseberry bushes herself. It was not until August that she was able to engage new immigrants recommended by John Hay and immediately liked by her: Annie Asher as her maidservant and William Hislop as her gardener. Annie stayed with her for several years, and Hislop later became a nurseryman in Christchurch.

Companions and calamities

Whenever possible after John's death, friends stayed with Jane at Riccarton to keep her company, doing 'their best to cheer me up and encourage me in my responsible undertaking'. Throughout the next 20 years, she was to continue finding it difficult to be alone, apart from her current maidservant and her growing son. Her letters often refer to her loneliness during that time. Yet a constant stream of friends came to spend days or weeks with her whenever they could. Mary Williams (now Mrs Cass) and her grown daughter Mrs Innes, Mary Gebbie, the Reverend Charles and Jane Fraser, the Lyons and a Mrs McDonald, whom Jane refers to as 'my New Zealand mother', were among them.

In that first difficult year, William Lyon made several trips from Wellington to visit Jane, eventually bringing his 10-year-old daughter Grace to keep her company in the cottage until her brothers could arrive. Before long, he also left his seven-year-old son Willie with her. The care of lively children as a cheering distraction may have been his motive for doing so, but red-headed Willie soon proved a disastrous responsibility.

Jane found him 'a difficult boy to manage', and she 'could not keep him away from the river'. In February 1856, Willie was playing

near the bridge with John Pierce, the son of one of the harvesters. No sooner had Jane turned her back to fetch vegetables from the garden for dinner than the two boys fell into the river, dangerously swollen and muddy after three days of rain. Summoned by a frantic Grace, Jane ran to the sluice. She plunged in, thinking she could see Willie's red head floating down the river towards her. But it was merely the Noah's ark the boys had been playing with. Both boys had already sunk below the surface. They drowned before the farm workers could reach them.

A distraught Jane sent Grace home to Wellington in early March. Mary Gebbie came to stay with her to help with the move into the new house, far from finished but now habitable. The move was urgent as the McIlraith brothers had reached Melbourne and were expected any day. The three-roomed cottage could not possibly accommodate them as well as Jane and Johnnie.

The plan was for the cottage to now become the home of Douglas Graham. He was expecting the arrival of his bride-to-be, Helen Eaglesome, who was coming out from Scotland. Once Jane had moved into the new house, the McLachlans were directed to clean the cottage thoroughly in preparation for its new occupants. As he was about to sweep the chimney, John McLachlan was seized by a violent pain in his side, requiring urgent medical attention in the form of a 'fly blister'. His alarmed wife's reaction served to reinforce Jane's disapproval and dislike of her:

The pond above the sluice gate where Willie Lyon and John Pierce drowned in 1856.

The ploughman's cottage, where the unsatisfactory McLachlans were living 1855–56.

His wife thought he was going to die, and instead of attending to him, thought fit to scrub out the other house for Mr Graham, and made so free with his whisky ... that by the evening she was mad drunk, and it took four men to put her to bed beside her poor husband ...

Next morning, when Mary Gebbie and Jane called at the ploughman's cottage to enquire after McLachlan's health, the woman was still in bed, still drunk and belligerent. Her husband, 'lying with his side uncovered, showing the raw flesh where the blister had been taken off', was trying to pacify her. Jane had to send her maid Annie to cook for the farm workers, while she and Mary Gebbie fended for themselves.

The shock of such a sight and its aftermath was too much for Jane, coming so soon after the boys had drowned and the stress of her own shift into the unfinished house. She collapsed, possibly with some sort of nervous breakdown that she described as 'one of the worst illnesses I ever had'. After Mary Gebbie left, the Frasers stayed with her for several months, overlapping with the arrival of Hugh and George McIlraith in May 1856.

Jane's joy at the welcome presence of her young half-brothers was immediately tempered by foreboding. Hugh, aged 20, had caught a cold that threatened to settle on his lungs, and it was not until the spring that he regained his health.

In September, the brothers rode out to the Malvern Hills to assess the new sheep run and plan a site for a house, the timber for it to be delivered by dray from the bush at Riccarton. Jane and Johnnie accompanied them in the dog cart, and stayed at Homebush with the Cordys for a second time (they had visited with William Lyon and his children the previous year). Not long after their return to Riccarton, James McIlraith arrived from Melbourne. For the next two years, one brother at a time would stay with Jane at Riccarton for stints of three months, the other two carrying on the work of setting up the sheep station.

James's arrival coincided with Jane's planned trip with Johnnie by the new steamer *Zingari* up the coast to Wellington to visit the Lyons, and the brothers insisted she continue with her plans. While she was away in Wellington for several weeks, she wrote a long, sisterly letter to her brothers that exhorted them to 'all get on as well as you can like good children'. Patronising perhaps, but excusable — she was after all at least 10 years old when James was born, and George, the youngest of the three, was still barely 18. Jane was already taking an active interest in the farming operations (keeping her own detailed stock record books from 1854 to 1874), so she gave them specific directions about the grazing of the stock at Riccarton. As well as these directions, her letter included detailed domestic instructions about laundry, groceries and meals since her brothers were looking after themselves in the new house at Riccarton:

> *There is plenty of bacon hanging in the kitchen, boil some of the cheeks or fry some of the side hams. There is also the beef ham, cut it in two and soak half of it in fresh water two days before boiling it. Let it boil slowly five hours and leave it in the pot till the water is cold. It eats better that way.*

With the boost to her morale provided by the constant company of one of her brothers (young George soon a favourite with Johnnie) and a successful stay with the Lyons in Wellington (although the steamer had proved no solution to her seasickness), Jane's spirit of adventure returned. She had the energy to embark on many excursions with Johnnie over the next few years, leaving some vivid accounts of her adventures.

Adventures and excursions

In March 1857, Jane, Johnnie (now three and a half), her brother George, the Frasers and two young women set out from Lyttelton in a whaleboat to visit the Hays at Pigeon Bay. Delayed at the port by a strong northeast wind and a heavy sea, they waited until late

afternoon for the sea to calm down. The boat was overloaded with passengers and luggage so the steersman was forced to sit with his legs over the stern. They were not far beyond the heads when he got cramp, and one of the young women bravely took over until he recovered. When they then encountered 'a jumping sea' off Port Levy, George manned an oar to help retired whaler Tom White row. By that stage, most of the passengers — including Jane and Johnnie — were violently seasick. It was well after dark before they at last landed at the Hays':

> We were a helpless lot, but they spared no pains to make us comfortable. I remember Mr Fraser (who suffered most) lying on the sofa in the sitting-room, your father [Johnnie] and I lying together on the floor till after tea, when we revived and sat up, but it took Mr Fraser all next day to recover.

After two pleasant days enjoying 'kind, warm-hearted hospitality', they left in calm conditions for the return trip. All went well until the boat was beyond the shelter of the bay, where they:

> ... met a strong sou'wester coming up which raised the sea

Pigeon Bay looking towards the heads, painted by Theodore Hurt c.1869.

tremendously, and we had to keep almost within an oar's length of the rocks all the way round to prevent being blown out to sea.

Only Tom White's seamanship and calm head kept them out of serious trouble, but they had to pull into a small cove once safely inside the Lyttelton Heads to give the exhausted oarsmen an hour's rest. Although they escaped the worst of the storm (the wind, thunder and lightning being more severe on the plains), their adventure was not yet over. The boat nearly capsized at the landing beach, causing observers on nearby ships in the port to wonder what madness had induced them to venture out to sea on such a day.

Later that autumn, Jane and Johnnie, accompanied by Jane Fraser, embarked on a less risky adventure, visiting the McIlraith brothers at their new house (named Te Pukiti Marama) on the sheep run, recently stocked with 1000 sheep. The undeveloped run was still 'very rough — all fern, flax, toitoi and tussocks'. The brothers had made some rustic furniture and their mattresses were stuffed with tussock. Since the visitors had brought their own blankets and other necessities with them in the 'commodious' dog cart, they were quite comfortable. They stayed an enjoyable fortnight, taking long walks over the hills:

I daresay the dressmakers were glad to see us back as we needed a new 'rig-out'… the rough fern fringed our dresses quite a finger length deep round the bottom.

A less comfortable return trip to the run in spring involved helping James rake tutu roots from the garden patch in preparation for

planting. The sandflies were bad, and their 'faces, hands and necks [became] a mass of red lumps, which were very painful'. Sheep had been camped on the patch over winter to kill the fern and manure the soil — a successful strategy. Everything grew so fast that the brothers had plenty of vegetables that summer and 'in two years they had abundance of fruit, strawberries, gooseberries, currants and peaches'. The journey home was cold, with hail showers, so the travellers were glad to take refuge from one in an old sod hut, Jane describing the experience with aplomb:

We lit a fire and made some tea in a billy with water from the wheel ruts. It was delicious.

But it was not long before fate dealt Jane Deans another unkind blow. In November 1858, George McIlraith was killed in a riding accident at the sheep station. His death meant she could no longer have the constant company of one of her brothers at Riccarton. As her new house was some distance from the farm houses, she often felt isolated.

Homebush photographed by Alfred Barker in 1863, with Robinson Clough's whare and yards in the foreground and the house built in 1854 by John Cordy adjacent to an extensive tree nursery and vegetable garden.

Even though Douglas Graham and his wife Helen would come to stay overnight with her whenever she expressed the need, Jane was again beset by loneliness. The company of her current maidservant Margaret Patrick was not enough. Jane was often unwell:

Not being very strong, the strain of loneliness was becoming too great for me, and there was no one in the place that I could have permanently as a companion, though seldom without someone.

Changes on the estate

In the midst of so much tragedy (those four deaths in less than five years), the alarms accompanying many of her excursions, her valiant attempts to keep young Johnnie active and occupied in his preschool years, and her own frail health, a lesser woman of her class in the mid-19th century would have retired permanently to bed. Jane Deans was made of sterner stuff. She continued to have a direct input into what was happening on both farms.

Much to Jane's relief, John Cordy asked to be released early from his seven-year term managing the cattle station at Homebush — she had been expressing misgivings about his stewardship for some time. James McIlraith took over the cattle station in 1859, leaving Hugh to look after the sheep station with the help of a married couple. Jane attended the handover of the cattle herself, driving up with Johnnie, then nearly six, to be joined in the dog cart by Mrs Cordy:

... we sat and saw the muster of the cattle on the Selwyn side, between Glentunnel and Coalgate, one day, and those on the other (Waimakariri) side another day. Over five hundred head in each mob. It was a fine sight ...

James McIlraith employed a married couple to run the Homebush dairy for him, but Jane was soon 'summoned in haste' to sort them out:

Every utensil had been allowed to go sour. They knew little about cleanliness and nothing of their work.

Experienced in dairy matters from her growing-up years at Auchenflower, Jane advised sacking them, then gave James a book on cheese-making so he could oversee the process himself, which

he did successfully for a year. But, eventually, the dairy venture was abandoned as keeping the cows in without fencing was too much trouble. By now the last of the McIlraith brothers — Alexander — had arrived to join James and Hugh. He worked at both Homebush and Riccarton wherever needed until he found a permanent position on Haldon station.

Any profit made on either property during these years (topped up by continued financial contributions from James Deans back in Scotland) was now used to freehold run land or make improvements on land that was already freehold. By 1874, nearly 11,000 acres (about 4400 hectares) had been freeholded at Homebush.

At Riccarton, James Johnston had been continually employed with his workers between 1853 and 1860 to build new barns, sheds and stables, as well as the new house. Improvements were made to the mill race, a new culvert was built and the bridge was strengthened. New machinery was bought — in keeping with John Deans's expressed desire that Riccarton should continue to be at the forefront of farming in Canterbury. Jane had developed a good eye for stock, so breeding for quality meant both cattle and sheep from the Deans's properties continued to have an excellent reputation throughout Canterbury. Southdown ewes bought from England by the trustees in 1862 became the basis of a well-known stud flock at Riccarton. Exhibits of stock and produce from Riccarton regularly won prizes at the Canterbury agricultural shows, which were held each year from 1862 onwards.

During the early 1860s, prices for wool and sheep meat were high. As a result, when in 1864 the McIlraith brothers fell out with James Deans for a final time over the terms of their lease of the sheep station and asked to have their interest bought out by the trustees, their agreed proportional share of the carefully evaluated improvements, stock and freehold land amounted to a tidy sum. Indeed, such a tidy sum that James Deans, who had provided most of the finance needed for the development of the sheep station, felt hard done (if not deliberately duped) by the McIlraith brothers. He wrote his sister-in-law Jane an uncharacteristically stiff and unfriendly letter that must have caused her added grief. Perhaps James's displeasure was partly motivated by the considerable cost to the Trust — and therefore to his nephew's inheritance — incurred by this settlement with the McIlraiths. He promptly sailed to New Zealand to check for himself that all was in order. The initial valuation done by John Caverhill was modified as a result, but the payment to the brothers of £14,000 was still a considerable drain on the trustees' resources.

The McIlraiths bought a station at Culverden with the proceeds, then Hugh moved there to manage it with his new bride — none other than Grace Lyon, now aged 19 or 20. James McIlraith stayed on at Homebush, where he managed both parts of the station. As part of this joint management, he began the gradual switch from cattle to sheep that had been recommended in Caverhill's valuation report.

At the time of Hugh's marriage in June 1864, Jane was dealing with yet another crisis. Ten-year-old Johnnie had contracted scarlet fever, an often fatal disease. As a result, she was unable to travel to Wellington for the wedding. Johnnie was not a robust child and suffered frequent illnesses that required him to take time off school. Jane must at times have despaired of ever raising him to adulthood, when she could hand over her responsibilities. Yet her letters to her grandchildren are full of the social events in which she and Johnnie took part with evident enjoyment. Among these were a royal commemoration in 1863 to mark the marriage of Albert, Prince of Wales, a royal visit (the Duke of Edinburgh) in 1869, frequent dances and parties, visits to the McIlraiths at Culverden and regular holidays at Homebush, further trips by steamer to Wellington (despite continuing seasickness) to stay with the Lyons and the Parks (Robert's friendship with William Deans had now extended to widowed Jane), and numerous forays to visit her oldest friends on Banks Peninsula and throughout Canterbury — all of them Scots.

Throughout the 1860s, Jane Deans's load of duties and activities continued to increase. As well as her determination to provide Johnnie with a full and stimulating upbringing, she was actively involved in local Presbyterian affairs — the new St Andrew's Church built in 1857, the associated Boys' High School run by Charles Fraser, and the purchase of land for a Presbyterian cemetery. She was busy trying to bolster the financial viability of the estate during the onset of what was to be a lengthy depression in agricultural fortunes. As well as struggling to keep the peace between her warring brothers and brother-in-law over the sheep station lease, she was also having to prevent ever-recalcitrant city officials from disputing Riccarton's boundaries and encroaching on Deans's land for drains and roads. At the same time, the Trust was embarking on what was to be a lengthy legal dispute over the lease of Riccarton land to William Wood for his flour mill, which had caused trouble with the mill's neighbour (HB Johnstone) over the diversion of water for the mill. All of this required her to maintain lengthy correspondence with co-trustee James Deans for legal advice as

Jane Deans with Johnnie, aged about 10 years, c.1863.

well as keep meticulous records so she could fight her corner, which she did with firmness but unfailing courtesy.

By the end of the 1860s, this load was exacting an enormous toll on Jane's health. Plans for her to take Johnnie, now 15, to Scotland to complete his education were abandoned on the advice of her doctors. Instead he stayed on at the Presbyterian-run Boys' High School in Christchurch to the end of 1869, then joined a firm of solicitors as an articled clerk, leaving 18 months before he came of age. Jane's visit to Homebush in 1871 to inspect the newly discovered coal seam (which was later developed into the family-owned coal mine at Glentunnel) was the last she would make for some years:

> *From the visit to Homebush in 1871, I was not strong enough to risk the fatigue of the journey until spring 1874, so that many of my pleasant visits to old friends had to be discontinued.*

A spate of deaths among her oldest and most loyal friends further sapped her strength. During 1870 and 1871, Mrs McDonald (her 'New Zealand mother'), Robert Park, James Johnston (the builder) and several others all died. Then in March 1872, her cousin and faithful manager at Riccarton, Douglas Graham, also died, suddenly and unexpectedly of a heart attack during an operation to amputate a little finger that had been damaged in a horse accident. His wife Helen, weak and yet to recover from a severe illness, was devastated. It was Jane who bore the brunt of tending her through the early stage of her grief:

> *Mrs Graham stayed with me for about three months after her husband's death. She was dreadfully broken down in health and spirits. I don't think during all that time anyone could mention her husband's name in her presence without calling forth a flood of tears.*

The new Scottish church, St Andrew's, built in 1857.

At that time, operations at Riccarton were already changing because of the depressed prices for grain crops (by 1874 only 3 per cent of the estate's income was coming from crops). With Douglas Graham's death only a few years out from Johnnie's taking over of the estate and little enough time or money to employ and train a new manager, it was all too much for Jane:

> ... *my health not being robust enough at that time to look after everything properly* ...

James McIlraith took over managing both Homebush and Riccarton for her, with the assistance of James Webster, the Riccarton overseer. For the last few years of the trusteeship, the farm at Riccarton was kept merely ticking over to reduce running expenses, with crop cultivation restricted to what was needed to feed the cattle and sheep brought in from Homebush for fattening. Jane remembers that 1873:

> ... *was spent much as usual, looking forward, sometimes with hope, not unmingled with fear lest any other untoward event should occur before delivering up our charge and giving an account of our trusteeship to your father* [Johnnie], *the heir.*

A ball held at the Land Office in December 1852 to celebrate the second anniversary of the Canterbury settlement.

· 8 ·
House and Garden

Along with Deans Cottage, Riccarton House and its woodland surroundings would become evidence of the Deans family's progressive contribution to the social history and heritage of Canterbury. First built in 1856, Riccarton House would undergo three main phases of construction, with two of these taking place under Jane's command. The main plantings of the extensive grounds around the house would also take place during those years. The array of now-protected heritage trees still growing here are survivors of one of New Zealand's earliest colonial landscape plantings.

A suitable family home

The sturdy cottage built in 1843 by Samuel Manson for the bachelor Deans brothers was inadequate as a home for a family of standing in a colonial community. Before John left for Scotland to fetch his bride in 1853, he was already talking of a new house being needed at Riccarton. He chose a site upstream from the farm cottages that, like them, overlooked the Avon River with the shelter of the bush behind. Although the site was prepared before John died, no start had been made on building a more suitable house for his wife and child. Early the following year (1855), with the knowledge that her McIlraith brothers would be coming to expand her household, the recently widowed Jane hastened to get the house under way. She may also have been influenced by the growing number of substantial houses already being built in Christchurch; it would not do for Riccarton to be outclassed by English latecomers.

It seems that house plans had not been decided on before John died. Jane and her advisors, with the help of James Johnston (the builder already doing substantial work on the farm buildings), drew up plans and specifications for a modest two-storeyed house, comprising parlour and morning room (with a marble mantelpiece), lobby, kitchen (with brick oven and boiler) and two bedrooms downstairs, with more bedrooms, a 'jam closet' with shelves and a bathroom upstairs. Of this house, what survives today are two rooms upstairs (Jane's bedroom and the night nursery), and two down (the morning room and back parlour). Jane was to occupy this bedroom throughout the rest of her long life, and the morning room remained her favourite place in the house.

Although the original plans mentioned by Johnston in his detailed specifications and by Jane in her letters to her grandchildren have disappeared, much can be determined from the specifications and Jane's own description of the house construction.

All the timber for the weatherboard-clad house was sawn from Riccarton Bush and stacked on the lawn to season. The sawyers caused Jane to lament:

There was frequent trouble with the sawyers in the Bush. There was no means of preventing them from wastefully destroying fine trees that might have remained standing. They usually clear all before them.

Framing for the house was black pine (matai), and the weatherboards

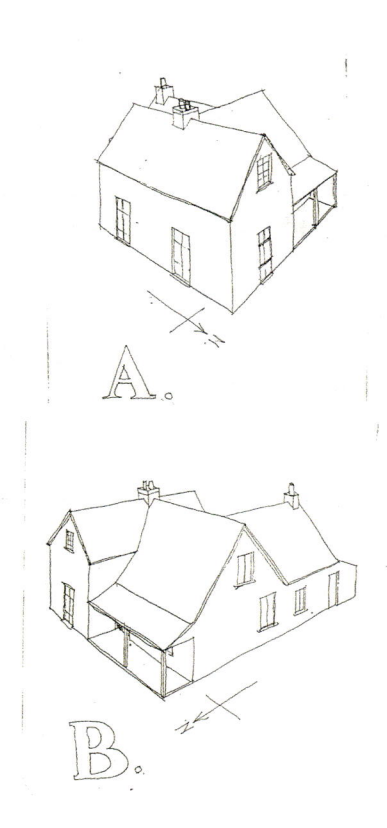

were kahikatea. The roof covering was made from shingles of 'sugarloaf white pine' (kahikatea) split in the bush. Six doors, including the front door, and four French windows were bought from John Watts Russell, imported from England and surplus to requirements for his own house at Ilam. The other doors and windows were made to match from totara cut from the bush. Flooring was close-fitted kahikatea planking, one inch (2.5 cm) in thickness.

The site was marked out for concrete foundations, then trenches were dug to a depth of 12 inches (30 cm). The foundations were to have an above-ground height of nine inches (about 22 cm). The gravel to make the concrete was brought by cartload from the Avon below William Wood's house. Jane tells of a mishap with a horse that backed its load into the river beside the house site and nearly drowned, requiring the muscle of half a dozen men to extricate it and the heavily laden cart. Lime for the concrete was unavailable so Johnston and his team gathered shells from the beach at Sumner, then burnt them in a kiln dug into the riverbank near the stables. The kiln was filled with alternate layers of shells and matai logs, the fire then being left to burn out before the lime was scraped out through a hole dug lower in the bank:

The odour from it was not always pleasant, but it had to be done, and there was no use fretting.

Jim Espie's sketch plans of the profiles of the 1856 house built for Jane Deans.

The new house painted from the east by an unknown artist in the early 1860s, seen across lawn, shrubberies and a circular flower bed, with Riccarton Bush beyond the house.

Bricks were hand-made on site in a newly cleared corner near the bush, then baked in long, shallow pits after being sun-dried for a few days. Rows of bricks were alternated with matai logs, then once the fire was lit and burning well, the pits were covered in earth to keep the heat in. Sand for mortar probably came from the Waimakariri riverbed. The exterior walls of the house were brick-

Riccarton N Z
Dec 27 1863.

nogged (Scottish brick-knagged); the outer weatherboards being lined with brickwork built up between timber frames. Internal partitions were also specified as being lined with brick, but an exposure in the morning room shows the internal walls ended up being lath packed with clay.

Downstairs, interior walls and ceilings were finished with lath-and-plaster. Despite the walls getting two coats of 'best plaster' and the ceilings three, Jane reports difficulty getting enough horsehair to bind the plaster:

> *At length half a sackful was got to do the whole. A touch would make the walls crumble. The* [wall] *paper has been a great support to them.*

Some of the wallpapers were those John and Jane had brought with them on the *Minerva*. James Johnston paid close attention to the workmanship, doing much of the finishing work himself. Timber linings used in the passages and roofs were finished to a high standard that met with Jane's approval:

> *He took great pride in making it look nice.*

The house photographed from the drive by Alfred Barker in 1863, with the hawthorn hedge that bordered the garden well into the 20th century.

The house took over a year to build. Expecting her brothers to arrive any day, Jane moved in on 7 March 1856 when it was far from finished. Her large wardrobe and boxes for the bedrooms upstairs had already been hauled up through the upper window spaces before the windows were installed. Downstairs, not all the doors or windows were in place, and seasoned planks for the floors had run out. Fortunately, it was possible to acquire the floor of a pavilion that had been built at the Royal Hotel for a ball during Governor Gore Browne's visit to Christchurch that January.

Jane's premature move into the house was partly to hurry the tradesmen along (they finally left in mid-April), but it may also have been partly precipitated by the Maori potato harvesters. After the house gained its roof, they burnt their huts on the island in the expectation they would be allowed to occupy the new house:

> *I stood firm in resisting their petition to do so, but allowed them the use of the 'old barn'* [the first cottage] *till they erected other huts down the riverbank near the* [eventual] *railway bridge.*

This 1856 house stood amongst an established garden and orchard, plantings that had been initiated soon after the arrival of the Deans brothers in 1843.

Establishing a garden

For John and William Deans, planting a garden with fruit and vegetables was an early priority, as it was for all colonial settlers. They wasted no time in clearing approximately one hectare of ground in the lee of the bush (behind the site of the 1856 house). Their first sowing of a variety of vegetables was flourishing there by January 1844 (see Chapter 3). They were also busy grafting a great many fruit trees, some of which were successfully planted out in 1846. It is likely that slips for these fruit trees were sourced from Sydney nurseries at the same time John acquired their first farm stock in 1843 (see Chapter 1). The following summer (1847), the brothers were able to pick quantities of fruit:

> *We have this year more than a dozen apple trees loaded with fruit, a good many plum, cherry and peach trees, all with more or less fruit, and a great many young ones coming on.*

One of the fruit trees planted in 1846 is still flowering and fruiting today — a Durondeau pear (labelled Tree 19). This is now the oldest exotic tree in Christchurch and one of the oldest fruit trees in New Zealand. Other survivors from this first orchard are a huge Jargonelle sugar pear planted in 1850 (Tree 23), and two other pear trees.

This garden and orchard were protected by a paling fence, with a hawthorn hedge planted inside that, which grew 'astonishingly fast'. Throughout the next few years, the canny brothers continued raising as many fruit trees as they could, intending to sell any surplus trees to the Canterbury settlers they expected to arrive any day.

At the same time, the brothers set about acquiring stock of the ornamental trees considered appropriate for a gentleman's estate of the times. Late in 1848, brother James in Scotland was asked to send them a selection of seeds of English trees, although in the event these did not arrive until the end of 1850. As well as haws to establish hedges, the selection comprised seven pounds' weight (about 3 kg) each of seed from Scots fir, larch, spruce and alder, and four pounds' weight (just under 2 kg) of birch. As John explained to his father, as with the fruit trees, any surplus would be:

> ... a great thing in the early stage of settlement. If they grow well we will have a good chance of disposing to advantage of those we don't require for ourselves.

Some oak trees were already planted at Riccarton: gifts from Sir George and Lady Grey during their stay at the cottage in 1849. Progeny from these trees provided most of the oaks grown later at Riccarton and Homebush, as well as many others throughout Christchurch. Three of the 1849 oaks still survive in the grounds at Riccarton House today (Trees 7, 8 and 9). Known to the family as 'Cape oaks', these may have been English oaks naturalised at the Cape in South Africa. As Cape Town was on the shipping route, it became a common source of horticultural specimens brought to colonial New Zealand. Charlotte Godley refers to this practice:

> Those settlers who came out in ships touching at the Cape, generally brought supplies of flowers and shrubs from there, and they all do uncommonly well, and even bear the wind pretty well, which the roses do not.

The oaks were not the only connection between the grounds,

The oldest exotic tree in the Riccarton grounds, the Durondeau pear planted in 1846.

Governor Grey and South Africa. Sir George took a continuing interest in Riccarton, sending the brothers a hive of bees and promising to send seeds and plants from Auckland. When Bishop Jackson (the Canterbury bishop-designate with whom John Deans had hoped Jane would travel out to New Zealand) made a hasty return to England in 1851, he gave Sir George (by then Governor at the Cape) a list of trees to send to the Deans brothers. These duly arrived in a Wardian case at the end of July 1851. Sealed terraria constructed of wood and glass, these cases were designed to help living plants survive the long journeys on 19th-century sailing ships. They were used extensively to import plants to Christchurch in the early 1850s, and there is an example on display in the visitors' centre in the Botanic Gardens. Although Jane Deans later reported that most of the plants sent from South Africa had survived and done well, none is alive today. As well as ornamental trees, they included semi-tropicals like oranges, guavas and loquats.

When the Godleys arrived in 1850, ahead of the Canterbury settlers, Charlotte took advantage of the ever-obliging Deans brothers and their well-cultivated ground at Riccarton:

> [The Deans's garden] *which stands between the bush and the river, is most flourishing, and in it we planted half of all our English seeds, most fortunately, as the other half, sown here* [Lyttelton], *have all of them failed. It is unusual for them to grow at all here, but ours have a good many of them come up at Deans'.*

Surveyor Charles Torlesse likewise planted seeds at Riccarton in winter 1850, planting the rest at the Godleys' and Dr Donald's in Lyttelton. He also intended planting more 'tree and other seeds' at Riccarton, after finding an apparently mislaid box of seeds 'by the merest accident' — Torlesse's habit of losing his possessions (see Chapter 4) seems to have continued.

Certainly, the Deans brothers expected to benefit from exchanging some of their stocks of plants for other useful seeds brought by the arriving settlers. It is likely that this practice of swapping seeds and plants contributed to many of the gardens being established early in the settlement of both Lyttelton and Christchurch. Establishing a garden and becoming self-sufficient in food production was seen as a priority and a duty, encouraged by both the Canterbury officials and editorials in the first local newspaper (*Lyttelton Times*). By early 1852, there were already 60 acres (24 hectares) of fenced garden in Christchurch.

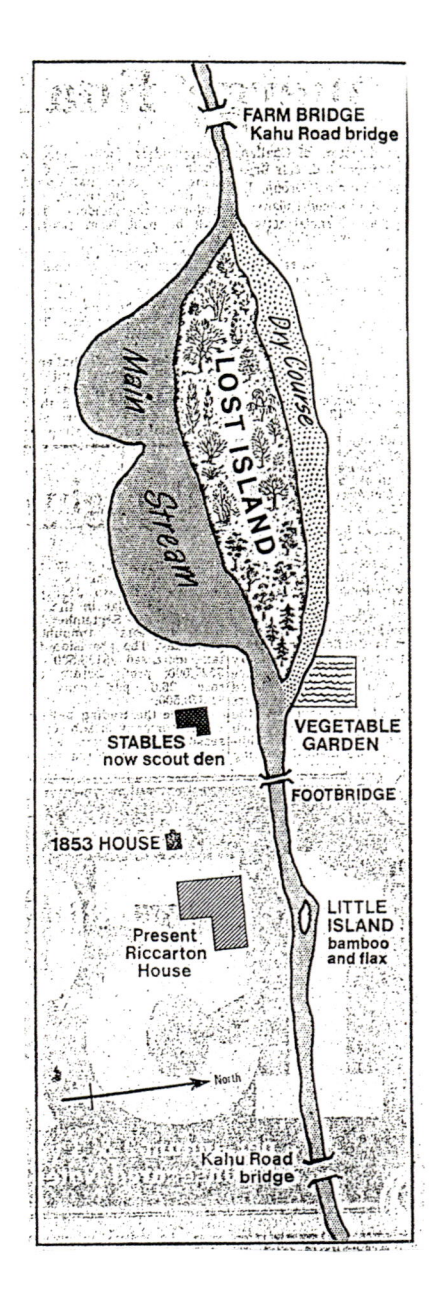

Sketch map of Jane's 'island' printed in *The Press*, 8 November 1979 (see p. 140).

Before John Deans left for Scotland in 1852, he added willow and poplar slips to the expanding tree nursery at Riccarton. By then at least some flower seeds had been planted at Riccarton, by either the Deans brothers, Charlotte Godley or Charles Torlesse. Canterbury agent Henry Sewell, visiting Riccarton on his arrival in February 1853, mentions 'a pretty little bit of flower garden'. Perhaps John had planted a decorative bed in anticipation of his bride's arrival (they had returned on the same ship as Sewell), but Jane herself mentions admiring only the fruit trees on her first walk in the flourishing garden.

The Deans brothers' garden was a welcome sight for arriving Canterbury settlers, who visited in droves. The success of the garden at Riccarton, particularly the burgeoning orchard, encouraged wavering settlers to persevere with their own efforts to establish gardens. Garden historian Thelma Strongman would later claim, with some justification, that this first productive garden at Riccarton was probably the most significant of any garden in the history of gardens in Canterbury.

Passionately fond of planting

Planting was also one of Jane Deans's many preoccupations during the 20 years of her own management of the estate. The transformation of the grounds at Riccarton during her years in charge both reflected and contributed to the social and cultural changes that were taking place in Canterbury in the second half of the 19th century.

After John's death, Jane inherited his nursery of young pines and Scots fir. Although her early attempts at planting these out were mostly unsuccessful as many succumbed to blight, she had acquired a considerable knowledge of tree-planting from her father at Auchenflower. She went on to plant a great variety of trees at Riccarton.

At the time, tree planting was seen to be a gentlemanly occupation and the growing of flowers the province of a lady, but flower gardens do not feature in any of Jane's letters. She seems to have left such plantings to Willie Hislop (her first gardener) and his successors. The watercolour of the house painted in the early 1860s does show a circular flowerbed typical of Victorian gardens, and splashes of colour along a border may have been roses. But it was trees, not flowers, that interested Jane. True to her independent spirit, she set

about pursuing this interest.

With the expert help of Willie Hislop and with an eye to her son's inheritance, Jane continued the transformation of the south-eastern area between the bush and her new house into grounds that would befit a gentleman's estate. Many of the trees planted in this area were conifers, forming a type of 'gardenesque' arboretum that was popular at the time. Based on Scottish landscape gardener John Loudon's ideas, specimen trees were planted as spaced individuals set amongst groomed lawns, emphasising the art of the gardener in contrast to natural vegetation. Most of the heritage ornamental trees still growing in the grounds at Riccarton were planted in this style under Jane's direction from the mid-1850s to the late 1860s. As well as half a dozen unusual conifers, these include the rare weeping lime south-east of the house (Tree 27, planted in 1855), the huge blue gum near Deans cottage (Tree 15, planted in 1857) and the magnificent English elm near the entrance to the grounds (Tree 2, planted in 1867).

Further plantings were made throughout the 1870s and 1880s, many oaks among them. As well as purchases from nurseries, both local and Scottish, some seeds or seedlings were provided in 1873 by John Armstrong (curator at the Botanic Gardens 1867–89), and others came from a collection of seeds provided by the Canterbury

One of the many English oaks (Tree 24) planted by Jane Deans on the south-eastern side of the house to create a 'gardenesque' arboretum.

The biggest exotic tree at Riccarton is this blue gum (Tree 15) near Deans Cottage, planted by Jane Deans in 1857.

Museum in 1876. A local reporter visiting for *The Press* in 1878 noted that Jane's custom of planting a tree to commemorate every event was perpetuating local history in the plantations growing up around the house. In 1882, Jane herself claimed that over 100 varieties of trees had now been planted at Riccarton, with a success rate of 80 per cent, giving substance to her comment that:

I am passionately fond of planting ...

Somehow, amid her many and onerous duties managing the estate and bringing up young Johnnie (see Chapter 7), Jane Deans also found time to design two ambitious planting programmes to 'beautify the property'. The first of these was planting the island in the Avon in 1865 to represent the history of Canterbury. Patterned and patriotic plantings were not an uncommon feature of Scottish gardens of the time, but Jane added her own interpretation in extending this concept to represent the social elements of colonial Canterbury. Her design for the island was inspired by it being 'shaped like the shadow of a tree':

I made the narrow end the root and planted it with Scotch and other firs and pines, and evergreens, as the so-called prehistoric

The drive planting, c.1905.

settlers (those who were here before 1850). A straight trunk was planted with bluegums: these were to stand for the runholders and Australians to give backbone to the branches which were planted with oaks, elms, ashes and sycamores as the farmers and other settlers, and some ornamental trees and shrubs round and round to represent the professional and other ornamental people.

Well-pleased with the overall effect of the 'masses of different colours together', Jane reports that this planting was pretty when young. To her evident gratification, it was much admired by the Duke of Edinburgh when he visited in 1869.

Both the planting and the island have long since vanished. For many years, the location of this island, so often referred to in the Deans's letters, was something of a mystery. But in 1979, garden writer for *The Press* Rosemary Britten pinpointed its position in the Avon with the help of one of Jane's grandsons, Douglas Deans, then aged 90. Bounded on its northern side by a dry channel, the island extended upstream from near the present site of the Riccarton scout den (north-west of the house) to near the junction of Kahu Road and Totara Street.

The success of Jane's representation of Canterbury history spurred her on to design a complicated, triangular-shaped plantation near the drive in 1867. This was to be both her 'masterpiece in the art of planting' and her 'memorial as a Scotswoman'. Wanting trees with foliage that would reflect the colours of tartan, Jane used crisscrossed lines of sycamores, elms, ashes and silver birches, filling the squares with oaks:

The remains of the drive planting, possibly in the 1920s.

It cost me a great deal of thought and many sleepless hours at night how to manage to bring out the colouring of the checks of tartan with trees to make them blend.

An outer border of firs, pines and silver birches represented Great Britain on one side of the triangle, with a corresponding border of gums and wattles representing Australasia on the other, meeting in a planting that reflected the colours of the associated patriotic flags. According to Jane, the colours were greatly admired by travellers on northbound trains when the plantation was at its peak of health and vigour, but thinnings and diseases meant it never quite achieved the look she wanted.

The drive itself, originally extending as far as the junction between Riccarton Road and what is now Straven Road, was lined with a backing of gums, poplars, Scots fir and silver birches, with limes and shrubs in front. Two years later, in 1869, the drive was formally opened by the Duke of Edinburgh, coming to take part in a pigeon shoot on one of the Riccarton fields. Unfortunately, as the drive trees matured, the gums and poplars had to be removed as they 'robbed the other trees of their sustenance' and created too much winter shade. Eventually, only the lime avenue was left. This still lines the entrance to Riccarton House today.

Keeping up appearances

Like all houses, Riccarton House needed maintenance and repairs from time to time. During a repaint of the weatherboards in 1867, it was discovered that the kitchen chimney was badly cracked and would have to be pulled down. In common with today's experience, Jane comments that tradesmen had to be 'taken when they could be got'. Unfortunately, the work coincided with an unexpected visit from Sir George and Lady Grey. The Governor was keen to see how the oaks he had given William and John Deans in 1849 were faring. With only a few days' notice (and this indirectly on the Friday via the newspaper), Jane was faced with having to deal with bare floorboards in the parlour and undressed windows, as well as a shambles at the back of the house. Dust from the dismantled chimney lay thickly, and the end of the passage was exposed both to the kitchen and the outside in preparation for adding on a lean-to pantry:

I had to hang up a tarpaulin at the foot of the stairs ... It did not look very picturesque, but I had nothing better.

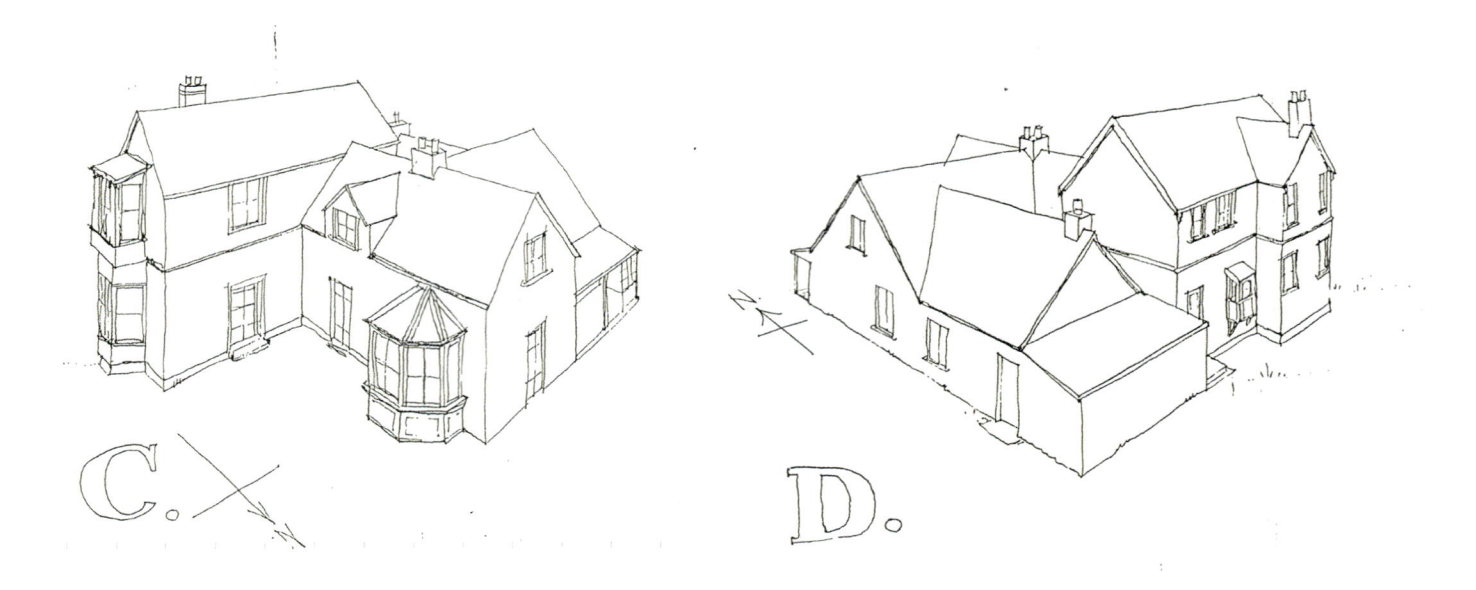

At least the man hastily booked to come to lay the carpet in the parlour and hang blinds on the lower windows duly turned up early on the Monday and completed his work at midday before the Governor's party arrived. But the other tradesmen, having just finished demolishing the chimney, were on their way to wash in the river as the regal party walked around to the back of the house, so had to be hastily 'ordered elsewhere'.

Sir George and Lady Grey enjoyed their visit, and admired the 'state of preservation' of the old cottage, now lived in by the Grahams. But Jane was embarrassed by the untidy paths (she was without a gardener at the time) and the rough vehicle access to the house (this was before the drive planting had begun). To add to her chagrin, a tactless Sir George sent a message back from his next port of call (Wood's mill) to say that Wood had 'a prettier place ...'

With Johnnie's coming of age looming in 1874, and the expected arrival of James Deans from Scotland for the occasion, Jane arranged for more extensive alterations to the house than the lean-to pantry added in 1867. Built to the south-east of the existing structure, the addition included a dining room and bathroom downstairs, and an extra bedroom and new bathroom upstairs. A dormer window was installed in her own bedroom and a bay window in the parlour downstairs. The work began in March 1874 and was finished in June — a bare week before her brother-in-law arrived:

Of course, the plaster was too damp to occupy these new rooms then, and we had to be content with the old.

Jim Espie's sketch plans of the profiles of the 1874 additions to Riccarton House.

Worse, being preoccupied with ensuring the estate was in good order and preparing for the celebrations to come, Jane had uncharacteristically left both the plans and the construction in the hands of an architect (William Marley) and his builder (probably George Rankin since many payments were made to him at this time). She was to regret her misplaced confidence in these necessary substitutes for the excellent but now-deceased James Johnston. Not only was insufficient headroom allowed for above the new stairs, requiring an awkward 'table contrivance' in the new, first-floor bathroom — something like a raised cockpit hatch — but also the timber used throughout the addition was inadequately seasoned and the workmanship was rough.

Nevertheless, this expanded 1874 stage of Riccarton House, with its ornate fireplaces, high ceilings and bay windows, was a suitable reflection of the substance and solidity acquired by the Deans's estate during the 20 years under the admirable Jane's capable management.

Riccarton House after the 1874 additions, seen from the drive in the 1890s.

• 9 •

A Gentleman's Estate

The coming of age of John Deans's sole heir would be celebrated with a grand public ceremony in the grounds of Riccarton House. It was not an inheritance to be entirely envied: the heir was young, the expectations were onerous, the times were tough, and his capable, disciplined mother would be a hard act to follow. But the new owner of Riccarton and Homebush had a social position to uphold and farming ambitions of his own, both of which he would pursue with diligence.

John Deans, the squire of Riccarton, 1881.

Handing over the reins

Soon after James Deans arrived from Scotland (his second visit to New Zealand) to attend young John's coming of age on 6 August 1874, the trustees belatedly decided it would be both appropriate and proper for some sort of semi-public celebration to be held in honour of the occasion. The proprietor of the Langham Hotel, JW Morton, was hastily commissioned to provide a handsome, sit-down luncheon for 200 guests, to be held in a marquee provided by him and erected on the lawn between the house and the bush. Morton also supplied the necessary waiters, table linen, crockery, glassware and cutlery. Jane was well satisfied with his efforts:

There were only ten days to do it in, but it was splendidly done for those days, when gatherings of that sort were less common.

It was certainly the grandest affair that had ever been held at Riccarton — and possibly in Christchurch at that time. Jane, writing about it for her grandchildren years later, recalls the celebrations in detail and with some pride. After the worry of three days of rain beforehand, the day itself dawned 'calm and bright and warm'. The day before, the men at Riccarton had worked hard to get the marquee up, and all was ready for Morton and his staff when they arrived early on 6 August. Cabbage trees had been planted on either side of the drive entrance, in keeping with Jane's habit of marking any commemoration by planting trees, and flags were flying. The guests all arrived on time, with much shaking of hands:

It gave me an idea of what a Governor's lady has to perform when holding a levee.

As the senior member of the Deans family present, James Deans took pride of place at the head of the table, with nephew John seated on his right, and sister-in-law Jane on his left. William Lyon and Thomas Duncan acted as 'chairmen' for the occasion, Charles Fraser said grace, and Archdeacon James Wilson gave final thanks. The main toast to John's health and prosperity was made by William Lyon, amid much cheering. John's brief and modest reply was greeted with acclaim, according to reports in the local papers (in a rather modern fashion, press reporters had been invited to attend as well as John senior's old friends and 'all ranks of the people').

The food itself was 'sumptuous', in Jane's words, and the menu reads like that for a medieval feast: meats, pies and poultry, including two 'splendidly dressed' boar's heads; jellies, tarts, cakes and pastries; fresh and dried fruit, and sweets and nuts. A large birthday cake on display at the head of the main table was cut and distributed among all the guests. Champagne, hock and sherry were on offer.

The luncheon was followed by a dance in the house that evening for about 50 people 'to warm up the new dining room'. The dancing was opened by Jane herself, performing a Scottish reel in partnership with Robert Wilkin, a family friend, stock dealer and landowner. Supper prepared from the luncheon leftovers was served by one of Morton's waiters.

The next day, repeat celebrations, including the 'speechifying', dance and supper, were held for current and previous farm workers and their families. Less egalitarian in her outlook than William and John Deans, Jane had not included them in her 'all ranks of the people'. This time, John took his place at the head of the table, presumably as his father's newly anointed successor.

For three nights, the house was full to overflowing with guests, some of whom Jane considers must have slept three to a bed or on the floor. The following week, on a warm nor'west day, a picnic feast was held for Riccarton's Maori employees under the trees in the plantation. The food for this was prepared at Riccarton, and the leftovers were given to the guests to take home. Jane was impressed by the impeccable manners of their Maori guests:

> *Lots of speeches expressing friendship with the family, etc., were made. They all sat round in a circle, and as each was helped he put down his plate until all were served. Then they sang a hymn and said grace most reverently.*

After these subtly and carefully structured social celebrations, everyday life at Riccarton resumed, but with the major difference that John Deans was now the head of the house instead of his mother. The trustees formally signed over the estate properties and assets to him, signalling the end of 20 years of their trusteeship. For Jane Deans, it was with overwhelming relief that the burden now passed from her shoulders. She confessed to her grandchildren:

> *Little did I think what I was undertaking when your*

grandfather [John senior] *gave me my choice of remaining here or returning to Scotland after his death.*

Although Jane claimed never to have regretted the decision she made, it is with characteristic piety that she took little credit for the consequent successful raising of her son to maturity or the satisfactory fulfilment of the trustees' duties:

> *It is of no use trying to describe the feeling of thankfulness I felt to my Heavenly Father for His great kindness to us both, in times of joy and sorrow ... for bringing us to such a happy consummation of such a long trusteeship ...*

It is not possible to recreate young John's feelings on now being in charge of a considerable estate, surely daunting regardless of — or perhaps because of — the long and focused efforts to prepare him for the role. The lavish and community-attended celebrations of his coming of age would have endorsed any feelings that his subsequent performance would not only be judged by his mother and the other ex-trustees but also inevitably be the subject of public examination and assessment.

John would not be left entirely to his own devices. At Homebush, he had the assistance and advice of his uncle James McIlraith, who had been manager there since 1859 and would remain so until 1895. At Riccarton, he had his mother on hand. But both had strong personalities and their own ideas about the future of the estate. According to Ian Deans (John of the third generation), great-uncle James McIlraith's kindness was balanced by a sarcastic tongue and a temper that was not always under control. Jane was highly intelligent with a firm grasp of the history of the estate and its management — and she adored the son for whom she had worked so hard and sacrificed so much.

John, by all accounts, was both shy and reserved and may well have been intimidated by his mother and uncle's high expectations of him. At the same time, his upbringing would have given him a sense of entitlement. Any decision he made and any direction he took during his management of the estate would inevitably be influenced by these two driving forces: expectation and entitlement. As a result, he would not always make the most prudent decisions for the difficult economic times in which he found himself.

A dynasty in the making

No doubt pressure of sorts, whether subtle or blunt (including that 1874 extension to the house), was soon brought to bear on John to marry and secure the continued succession of the Deans family. In 1879, he married Catherine Edith Park and set about achieving precisely that. Over the 17 years from 1880 to 1897, the couple would produce 12 children — eight of whom, satisfyingly, were sons.

Catherine Edith, usually known as Edith, was surveyor Robert Park's daughter, born to Marion Park in Wellington in 1856. With a father frequently absent on survey duty, two much older half-sisters (Robert's surviving children from his first marriage), and herself with an older brother and younger sister, Edith had grown up to be a capable young woman with a mind of her own, a sense of humour and practical organising skills. John Deans, who had known her from early childhood, may have seen her as the perfect foil to buffer his mother's continued influence and expectations of him. Many years later, Edith was to tell grandson David Deans that the only reason she married John was to 'even up the score a little' after a childhood incident in which he had succeeded in pushing her off the verandah at Riccarton House. This humorous comment alone would suggest their marriage was affectionate and far from merely functional.

Robert and Marion Park and their children had been frequent visitors to Riccarton in the years since John Deans's death. Marion, the same age as Jane Deans and from a good family with Scottish links, was surely a compatible companion as she was 'exceedingly pleasant in her manner, and … very clever and well educated', according to her Wellington friend Susan Strang. But flamboyant Robert Park seems an unlikely person to have won Jane Deans's wholehearted approval. Perhaps being a Scot was sufficient endorsement, and he did have a good singing voice (she liked nothing better than an evening filled with song). He was one of William Deans's friends from early Wellington days, and Jane had first met him during his visit to Christchurch in 1854, not long before John died. She certainly knew nothing of his colourful past, and probably neither did John.

By the time Jane met Robert, it was some years after his short-lived relationship with Terenui, Te Puni's relative, which took place between late 1848 and 1850. Not uncommon a liaison at the time between a European man and a Maori woman, this was probably an informal marriage and not sanctified by the church since no official record of it has been found. Neither Marion Hart, who arrived in

Robert Park, surveyor, artist and long-term Deans family friend.

New Zealand in late 1850 and married Robert Park in September 1852 after a year-long courtship, nor his two daughters from his first marriage were aware of this relationship, or that Robert had two children from it. Robert himself may not have known that Terenui died shortly after the birth of their son in December 1850. He seems to have had no contact with these children, who took his surname but were brought up by their Maori relatives. Robert's survey duties did mean he was mostly absent from Wellington during that time. It would not be until 1939 that the Maori connection with Robert Park resurfaced in public — and nearly another 50 years before the Deans family and other Park descendants openly acknowledged it.

Any lingering whiff of scandal would have subsided by the time Jane Deans visited Robert and Marion Park in Wellington while she was staying with the Lyons in 1856. The oldest child from their marriage, Robert (known as George), was a similar age to her John, and baby Catherine Edith had just been born. The following year, the Parks paid a return visit to Riccarton, bringing the children

Robert Park with his third wife, Marion, probably mid-1850s.

with them. Robert's two adolescent daughters were about to attend Mrs Thomson's recently opened Christchurch Ladies' School.

Jane was at first dubious about accommodating them all. She already had guests staying, including Helen Eaglesome and her brothers (awaiting her wedding to Douglas Graham), and was without a servant. Robert assured her they were quite capable of bedding down anywhere, having once 'slept under a flax bush'. Jane's brothers gave up their room for the Parks, and she ended up enjoying their visit:

> *He* [Robert Park] *was very merry, and we had such jolly evenings, songs all round … We had only the parlour for meals, but it was quite wonderful how elastic it was, and how good-naturedly people took what they got in those days.*

Everyone looked after their own bedrooms, Jane did the cooking, except for the bread (made by Willie Hislop's wife), and Marion Park and Helen Eaglesome helped her wash up.

Jane Deans liked nothing better than a musical evening, enjoying several such evenings with the Park family on their first visit in 1857.

The two older Park girls went on to spend many holidays at Riccarton while at school in Christchurch. In 1860, fiery Robert Park finally fell out with officials in Wellington and lost his job as provincial chief surveyor as the result of a series of letters in which he expressed unwelcome opinions in sarcastic terms. By 1862, he had moved Marion and his family to South Canterbury, where he leased his brother-in-law Robert Hart's sheep run at Winchmore, as well as taking on substantial southern survey work. The friendship with Jane Deans continued, and she and young John visited Winchmore on at least one occasion.

By 1869, John Deans and George Park were both senior boys at Christchurch Boys' High School. Edith and her younger sister were at Mrs Thomson's finishing school, now known as Avon House, following in the footsteps of Robert's two older daughters, who had since married. Presumably, Edith and her two siblings continued the tradition of spending holidays with Jane and John at Riccarton.

After a short illness, Robert Park died in 1870, aged 58, and Marion eventually returned to Wellington with her two daughters. It was during a visit back to Christchurch in 1878 with her mother that Edith became engaged to John Deans. Later that year, she spent several months in Christchurch, helping her younger sister during her first pregnancy and after the birth. Her own wedding took place in the new St Andrew's Church on the Terrace in Wellington in June 1879. It was a small but glamorous affair, the bride and her five bridesmaids in elegant satin or silk gowns of the latest fashion and wearing silk caps and gold jewellery that were gifts from the bridegroom. Twenty-four guests — all relatives of bride or groom — attended the wedding.

In her letters to her grandchildren, Jane Deans, who writes so fulsomely of her son's coming-of-age celebrations, makes no mention of his wedding a mere five years later. As the mother of just the one child and so early widowed, Jane may well have found it difficult to see her precious son move away from her sphere of influence into that of a young woman of such undoubtedly strong character. That from now on she would share her house and domestic responsibilities at Riccarton with her daughter-in-law must have caused at least some awkward moments until the two of them found an acceptable compromise. Perhaps it took the arrival of several grandchildren in quick succession, starting with Ian (the third John Deans) in June 1880, before Jane became wholly reconciled to the new regime at Riccarton.

The young couple, John Deans and Catherine Edith Park, after their engagement in 1878.

The squire of Riccarton

It seems unlikely that John Deans would have had the temerity to intervene in any tension between his mother and his new wife. By all accounts, including the family's own memories of him, he was a man of few words and not one to show his feelings. He was not physically robust, like his mother being prone to 'low fevers' and gastric upsets. That in his earliest years at school at least he had been subject to bullying can be surmised from Jane's comment in her letters to her grandchildren:

> *At first he only took a sandwich with him, which the other boys frequently took from him, and he would come home faint with hunger and headache.*

Although John had plenty of male relatives as role models in his formative years — his McIlraith uncles upcountry, Douglas Graham at Riccarton, and his uncle James Deans in Scotland — his mother was undoubtedly the dominant influence in his life. Like Jane, he remained devoted to the church, conscientiously dutiful and modest in his behaviour throughout his lifetime. He also took his cue from her in matters of deportment and dress, always being conservatively clad and sporting a style of semi-clerical collar and stock long after it went out of fashion.

It is not surprising perhaps that early in John's marriage to Edith, forthright Robert Hart (Marion Park's brother) expressed a lukewarm opinion of him in his weekly letter to nephew Douglas Maclean in England, a contemporary of his other nephew, George Park, and John Deans:

The first crop — the Deans family in 1889. Robert aged five or six, on rock at the back, next to the nurse holding baby William. Marion aged eight on the left, Ian nine, Catherine three, and James four.

I would not like to see you resemble the Laird of Riccarton. He is all very well in his way but to speak the truth is not by temperament or training fitted to perform the duties of a man of his property and stake in the country.

Admittedly, Edith's uncle acknowledged that he was dyspeptic when he wrote this and modified his opinion — slightly — in another letter to Douglas Maclean the following year, when John and Edith were leaving on a trip to Europe and England in July 1881. Baby Ian, barely a year old, was to stay behind at Riccarton:

The Squire of Riccarton and his wife are going to England leaving the heir in charge of his two grandmas [Jane Deans and Marion Park]. *I am heartily glad of this as he* [the Squire] *is to my mind one who may under wise guidance be made a good deal of but who's* [sic] *training hitherto has been altogether* [naïve?] *for the position which wealth makes it a duty upon him to assume. From what I saw of him at the wedding I believe him to be possessed of very good qualities.*

It is as well that Jane knew nothing of Robert Hart's disparagement of her dedicated efforts to raise her son to be well-equipped to manage his estate. And appearances can be deceptive. In the matter of securing the succession, John Deans soon proved his virility — and Edith her productivity. Ian was followed in quick succession by Marion (1881), Jane Edith (1883, who died in infancy), Robert George (1884), James (1885) and Catherine (1886). After a short respite until 1889, over the next eight years Edith duly produced

John Deans upcountry with John Wason, a friend of the McIlraith brothers.

William (1889), Alexander (1890), Douglas (1892) and Colin (1894), then, in a final burst, Violet (1896) and Stuart (1897).

While Edith was being kept fully occupied with pregnancies, babies and small children, John found time to enjoy some of the pursuits that befitted a Victorian gentleman of his standing. He was a keen fisherman, with trout released by an enthusiastic acclimatisation society now flourishing in the Avon on his doorstep, but his real skill was as a marksman. Many days of shooting were enjoyed at the upcountry station, where bags of ducks, pukeko and hares were joined by the more challenging targets of wild cattle and pigs. Some of these excursions included his sons as they grew old enough, but it seems likely that John was very much an austere and somewhat remote Victorian father figure, held in awe by his children who, in Ian's words, seldom questioned what he said.

On working days at Riccarton, John always carried a revolver with him to deal with any dogs that might be molesting his sheep (a problem that had beset the farm at Riccarton from early days). On one occasion in 1882, being confronted by an armed intruder skulking in Riccarton Bush, who promptly fired at him, hitting him twice (in the ribs and shoulder), John had the presence of mind to return the fire. Although badly shaken, he was not seriously injured. The incident received full coverage in the local papers, with implied indignation that a man of his status should be so treated. The culprit, a well-known criminal who had stashed stolen jewellery in the bush, was captured six weeks later, after John offered a reward of £200, and was sentenced to 14 years in prison.

A keen horseman, having ridden ponies in early childhood before progressing to horses, John Deans had the unusual skill of being a crack hand with a stock whip, which he was equally adept at using in either hand. His son Ian was to write:

> It was a revelation to see him on horseback cutting out cattle from a milling mob.

More sedentary gentlemanly occupations were, at the lightest level, playing an excellent game of whist, and at a more serious level serving on various boards of organisations, mostly related to the business of farming — the Canterbury Frozen Meat Company, the Central Dairy Company, and the Canterbury A & P Association. In keeping with his solid sense of social duty, John also served on the Canterbury College Board of Governors, the Christchurch Drainage Board, and, of course, he was fully involved with the affairs of St Andrew's Church.

As well as his early trip to Europe and England with Edith, in 1900 John made another similar 'pleasure trip', this time taking his oldest daughter Marion, now aged 19 — presumably as a type of coming out. Father and daughter were away for well over six months, travelling to Scotland via America with a visit to Yosemite. The trip included three days spent at the Paris Exhibition.

Pleasure trip this may have been, but John spent much of the time away investigating export opportunities for frozen meat and, as on his earlier trip to Britain with Edith, looking for breeding stock with an eye to further improving the stud herds and flocks he had been consolidating at home. Other trips had been made earlier to Australia for the same purpose. Although he clearly found time throughout his life to ensure his social standing as 'squire of Riccarton', John Deans's main preoccupation over the nearly 30 years of his reign was undoubtedly managing the estate to the best of his ability.

Marion Deans in 1900, shortly before her overseas trip with her father.

Managing the estate

At the time John Deans took over the estate, prices for wool were high and future prospects seemed positive. So positive that during James Deans's visit for the coming-of-age celebrations in 1874, he leased his half of Homebush to his nephew for three years at the princely sum of £1000 per year (later reduced to a more manageable annuity of £500, payable for James's lifetime). Although within the term of that initial lease, wool prices dropped steadily on the London market, the process of replacing the Homebush cattle with sheep (as recommended by John Caverhill's 1864 report, see Chapter 7) had been completed by 1876. From then on, the previous system of fattening Homebush cattle at Riccarton ceased, and the two properties were run more or less independently.

Leaving the day-to-day management of the sheep station and other Homebush ventures in the hands of his uncle James McIlraith, John Deans focused his own attention on the farm at Riccarton. He set about establishing a herd of pedigree Shorthorn cattle and a stud flock of Lincoln sheep, as well as improving the existing flock of pure-bred Southdown sheep first introduced by the trustees in 1862. From Jane, he had inherited a good eye for stock and a keen interest in stud breeding.

By the time John married Edith Park in 1879, he had already imported some expensive bulls and cows from Australia to add to the genetic potential being provided by a 'celebrated bull' with the incongruous name 'King of the Butterflies', acquired from Otago.

Cows at Riccarton, with Deans Cottage on its original site (right background) and the ploughman's cottage on the left.

Locally sourced, pure-bred Border Leicester sheep had been added to the flocks of Southdown and Lincoln sheep. The main purpose of the trip with Edith to Britain two years later, no matter in what social terms it may have been couched to her, was to acquire a prime bull that would enable him to establish a Shorthorn stud at Riccarton, which would, according to *The Press*, become 'the envy of the colonies'. Moreover, on his return an ambitious John expressed the hope that the splendid bull he had bought from the Wetherby herd in Yorkshire at vast expense would produce progeny that would 'ere long rival the celebrated Wetherby herd'.

Such an ambition had necessitated the earlier purchase, in 1880, of several pedigree heifers of sufficient calibre at equally substantial prices. During his time in England and Scotland in 1881, John Deans also bought two magnificent rams, one a Border Leicester, the other a Southdown, and five pedigree ewes of each breed, all of this precious cargo needing shipping back to New Zealand. He was spending thousands of pounds on pedigree stock at a time when wool prices were low and the overseas market was continuing to be stifled by a long slump. The frozen meat trade, which would boost earnings from both Riccarton and Homebush, would not be under way for a few years yet (carcasses from both properties were among the first shipments from Canterbury in 1883–84).

To a great extent, John was financing these purchases by selling off land. He was able to take advantage of a land sales boom in 1878–88, selling a 30-acre (12-hectare) paddock at Riccarton (between

James McIlraith (left), manager at Homebush, and brother Hugh, c.1900.

the railway line and Hagley Park) to be subdivided for residential purposes. Some of these sections fetched £900 an acre. Although a report in *The Press* a few years later claimed a boastful total of £29,000 was achieved from this sale, according to family records many of the sales fell through and much of the land was resold later for 'very poor prices, some as low as £40 for a quarter-acre section'.

It was not only the pressures of a slumped wool and meat market that continued to beset John Deans. In 1885, he bailed out an improvident Hugh McIlraith (in serious financial strife and in debt to both his nephew and his brother James McIlraith) by taking over his uncle's latest miscalculation, Broom Park. Renamed Waimarama, this sheep run was initially in poor condition, and John would exert a great deal of time and anxiety on its improvement. The two non-farming enterprises established at Homebush by James McIlraith, the coalmine and the brickworks, had become a constant drain on finances rather than the profitable ventures anticipated. An ailing James McIlraith retired in 1895, so John Deans was obliged to take on a closer managerial role upcountry. The constant travelling by rail and open gig to and from the two sheep stations in all weathers sapped his energy and eroded his already far from robust health. Added to his growing financial worries were a new brick homestead planned for Homebush and expansions needed at Riccarton to accommodate his now large family.

Sales of stud stock, although lucrative, were insufficient to cover the shortfall. With debts continuing to mount, John Deans felt obliged to sell more land, both at Homebush and at Riccarton. In 1896, a further 150 acres (60 hectares) of the Riccarton farm were offered

for sale. According to *The Press*, the demand for residential sites so close to the city now meant the land was considered 'too valuable to be used for rearing stock'. Only a few years later, the Mona Vale block was also sold. The combined sales since 1878 reduced the farm at Riccarton to less than half its original 400 freehold acres. Inland, the freehold land shrank from over 23,000 acres (9300 hectares) to about 19,000 acres (7600 hectares) (Homebush and Waimarama combined) in the 10 years from 1892 to 1902.

Towards the end of 1898, a considerable boost to John's finances was provided by James Deans in Scotland. Aware that his nephew was now dealing with substantial debt, he sent him a generous gift of £8500 (part of the proceeds from some land sales of his own in Scotland), with the proviso added a month later that the money should not go towards relieving John's debt burden:

> It [the money] *was solely to serve you and your family — not provide a fund out of my means for the satisfaction of your creditors ...*

Later that year (1899), John accordingly commissioned Robert William England, a notable Christchurch architect, to design a major extension to Riccarton House that would double its size. No one could argue that a larger house was sorely needed to accommodate his family. But John Deans also pushed on with other expensive projects that surely were less justified: commissioning plans to build a brick homestead at Homebush, taking his daughter Marion on the 1900 extended 'pleasure trip' to England and continuing to spend money on new pedigree sires for the now much smaller farm at Riccarton. Perhaps John could see signs that the poor economic conditions were at last about to improve. What he could not foresee was his own premature death in 1902 before any upturn in his fortunes could be realised.

John Deans's flock of Southdown ewe hoggets, at Riccarton c.1895.

· 10 ·
Victorian Splendours

Over the nearly three decades John Deans managed his inheritance, he would consolidate his family's presence and impact on the Canterbury landscape by embarking on several ambitious building projects, both agricultural and domestic. These projects would crown a built legacy that has ensured the Deans family a place in New Zealand's architectural history.

Building in brick

Between 1883 and 1885, John Deans replaced the old farm buildings at Riccarton with a substantial brick 'steading' more suitable for the housing and feeding of his burgeoning pedigree Shorthorn cattle herd. With his use of brick rather than timber, he was following the example of his uncle James McIlraith.

Since the 1860s, James had been building in brick at Homebush; some of it fanciful, like a lookout on the top of Little Racecourse Hill, but most of it functional. A brick stables built in the early 1870s was modelled on simple and practical structures he would have known in Scotland. It comprised stalls for draft horses, separate stables for riding hacks, a carriage house, and a vaulted loft for storing chaff and hay. James then built a magnificent brick structure to house and operate a special water-driven turbine he imported from America in 1879. The turbine drew water from the nearby stream through an underground brick-lined tunnel, and another tunnel drained the water away. James used this turbine to drive various types of farm machinery and to pump water to the homestead. The same year, he commissioned the distinctive, Romanesque-style, 20-stand brick woolshed that today is still the building most people associate with Homebush. More modest brickwork extended to pigsties and sheep dips, a laundry, dairy and bakehouse, and several Roman-style bridges. Many of these structures used bricks made in the family brickworks at Glentunnel.

At Riccarton, John Deans was not to be outshone by his McIlraith uncle's efforts at Homebush. The new brick steading became the most up-to-date complex of its type in Canterbury. Stable, barns and cattlesheds were followed by stock yards and a whole range of ancillary farm buildings that covered all the activities needed to manage his stock and house his increasing acquisition of innovative farm machinery.

The famous Romanesque-style woolshed built at Homebush in 1879.

Although conservative in his personal habits, John Deans was always at the forefront of trying new equipment and approaches that would improve farming efficiency. He trialled various harvesting machines, mechanical gorse-cutters and drain ploughs, and imported Canterbury's first Wolsey machine-shearing plant in 1888. Threshers, chaff and mangold cutters, grain crushers and other machinery needed to produce high-value, steam-processed nutritional feed for his stud stock were all driven by the power generated with the waterwheel imported and installed by his father in 1853.

The previously muddy yards were paved with stone and carefully drained. The two brick sheds built to house the stud cattle in 10 separate stalls during the winter were fitted with individual feed boxes and water troughs, supplied automatically from the Avon via a hydraulic ram. Each stall was equipped with a central drain that directed the liquid manure into a large sunken concrete tank, which also accumulated the effluent from the nearby piggery. This effluent was later sprayed onto the crop fields by a water drill. The operation of the steading installed at Riccarton in the 1880s would rival any modern attempt at efficient and environmentally sensitive farming. The complex was much admired by visitors and newspaper reporters, whom John, justifiably proud of his achievements, was happy to show around.

Although the farm at Riccarton shrank to half its former freehold size during John Deans's tenure, he succeeded in establishing prize-winning stud herds and flocks and running his overall operation

The brick steading at Riccarton, built for John Deans between 1883 and 1885.

with considerable efficiency. Every year, a convoy of cattle, sheep, pigs and horses would leave Riccarton for the Canterbury A & P show and invariably return laden with prizes. In less turbulent economic times, John's tactics may well have returned a profit. As it was, his continued expenditure on stud sires, buildings and new machinery, coupled with the less-than-profitable coal mine and brickworks initiated by James McIlraith at Homebush and the purchase of Waimarama from Hugh McIlraith, would leave his estate in considerable debt.

Plans for a family home

With the generous gift from James Deans in 1899 earmarked for family purposes, not debt repayment, John Deans was able to commission an extension to Riccarton House that would give the Deans's family home an appropriate air of solidity and substance. English-trained but Christchurch-born architect Robert William England was in a position to ensure that the additions, fittings and decorative elements embodied everything that was considered up to date for a Victorian gentleman's country house. Although his design for the house is often attributed to the architectural firm known as England Brothers, Robert England was not joined by his younger brother until 1906, well after Riccarton House was completed.

Many gentlemen of John Deans's standing would have demolished the existing structure and started afresh. Instead, John retained some of the modest, original 1856 part of the house, as well as some of the 1874 addition. Although the new extension was grand, it was not overblown for the times. There were far grander houses being built in Christchurch in the 1890s, including several designed by England. Holly Lea, designed by him for wealthy bachelor Allan McLean the same year as the additions to Riccarton House, could be considered grandiose rather than merely grand, with its towers, imposing flight of entrance steps, two-storeyed entrance hall and gallery intended to impress.

In comparison, the plans for Riccarton House were restrained and classical in form rather than flamboyant. To some extent, the reasoning behind retaining as much of the existing house as possible must have been financial. John Deans would have been mindful of his precarious economic situation. His uncle's gift would only go so far. Besides, ostentation would hardly suit his conservative style or his Presbyterian upbringing.

Holly Lea, Christchurch, the grand mansion designed by Robert England for Allan McLean and built in 1899.

Such constraints aside, the plans also surely indicated a respect for the past and a desire to retain as much as possible of the visible evidence of the family's successful history at Riccarton. In 1889, Deans Cottage, still on its original site and well-maintained, had been re-roofed and its timber piles replaced with concrete foundations. The earliest structure, the 'old barn', built with materials brought from Wellington to accommodate the Deans brothers and the families of their first farm workers, the Mansons and the Gebbies, had been reluctantly demolished in 1890 only because it was in danger of collapsing. In 1897, Jane Deans planted one of her commemoration oaks on the site of the 'old barn' and arranged for the installation of the memorial cairn that still stands on this spot.

Jane's continuing presence was another strong reason for respecting the history of both cottage and house. She had lived in the 1843 cottage for her first three years at Riccarton, her husband had died there, and John himself was born there. The 1856 house was built for her and her baby son, and she was responsible for the extension added in 1874. By the time the new plans were being commissioned, she had also spent 20 years writing about the family's history in Canterbury (see Chapter 11).

Jane's dutiful son would have been aware of the personal significance the old sections of the house held for her. Her two favourite bedrooms upstairs in the 1856 section would be retained, as well as the large 1874 bedroom occupied by John and Edith and the existing bathroom facilities. Downstairs, both the 1856 morning room and parlour would be kept, and the adjacent 1874 dining room.

England's plans incorporated these earlier sections into the northeast side of the house in a manner that was sympathetic to them. Oddly, considering the vast volume of papers retained by the Deans family, the name of the builder of this major extension to Riccarton House is not known and the original plans drawn by England have not been located.

The work started almost immediately. The first part of the extension was a large service wing built on at the back of the existing house to provide a day nursery for the children, store room, kitchen and pantry, and a dining room, bedroom and bathroom for the servants. Above this were six bedrooms and facilities for the younger children, spaced on each side of a long passage and reached by a modest staircase at the back of the house. By the end of November 1899, this new wing was almost ready for use when John reported on progress in a letter to James Deans:

We have been rather upset here all winter adding to the house, we are putting on a large addition at the back, principally bedrooms and rooms for the children … We hope to get into the first part in about a fortnight or three weeks from now.

Once that wing was completed, most of the western side of the house was demolished for the construction of a large drawing room and entrance hall, with an inner hall and main staircase that led up to the first floor. Three substantial north-facing bedrooms were built for the three oldest children above the new drawing room and entrance hall. All these new rooms, downstairs and up, had high ceiling studs, adding to their imposing proportions. The drawing room and the corner bedroom directly above it had squared bay windows on their western walls.

The finished house would be more than twice the size it had been, with a total of 11 bedrooms upstairs, the service wing, two halls and two reception rooms downstairs, as well as the dining room and what became known as the study:

The completed 1900 house, photographed from across the river after a snowfall, in c.1905.

The house was getting very crowded so I hope we will have a little more room when it is all completed ... Edith and the children are very excited over the building ...

Excited during the first stage of the extension perhaps, but living in confined quarters for something in excess of 18 months amid the chaos of such a massive building project must have become trying for a family with 11 children ranging in age from 20 down to barely three. John and daughter Marion escaped by being overseas for more than half of 1900, returning only at the end of October when the worst was over. Jane, now a frail woman of 76, Edith and the other children were left behind to cope with the disruption at home as best they could.

Exterior and interior embellishments

The completed house achieved all the design features considered necessary for a turn-of-the-century villa of its type. The northern facade, while grand, still managed to complement the modest gable-topped 1856 structure that stood at its eastern corner. England linked this old part of the house to the new wing with an open double verandah. On the ground floor, this stretched from the main entrance to the western end of the new drawing room. It was matched upstairs by a verandah of the same length. French doors opened out onto these verandahs from both the drawing room and two of the upstairs bedrooms. Two large 'pagoda-like' gables extended over the verandah from the first and third bedrooms. A third gable was set back over the second bedroom. Decorative brackets, carved cornices and friezes tied the whole upper storey together. A clover motif was used in the apices of all three gables and elsewhere on the eastern and western sides of the house.

As well as the gables and verandahs, the other grand element was the symmetry added by the use of large totara posts, cut from a tree destroyed in the bush by an 1897 gale. These posts took the form of paired chamfered columns on the upper verandah, with matching sets on the ground floor. The gables, verandahs, columns and the bay windows are the features that still give the exterior of Riccarton House its distinctive appearance today.

The interior layout conformed to the Victorian attitude that servants and young children should be neither seen nor heard. Their modest quarters were grouped at the back of the house with

their own upstairs access. At the front, where visitors and the adult members of the family would congregate, were the reception rooms, the entrance and inner halls, and the main staircase leading to the upper hall and the main bedrooms. The interior decorative features also reflected this division between the more public, adult section of the house, and the domestic section hidden from view.

Timber finishing details were used throughout the house, giving it a warm and welcoming atmosphere. This use of timber reached its greatest expression in the main entrance hall, where the walls and ceiling were fully panelled in oak. The walls of the inner hall were also oak panelled, and the main staircase was built in oak. Apparently, it took two builders a full year to complete all the oak panelling. Jane Deans refers to her grandparents' house at Knockdolian being lined with oak panelling throughout, so the incentive to use oak may have come from her. She may also have been responsible for the adoption of a Scottish baronial style for the entrance hall to acknowledge the family's heritage. Neither the design nor its scale were modified for the colonial setting, as architectural historian Jenny May discovered when she gave an illustrated lecture on the house to heritage groups in Scotland:

People kept telling me they recognised the design from entrance halls of similar scale in several Scottish country houses, right down to the display of mounted animal heads.

The oak used was milled at Riccarton from a tree planted in 1849, according to exotic tree expert Derek Rooney. If correct, this was presumably one of the trees given to the Deans brothers by Governor Grey. John Deans's 1899 letter to his uncle James seems

The oak-panelled entrance hall at Riccarton House with its original furnishings, photographed c.1905.

to claim provenance of trees that surely were planted by his father or uncle well before he was born:

> *... I have been cutting up a lot of my own grown oak to panel the hall with and the stairs and doors are to be made with it also.*

Although at this time exotic timbers were often imported, this use of oak grown on the property (whatever its provenance) was possibly first example of New Zealand-grown exotic timber used for such decorative purposes. John's understandable proprietary pride is revealed in the acorns carved on the newel posts of the main staircase to draw attention to the identity of the timber.

Upstairs and elsewhere in the house, panelling took the form of a more modest dado covering the lower third of the walls, the rimu timber used being carved into a pattern of diagonal lines. In the main bedrooms and the drawing room, high timber skirtings with elaborate mouldings contrasted with much plainer skirtings in the children's wing and the older bedrooms.

In keeping with the fashion of the time, timber mantelpieces adorned all 16 brick fireplaces. Those in the most important rooms consisted of elaborate timber surrounds with niches for ornaments and inset mirrors — an off-the-shelf, contemporaneous design often used by England. The timber structure of the drawing room bay window and the inglenook in the 1874 dining room (another popular element which seems to have been added during these later additions) had archways and other decorative features.

As well as the carved acorns on the newel posts, stylised plant motifs provided finishing touches to the timberwork throughout the interior of the house. These were presumably a reference to

Dado with rimu panelling on the upstairs landing.

One of the acorns carved on the newel posts of the main staircase.

the all-important bush and the Deans family's abiding interest in tree planting, but were also a gesture towards the Arts and Crafts movement of the times, with its emphasis on natural forms.

The interior walls were papered in the latest William Morris and Sanderson styles, which were also part of the Arts and Crafts movement. Plastered ceilings in the main rooms were adorned with delicately tinted, French-revival ceiling roses and elaborate chandeliers.

John Deans's interest in innovation extended to some of the practical elements installed in the house. The kitchen was equipped with one of the first Shacklock coal ranges. As was typical at the turn of the century, the main kitchen was flanked by several small rooms with specific purposes. At Riccarton, these were a scullery, pantry and coal room (coal was brought in from Homebush). But there was also a cleverly designed cold room with a concrete floor. This was accessed from the pantry by three steps down to below ground level, which in itself kept the room cooler than above-ground temperatures. The hydraulic ram that filled the tanks used for the house's water supply also channelled cold water from the river through a two-chambered concrete tank in this room. The tank was equipped with heavy, hinged wooden lids that could be held open, ensuring the air was reduced to even cooler temperatures. Perhaps the most innovative feature John installed was electric lighting, provided by a series of lead batteries. Later, these also operated an electric bell system for summoning the domestic staff. The power for charging these batteries was generated by the 1853 waterwheel:

As I have the waterpower down at the farm I am going to have it [the house] *lighted with electricity, as it will be much safer and the kerosene and candle oil is a heavy item with us now.*

The dining room inglenook added in 1900, after restoration in 2014.

The Riccarton House that emerged from the builders' dust and debris of 1900 was a comfortable family home that embodied simplicity and practicality yet also paid attention to craftsmanship and elegance.

A bright flower garden

Gardening fashions in Canterbury in the late 19th to early 20th century continued to change as the settlement developed. The emphasis on productive fruit and vegetable gardens that had prevailed through the early years had given way to the Victorian arboretum and shrubberies favoured at Riccarton during Jane's time in charge (see Chapter 8). Now the focus turned to providing areas for recreation and entertainment. Most of the original orchard trees established behind the house by the Deans brothers in the 1840s to 1850s were removed at some stage to create space for a tennis court, popular from the 1870s onwards. A new vegetable and fruit garden was developed further north of the house, out of sight across the river and reached by a swing bridge (see map, p. 137).

The ornamental plantings surrounding the house were now receiving more attention. Unlike her mother-in-law Jane, Edith

In the early 1900s, delphiniums and sweet williams lined the path on the south side of the house leading to the tennis court.

The rose garden west of the house c.1905.

Riverside plantings on the bank below the house in the early 1900s, looking east down the river.

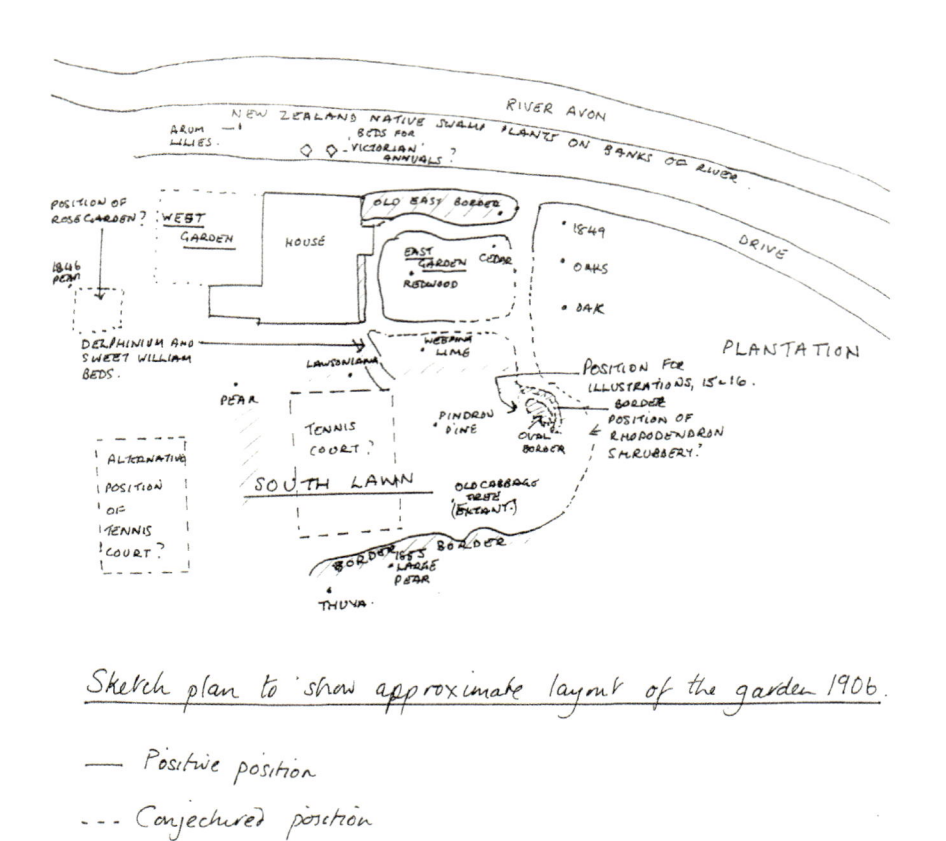

Sketch plan to show approximate layout of the garden 1906.

— Positive position

--- Conjectured position
Flower border

Deans had an interest in flowers — Jane refers to 'Mamma's flower garden' in a letter to her grandchildren written in 1886. Although tree seed continued to be ordered, nursery lists for Riccarton now also contained flowering shrubs like roses, camellias and French heathers. As early as 1882, a visiting reporter commented:

> *The effect of the various belts of plantations … when seen from the southern side, is very pretty, as also is the view of the house, with its bright flower garden.*

Mixed borders became fashionable early in the Edwardian era, so Edith's gardeners developed more informal borders of shrubs, perennials and bulbs to the south and east of the expanded house, including flower beds around the tennis court and under the specimen trees. Photographs taken in the early 1900s show camellias, rhododendrons and roses, with many perennials like delphiniums, offset by lawns and grassed pathways. The banks of the Avon in front of the house were bordered by flax, arum lilies and rhododendrons. The expansive gardens became the setting for Canterbury's jubilee celebrations in 1900. Many other public events were held in the grounds in the first few decades of the 20th century (see Chapter 11).

Thelma Strongman's sketch plan of the probable garden layout in 1906.

The completed family photographed in 1900, the year before first Violet, then Catherine died. Left to right, back row: Robert, John, Marion and Ian. Middle row: William (leaning on Jane's chair), Jane, Violet, Edith and James. Front row: Colin, Stuart (Max, the youngest), Douglas, Alexander (Alister) and Catherine.

End of an era

With a newly commodious house and a garden adapted for the more relaxed lifestyle and recreational needs of their now complete family, and with the hope of improving economic prospects, John and Edith Deans would have been looking forward to a middle age of less stressful years. But it was not to be. Within a year of John's return with daughter Marion from England towards the end of 1900, both their other daughters died — first five-year-old Violet, and then 15-year-old Catherine.

The family had barely time to recover from these losses when John himself fell ill. In mid-June 1902, he contracted what seems to have been meningitis. Never robust, his health had probably been compromised by the stress of managing a large estate during a time of economic depression and the financial strain accompanying his determination to continue improvements to both farm and family property. He died a week later on 19 June, just short of his 49th birthday.

John Deans's sudden death was mourned throughout Canterbury, with flags being flown at half-mast in Christchurch. His funeral cortege comprised 120 carriages and stretched nearly a mile and a half (about 2.4 km) from Riccarton House to the cemetery in Addington. Several fulsome and appreciative obituaries were printed in local papers, emphasising not only John's own significant achievements in agriculture but also the Deans family's overall contribution to the history of Canterbury. In the words of one of these obituaries:

John Deans in 1900, two years before his death.

Mr John Deans ... grew up with the city, arrived with it at man's estate, and in his quiet unassuming way, helped it along on the road of progress. He was no strenuous politician, but a retiring modest gentleman, who, though he did not neglect his public duties, avoided publicity, and sought rather to hide his good deeds than to publish them abroad. Such men are rare enough; we cannot afford to lose them.

As with his uncle William before him, John's premature death meant he did not leave a will. His oldest son Ian (the third John), at the age of 22 was left to contend with a diminished estate and substantial mortgages and debts amounting to nearly £60,000. At least the family still had an estate — 22 Canterbury stations had passed into the hands of banks and finance companies between 1879 and 1890. At the time, a Liberal government was also busy breaking up large estates. The passing of the Land for Settlement Acts 1892 and 1894 had been causing the family some concern, Jane herself writing a substantial letter to her grandchildren in March 1895 to ensure the history of the Deans's land holdings was clear in the face of this threat. On John's death, Homebush was targeted for purchase. It was only a concerted effort by Ian and the other trustees that retained the property for eventual division among John and Edith's surviving children. Edith herself would have a life interest in a large part of the remaining land at Riccarton as her marriage settlement (effective after Jane's death, see Chapter 11), with the eventual right to dispose of the capital to family members as she wished.

By 1906, high graduated land taxes forced the splitting up of Homebush and Waimarama into family holdings of nearly equal value (as much as was possible). The older members of the family took up their blocks at this time. Those formed from Waimarama for the younger members were leased out, then later sold. The properties subdivided from Homebush, with the names Kirkstyle, Rowallan, Homebush, Sandown and Morven, each eventually with substantial homesteads, would continue to remain in Deans family hands for several generations.

At Homebush, despite his precarious financial situation, John Deans had pushed ahead with commissioning plans to replace the modest timber homestead with a grand, three-storeyed house to be built with bricks from the family brickworks at Glentunnel. His reasoning remains obscure, since any prolonged family occupation of the

homestead amounted to the children's holiday visits. A brick mansion was hardly the type of accommodation anyone would build for a farm manager, however admired (at this time John Cochran). Perhaps John Deans had an eye to the future when one of his sons could be expected to live permanently at Homebush to run the sheep station. Perhaps he was influenced by the grand homesteads being built on surrounding stations. It would not do for the Deans family to lag behind others of their social standing, and he may have felt the Homebush homestead needed to match the status achieved by the new house at Riccarton.

John died before the building could proceed, but a start was made in 1904. The handsome, six-bedroom brick homestead was eventually built in two stages, with a balcony and verandah added in 1924. The attic was originally divided into further bedrooms for the Riccarton children to occupy during holiday visits, and the grand reception rooms downstairs were in scale with the overall architecture of the house. Several of John and Edith's sons, then successive generations of their descendants, would indeed live in this house and run Homebush. It would remain a Deans family home until 2010 when it became the victim of Canterbury's September earthquake, its triple-brick structure partially collapsing in spectacular fashion.

Until its resulting demolition, the homestead at Homebush joined with the dwellings built at Riccarton by the Deans family in encapsulating the European social history of Canterbury. Together, the 1843 modest settler cottage, the 1856 timber homestead and its 1874 extension, the final grand 1900 timber-built town house at Riccarton, and the handsome brick homestead at Homebush reflected the family's progression from hard-working settler farmers to well-established landed gentry, a progression that underlay and represented Canterbury's own.

The brick mansion built at Homebush, soon after its completion in 1904.

· 11 ·
Matriarchs at Riccarton

Two women of strong character with different backgrounds dominated the domestic scene at Riccarton for a combined total of 80 years. Jane Deans lived in Riccarton House for 55 years. For 32 of those years she would share the running of the house with her daughter-in-law Catherine Edith, both of them as widows for the last nine. After Jane died in 1911, Edith in turn became the matriarch at Riccarton until her own death in 1937. Both women, of Scots background and proud Presbyterian faith, would make their mark on the social life of Anglican Christchurch.

A Scottish upbringing

Jane Deans grew up at Auchenflower, the well-run estate of the McIlraith family. The McIlraiths had considerable standing in Ayrshire, where Jane's father James was much respected and admired. Immensely proud of her father's status as laird, magistrate and supporter of major public enterprises, Jane developed notions about her own station in life that would influence her opinions of people, her choice of friendships, and her participation in public social events throughout her many years in New Zealand.

Both Jane's mother and grandmother had died in 1832, when she was nine. It was her father and beloved grandfather who had the greatest influence on her, and she adopted their attitudes and principles in her own approach to life. James McIlraith ruled with a firm hand, although his daughter says he was also loving and kind. A special bond with her father was their shared interest in establishing plantations of trees, which James extended to plantings on neighbouring properties as well as at Auchenflower.

Brought up strictly with a strong adherence to the Free Church of Scotland, Jane trusted implicitly in God's will. Sundays and the associated church services would remain important to her all her life:

*Sunday was the day of days for us ... No rioting was ever allowed, we were taught to **walk softly and reverently in respect***

Auchenflower in Ayrshire, where Jane McIlraith grew up.

to God's Holy Day ... It was a delight, holy and set apart from other days ... In the evenings we were all collected for an hour to read the Scriptures, repeat hymns and catechism, taking alternate questions and answers round the family.

Reference to their 'own quiet Sabbath service' at Riccarton indicates that Jane and John continued this regime, at least initially. Although it may have softened once the family had their own church of St Andrew's to attend, Jane still expected her grandchildren to respect 'God's Holy Day'. John and Edith's three oldest sons were greatly influenced by their grandmother, becoming serious, sober and dutiful adherents of the Scottish church. Less influenced by Jane's strict practices, Douglas, one of her youngest grandsons, still retained memories of not being allowed to whistle on Sundays and having to remain quiet in her presence.

Jane's father was not well off and had five sisters to support with annuities from the estate, as well as his own expanding second family, so his children were taught to be frugal. Once Jane and her two younger sisters finished their schooling (when they reached 16), their father expected them to contribute to the running of the house:

Our father gave us to understand that he could not afford to keep us idle like mere supernumeraries and that we must take our share of domestic duties including charge of the younger children and do without the nurse, cooking, sweeping, etc., ...

Life was not without simple pleasures — picnics, family gatherings at Christmas, New Year and Easter. In Scotland, all family gatherings were accompanied by singing, and Jane remembers being moved to tears by one song while still a small child sitting on an aunt's lap:

It was always the height of enjoyment to hear my aunts sing. They knew an endless variety of songs from grave to gay ...

Jane tried to recreate all of these gatherings in New Zealand, and she herself accompanied many musical evenings on the piano, occasions for both family and friends.

As well as helping look after their ailing grandfather for the last three years of his life (he died in 1845), Jane and her sisters were frequently sent to assist one or other of the five McIlraith aunts. They alternated these visits with running the dairy at Auchenflower.

For the whole of her twenties, while waiting to hear from John far away in New Zealand, Jane was busy looking after various relatives. She spent the last five years before her marriage with Aunt Rodger, 'who was like a mother to me'. This was very much the life of a spinster, yet she termed these years as 'very happy'.

In keeping with one of her father's maxims, Jane always said there was no room in the world for idle hands, and she never sat without knitting, even mere months before her death. She also frequently quoted another of his maxims — that whatever was worth doing was worth doing well.

Elements of this upbringing, its firm grounding in practical domestic skills and frugality, and Jane's pleasure in assisting her father with aspects of tree management are reflected in all that she accomplished and how she accomplished it in her long, productive life at Riccarton. Above all else, she attributed her lifelong habit of self-denial to her father's influence, claiming this was a habit that proved:

> … one of the most necessary requisites for a happy contented colonial life …

A colonial background

Catherine Edith Park's upbringing was vastly different to Jane's. The middle child of Robert Park's third family, she grew up in a colonial household in which her surveyor father was seldom present. Her mother and her two older half-sisters were therefore the dominant influence in her growing years. Depending on where his survey work took him, Robert Park moved his family many times — from Wellington to Hawke's Bay, then to Dunedin, and later to Winchmore (South Canterbury). Modest cottages were their usual accommodation, sometimes ill-furnished and rudimentarily equipped. During her school years in 1860s Christchurch, Edith may have looked forward to the regular holidays spent in the ordered calm of Riccarton House under Jane Deans's austere but kindly eye as welcome relief after the more tempestuous household that probably prevailed at home whenever her father was in residence (see Chapter 9).

After Robert Park died in 1870, Edith moved back to Wellington with her mother and younger sister. Similar to Jane's role as an umarried young woman in Scotland living with her aunts, Edith would spend the next seven years living with her widowed mother, helping run the house as a dutiful daughter should. Once Edith

A serene Jane Deans in old age, c.1895.

renewed her contact with Jane and John Deans on visits to help her newly wed sister in Christchurch, the appeal of married status, a steady, quiet husband, and a more independent life at Riccarton exerted its pull. Edith was well used to a female-dominated regime, and a degree of affection between her and Jane had probably developed already during Edith's childhood and school years. The prospect of her mother-in-law's continuing presence clearly proved no deterrent to Edith agreeing to marry John.

Marion Park wrote to friend Annabella McLean, lamenting that she would miss Edith's organising skills, but acknowledged that she was lucky her older daughter had stayed with her so long. It is unknown to what extent Edith was able to apply those skills at Riccarton, where Jane as her senior was probably firmly in control of the household, at least during the early years of the marriage. Moreover by the terms of her husband's will, Jane had the added authority of life tenure of the house and land at Riccarton. Although these became part of her daughter-in-law's marriage settlement, they would not pass to her until Jane's death. With the greater flexibility and less formality of her colonial childhood, and being the younger of the two women at Riccarton, Edith no doubt accepted her lesser status with forbearance if not equanimity. Besides, becoming pregnant soon after the marriage, she was probably happy to leave the running of the household in Jane's hands.

Despite their different backgrounds, Jane Deans and her daughter-in-law shared some characteristics. As well as practical organising skills and a great deal of sound pragmatism, they both had a sense of humour, though Jane's wit was dry and less whimsical than the brand Edith was credited with by her contemporaries and her grandchildren. Both women had a strong attachment to the Presbyterian Church. Portraits of both women reveal a certain calmness and serenity.

Where their similarity parted company was those habits of frugality and self-denial that were the linchpins of Jane's outlook on life. These habits applied to her daily routine and the subordination of her own wants to those of others. One of her few indulgences seems to have been a hot whisky toddy drunk each night before bed, mentioned several times in her writings and continued throughout her life, as remembered by grandson Bill Deans. Despite her frugality, Jane was not without means; her lifetime annuity from her husband's estate was £300 (for comparison, the Riccarton cook was likely to have been paid £75 in 1893 — the first year such

Catherine Edith Park, a few years after her marriage to John Deans.

statistics were officially collated — rising to £100 in 1910). And she certainly spent this amount each year, stating in her will that she would have no money left to bequeath.

By all accounts, Edith was anything but frugal. She relished her status as wife of the Squire of Riccarton, making the most of the lifestyle that went with the expanded grand house. Photographs of Edith in evening dresses abound, and her grandchildren got the impression she liked to be waited on. Jane's maxim of never sitting with idle hands possibly fell on deaf ears. Edith and John employed two nursemaids to look after the growing throng of children, and there was an increasing number of domestic staff; cook and maids as well as gardeners. What her mother-in-law thought of Edith's tendency towards extravagance is unknown. Nevertheless, that growing throng of children would have endeared her to Jane's heart, for Edith more than fulfilled the main requirement of her — to ensure the Deans family succession.

Daughter-in-law and mother of Jane's grandchildren, Edith c.1900.

Edith in evening dress, possibly between 1900 and 1910.

Edith in evening dress with a train, wearing a tiara. This may have been on the occasion of the visit of the Prince of Wales (later Edward VIII) in May 1920, when a citizens' ball was held in his honour at the King Edward barracks.

Becoming a grandmother

The steady arrival of grandchildren transformed Jane Deans's life. Under the strain of raising her son to maturity and at the same time managing his estate in her role as her husband's main trustee, Jane's love and affection for her boy were constantly tempered by the responsibility she bore (see chapters 7 and 9). But as that son and her daughter-in-law continued to produce healthy sons — three in five years, she was able to relax. By 1885, the succession was firmly secured.

As well as those first three grandsons, Jane had the pleasure of a first granddaughter, born soon after John and Edith returned from their trip to England in 1881. Although the sadness of losing a third grandchild in infancy (in 1883) was surely compounded for both Jane and her daughter-in-law by the child being named Jane Edith after them both, healthy babies continued to arrive. By the time Jane was in her mid-seventies, she had 11 surviving grandchildren, eight of them boys. They were all born at Riccarton House, where they lived with her and their parents. An old friend of Jane's was quoted in the paper after her death as saying:

She passed through many trials and troubles, not least being the early death of her husband, but when her grandchildren came, she appeared to take a new lease on life.

The expanding family in 1890. At the back, John Deans, Jane Deans holding William (born 1889) and Edith. In front, from left to right, Catherine (born 1886), Robert (born 1884), James (born 1885), Ian (born 1880) and Marion (born 1881).

For Jane, being a grandmother had little of the stress or responsibility associated with bringing up her son. Although she was strict and undoubtedly set rigid standards of expected behaviour, she became much loved by her grandchildren. Her long years of loneliness were over. The big house was filled with the life and inevitable noise and laughter that accompany any large brood of children. She recorded in her McIlraith account:

> *My son has grown up and married Catherine Edith Park and they have a family of eight sons and three daughters alive and we all live happily together in the home at Riccarton.*

With Edith distracted by being either pregnant, about to give birth, or dealing with a new baby, the older children saw more of their grandmother Jane than of their mother. On at least one occasion (in 1885), Jane was left in charge while John was away on farm business and Edith was in Wellington visiting her mother, Marion Park:

> *Recruiting her health after the fatigues of the Volunteer Bazaar, which she assisted at …*

Edith can hardly be blamed for seeking the occasional respite —

The first three sons born to John and Edith Deans, photographed in 1896. Robert on the left, Ian (John) at the back, and James on the right.

Jane with two of her granddaughters in c.1900, Marion aged about 19 and Violet, four. Edith on the right.

17 years of pregnancies and infants would be enough to tax even the most maternal of mothers. With the backing of her mother-in-law and a large domestic staff, she was able to develop interests in various women's social and cultural movements early in her marriage. Such interests were, of course, seen as highly appropriate for someone of her social standing.

With all the joys that being a grandmother brought Jane, there were also accompanying sorrows. She was to lose more of her grandchildren. As well as the baby who died in infancy, her youngest granddaughter Violet died at Waimarama in 1901 aged only five, then Catherine died later the same year, aged 15. Added to that grief was the unexpected death of her son John the following year, in 1902 (see Chapter 10). Then grandson Robert, Bob Deans of All Black fame, died of peritonitis in 1908. Jane had outlived not only her husband but also her son and four of her grandchildren. Despite her own fragile health, she would live to the great age of 87.

Small wonder then that the ghost of Jane Deans is thought to have kept a close eye on the new generation of children being born at Riccarton House once her surviving grandchildren grew up, married and started having babies of their own. A nursemaid attending to baby Austen, born early in December 1915 nearly five years after Jane's death, reported seeing a small elderly woman dressed in black, standing gazing into the cradle the day after his birth. One of Austen's cousins also later saw a small figure in black who fitted Jane's description walking in the upstairs passage. And Graham Hemming, manager at Riccarton House for many years (until the mid-1990s), several times heard the rustle of taffeta in the hall outside his office, and saw a small woman in a long black dress wearing a white cap walking away from him. He had no doubt that it was Jane.

No sitting with folded hands

Within a few years of her son taking over the estate, Jane Deans turned her efforts to writing the first of her several accounts of family history. Widely read, she had always been interested in history. Her own book collection contained many volumes of Scottish and church history, as well as the 12 volumes of Gibbon's *Decline and Fall of the Roman Empire* and some New Zealand history (Hocken's *Otago*, for example), all of which were left to

her older grandsons. She also left them all the papers, letters and documents in her possession that pertained to William and John Deans 'in hope that they may compile them into book form' — a hope that was duly and dutifully fulfilled by her oldest and closest grandson Ian (the third John) in his two books on the early family history in Canterbury.

Over a period of nearly 30 years, Jane wrote steadily, leaving an invaluable record. Sadly, her first known effort, entitled 'Scraps of Family History' (written in 1878) seems to have been mislaid, although Gordon Ogilvie quoted from it in his 1996 book. She followed this in 1882 with an extensive article about the Deans brothers' early years at Riccarton, first published in the *New Zealand Country Journal*, then reproduced in full in several other sources later. This was written so vividly that extracts are often quoted as though they were an eye-witness account of William and John Deans's arrival — a full 10 years before Jane herself reached Riccarton.

Irked by continuing misinformation from recorders of Canterbury history about the role of the Deans brothers in the early days of settlement and their right to compensatory run land, Jane next embarked on setting the record straight by writing a series of extended letters to her grandchildren. She started writing these on the 35th anniversary of the Canterbury settlement (1885), then continued them at yearly intervals for the next two years. Focused mostly on her personal experiences, from her arrival at Riccarton in 1853 until her son came of age in 1874, these were later published in book form, providing a rare and detailed social history written from a woman's perspective. In March 1895, she wrote a separate, lengthy letter that specifically detailed the brothers' dealings over land, drawing on the extensive family papers. This was also the period during which she wrote her unpublished account of Auchenflower and McIlraith history (undated, but written after 1897, when her youngest grandchild was born, and before 1901, when two of her granddaughters died — see earlier quote under 'Becoming a grandmother', in this chapter).

In all of these writings, Jane Deans's probity and dislike of those who did not adhere to the same standards are clear. The Anglican authorities of early Christchurch came in for particular censure, not just for their protracted and difficult dealings over land entitlement. Among a long list of offences, the church authorities had created difficulties about Scots buried in 'their' cemetery being allowed the

Jane never sat without occupation. If she was not busy at her desk writing, she knitted.

Presbyterian form of service, including the very John Deans from whom they had received so much help and hospitality. Her own tart words sum up her opinion:

I hoped the Church of England might some day learn wisdom and become more charitable to those who, on good and substantial grounds, have chosen to differ from them.

Jane's disapproval of much about the Anglican Church no doubt reinforced her lifelong staunch support of the Presbyterian Church in Christchurch, represented by St Andrew's (opened in 1857) and all its associated doings. Five years before her death, she was asked to record her memories of the founding of St Andrew's, which were duly published under her name as *A Sketch of the Early History of St Andrew's Church 1856–1906.*

As well as the more substantial writings mentioned here, Jane continued to write letters and record her memories, snippets of family history and various observations almost up to the time of her death. In none of these writings, despite their focus on the history of the Deans's establishment and land holdings in Canterbury, does she comment on her son's management of the estate during what proved to be difficult years, but surely she would have been distressed by the continual whittling away of that hard-won land in the sales that John found necessary throughout his tenure.

Presiding at Riccarton

Although on the surface, Jane Deans remained unfailingly polite and continued the tradition of extending hospitality to all comers at Riccarton, she kept herself aloof from the many competitive squabbles that beset the pioneer Christchurch community. This approach had reaped early rewards. When the Duke of Edinburgh visited in 1869, he took part in a pigeon shoot at Riccarton. Jane notes with evident satisfaction that this venue, chosen by Lieutenant-Colonel Packe, was the only one possible:

… the Prince could not have been taken anywhere else without arousing jealousy. No one was jealous of me, for I never entered into rivalry with any, but tried to be friendly and civil with whoever was the same to me.

In later years, Jane, with her son and his wife, enjoyed hosting the increasing number of public social events held at Riccarton and the status this gave them — from regular Sunday school outings for St Andrew's Church to adult garden parties. As well as organised occasions, the Deans family continued to hold open home for visitors. From the time Jane's son attended Christchurch Boys' High School, his fellow schoolboys were regularly invited to Riccarton on Saturdays, occasions fondly remembered by many. Once John and Edith's sons, in turn, began attending the school, the habit probably continued. The annual Sunday school picnic at Riccarton was accompanied by sports events, for which Jane presented the prizes right up to her death.

The grandest event ever held by the Deans family at Riccarton was undoubtedly the 1900 Canterbury jubilee garden party, attended by 1200 guests. Refreshments were served and a band played. The current Governor, William Rolleston, and his wife attended. An animated Jane received the guests, seated characteristically upright on a chair on the lawn, from where she continued the reminiscences with many of the early settlers begun at previous celebratory events.

The largest public event held at Riccarton in Jane's lifetime was the garden party held in 1900 as part of the Christchurch jubilee celebrations and attended by 1200 guests.

Jane Deans presiding at the 1900 garden party celebrating the Pilgrims Association 50th anniversary. Charles Bowen is seated to her left, her son John to her right, with William Rolleston (recently retired from Parliament).

All commented on her remarkable memory. She had, of course, been busy writing up the family history, so had many details at her fingertips.

After John's death in 1902, garden parties and fundraising fetes continued to be held regularly at Riccarton, jointly hosted by Jane and Edith. The anniversary of the Canterbury settlement was celebrated each year with a garden party at Riccarton until Jane's death in 1911. Hosting such events was a tradition that Edith continued throughout her own reign at Riccarton, in particular providing the venue for further 'early settler' gatherings and annual meetings of the Victoria League as well as the ongoing Sunday school picnics. She served as president of the Victoria League for a total of 12 years from 1921, remained a benefactor of St Andrew's Church, and endowed a scholarship at Christchurch Boys' High School, where she continued to present annual prizes. Since 1926, the school had been located nearby on what had been Riccarton farm land, sold to the Ministry of Education in 1923.

By the time Jane died in 1911 she had become a renowned figure in Christchurch, despite her continuing modesty. She was not only much admired and respected, but also remembered with affection by more than the Scottish families who continued to be her preferred personal friends. Her funeral was well attended and fully reported in *The Press*. Jane was buried alongside her husband John in the Anglican cemetery on Barbadoes Street. The memorial stone erected by the local Scottish community bears witness to her standing:

> *Greatly beloved for her many virtues she lived a noble Christian life and left behind her a gracious and enduring memory.*

Meticulous in her business dealings to the end, Jane had updated her will in August 1909. First named amongst her executors was 'my dear daughter-in-law Catherine Edith Deans, widow of my late dear son...' That Edith continued many of the routines established by Jane at Riccarton can perhaps be seen as recognition of the relationship that had developed between them, centred on the bonds wrought by the arrival of Jane's grandchildren. Over a period of more than 30 years, the two women had shared much joy and sorrow.

Last years at Riccarton

Not long after Jane died, her oldest grandchildren moved to take up the properties subdivided from Homebush. Edith was left alone at Riccarton House with the younger children. The family memory is that she was not particularly interested in her children when they were youngsters, much preferring them once they were older. Then, as often happens with the youngest in any large family, the last three boys (born between 1892 and 1897) became unruly and mischievous in Edith's eyes. Eventually, she had had enough so all three were sent away in turn to complete their schooling as boarders at Waitaki Boys' High School. Douglas, the eldest of these three, gets the blame for this. A keen fisherman, walking to Christchurch Boys' High School along the route of the trout-stocked Avon proved too big a distraction. He was often late, if he arrived at all. With school holidays being spent at Homebush or Waimarama, the youngest member of the family, Stuart (known as Max), later said he hardly ever saw their mother — only when he was being outfitted for new school uniforms.

Edith was to live on at Riccarton for another 26 years. She still had many years ahead of her of having children at home. As well as her own younger brood, she fostered her niece 16-year-old Molly Park from 1905, after the death in quick succession of both her parents

(Molly's father George Park was Edith's older brother). Her 14-year-old nephew Reggie Park followed in 1907 when he went to school at Christchurch Boys' High. Both Edith and her oldest son Ian had been named in George's will as his children's guardians — an indication of the retention of close ties between the Deans and Park families.

As the older Deans children left home and married, it was expected that they would return frequently to stay with Edith at Riccarton, with bedrooms being set aside for their use. In adulthood, her sons were required to contribute to her monthly upkeep. Bill, one of the middle sons, was often unable to comply so he made a point of indulging her in other ways, such as taking her to the races. Although Edith was probably a daunting prospect for new daughters-in-law, with her rigid ideas of protocol and social niceties (some inherited from Jane), she made them welcome. A foolish friend once asked which of her daughters-in-law was her favourite. Her reply revealed the tact and humour for which she had become known:

Whichever one happens to be staying with me at the time.

Edith continued to retain a large domestic staff, including a chauffeur. Her granddaughters later remembered trips in the Daimler to Ballantynes to shop with Granny. She also employed a lady companion to help her organise the household and the

Edith in old age at Riccarton, taken from an undated newspaper photograph.

increasing number of social events in which she was involved. The family consider her insistence on having lady companions after Jane's death an indication of her sense of entitlement, but she may well have been acting on her mother-in-law's advice. Jane had intensely disliked being alone at Riccarton. In her letters, she often laments that she could not have a permanent companion living with her. After all, she had herself served in this capacity for her aunts in Scotland.

The regular family dinners held in Edith's time were formal affairs, with any daughters-in-law in residence seated around her at one end of the long table set with a white linen cloth and full array of silver cutlery. Her sons were arranged in order of age down each side. This placed the three youngest unruly ones at the far end, where they tended to swap dubious stories. Once their laughter aroused Edith's interest, she would demand to know the reason for it, so the young men would take it in turns to sanitise the current story sufficiently for her ears.

Before Jane died, Edith had become a grandmother in her own right. She ended up with 26 grandchildren, 17 of them boys. Sunday lunches became an institution for the country grandsons while they were at boarding school in Christchurch (first Medbury, then Christ's College). After lunch, the boys would change into old clothes kept at Riccarton to play in the grounds and the bush. Adrian Deans considered that these substantial meals once a week saved him from starving at school during the Depression years.

During Edith's reign, with her adult children moving to take over the subdivided inland stations, the rest of the Riccarton farm land was sold off. By her death in 1937, all that remained in family hands at Riccarton was the grand house, its current grounds, and the triangle of land between the drive and the Kahu Street bridge. The bush itself had been gifted to the city in 1914 (see Chapter 12).

Historians have long acknowledged that the first Deans brothers, William and John, and their establishment of the early farm at Riccarton influenced the history of the Canterbury settlement. But two women, the matriarchs of Riccarton, contributed substantially more to that history. It was Jane Deans and her astute management of what the brothers had begun who ensured that Riccarton and its legacy of unusual ecological and human continuity would survive into the 21st century. And it was Catherine Edith Deans who made sure there would be a close-knit Deans family, whose descendants continue to contribute in substantial ways to the social and cultural life of Canterbury.

• 12 •
A Link 'twixt Past and Present

The ecological and cultural significance of Riccarton Bush would be recognised early in the history of Christchurch. Throughout her life, Jane Deans made sure the bush was conserved as her dying husband had wished. At the beginning of the 1900s, her efforts would be extended into the public arena by several notable botanists and conservationists. After Jane's death, her family gifted the remaining bush to the city, but members of the Deans family would continue to be involved with its preservation and management under the auspices of the Riccarton Bush Trust. Within a few decades of the establishment of the Trust, its purpose would be expanded to include the preservation of historic Riccarton House.

An early conservation effort

The few remnant forest patches isolated on the plains received close attention from arriving surveyors and settlers. In 1851, Charles Torlesse recorded a first general description of their nature, most of which applied to Riccarton Bush:

> *The timber in them is chiefly Kaikatea* [kahikatea or white pine], *Mahi* [matai or black pine], *Remu* [rimu or red pine — not present at Riccarton], *Pokaka, Kowai and Totara ... There are some beautiful creepers ...*

This brief description was enlarged on in 1870 by John Armstrong (curator of the Botanic Gardens), who published the first complete listing of the plants present in Riccarton Bush. Today, the bush still retains the main elements and characteristics described by Armstrong, despite the loss of some 40 species. Some of these were probably always uncommon, some were crowded out by vigorous interlopers, and some were lost to disturbance or mismanagement. Although it would be 1914 before the bush became legally protected, the efforts of the Deans family to preserve what remained after John Deans's death in 1854 lend substance to the claim that Riccarton Bush is one of the oldest protected areas in New Zealand.

The Deans family's interest in trees was not restricted to those they introduced and planted at Riccarton (see Chapter 8). Within two years of the arrival of the Canterbury settlers, John Deans became only too aware that what was left of the iconic patch of native bush at Riccarton could easily be destroyed. The half allotted to the settlers had been completely felled before the end of 1851. The other patches of bush present on the plains were also rapidly disappearing under the onslaught of settlers desperate for timber and firewood. When the permission given to 'poorer people' to gather fallen timber for firewood in the Deans's half of the bush at Riccarton resulted in live trees being felled, John published a public notice in the *Lyttelton Times* in July 1853 warning that future trespassers would now be prosecuted.

Direct human interference was not the only threat facing the remaining bush. The exposed new southern boundary soon revealed the vulnerability to wind damage of what had previously been the interior. Accidental fires in 1851 and 1852 had already scorched trees on the fringes of the bush when, early in 1854 John, now terminally ill, was confronted by yet another accidental blaze.

One of the ancient kahikatea towers skywards.

The presence of the bush at Putaringamotu had been vital to the Deans brothers' decision to settle here. Like Maori before them, they relied on the bush for shelter, food and timber. Its presence was fundamental to the establishment and ongoing success of their farm at Riccarton. It is no surprise that on his death bed, John Deans expressed his wish to Jane that the remaining bush at Riccarton should be preserved to whatever extent was possible.

The Deans brothers had, of course, themselves extracted timber from the bush for the farm cottages and buildings, fencing and yards at Riccarton and the inland run, but they had done so with care not to be extravagant. As Jane was to record, their firewood use was restricted to waste wood from the bush and roots from felled or burnt trees. Considerable effort was also made to salvage the hundreds of historically burnt stumps and logs as well as those left on the section of the bush cleared by the settlers — for Riccarton use, and for sale (see Chapter 6).

At about the time of John's death, more serious inroads were being made on trees in the bush. A large amount of timber (kahikatea, totara and matai) was taken for the building of more substantial houses at Homebush (first for John Cordy and later for the McIlraith brothers at the sheep station), and then for the new house for Jane at Riccarton in 1855. Jane Deans's dismay at the contracted sawyers' wasteful destruction of trees has already been quoted in Chapter 8. She had the resulting cleared areas planted in oaks as a conservation measure. After that, no further timber was removed from the bush, except for fallen logs used for fencing. From the late 1860s onwards, Jane ensured that any gaps created by felled or fallen trees were planted with exotic trees raised in the tree nursery at Riccarton — oaks, ash, elms and gums, whichever seemed suitable for the soil. The aim of this gap-filling was to preserve the remaining bush as long as possible. With some pride, she points out that:

This was done before Sir J. Vogel enunciated his 'Native Forest Preservation' scheme [Vogel's failed 1874 attempt to pass an Act protecting the remaining native forests].

A reporter visiting Riccarton for *The Press* in January 1878 refers to these plantings amid the remaining 'black and white pine' (matai and kahikatea), saying that 'young John Deans' told him their presence was to 'supply the places of the native trees' because:

Notwithstanding the preservation and care exercised, the native trees are gradually dying out.

In addition, a border of oaks was planted along the periphery of the bush, within the already existing hawthorn hedge, with the aim of protecting the native trees from further wind damage. It was maintaining a canopy that was important in Jane's mind. It mattered little that the replacements were exotic species, and she had found that native trees were less easy to propagate and transplant. Although the use of exotic trees in this early attempt to enhance and preserve the bush was well intended, by 1882 Jane herself recognised it had been a mistake:

The planted trees have done well, but the result was not what was desired: for, instead of protecting the young native trees, they have smothered them out, in summer by their shade, and in winter with fallen leaves.

Even so, in that same account, written eight years after Jane Deans handed over the estate to her son John in 1874, she was able to claim with considerable justification that:

The remaining part of the Bush has been preserved as well as possible, in accordance with the late John Deans' wishes ...

Although Jane was no longer responsible for managing the estate, she undoubtedly maintained a firm grasp on what happened to the bush, including encouraging her grandchildren to honour her own concern for its preservation. It was her oldest grandson, the third John Deans, who was instrumental in the family gifting the bush to the people of Canterbury three years after Jane's death in 1911.

Jane Deans planted many oaks in the bush, first in gaps where trees had been felled and later around the margins to provide wind protection.

Pressure for public preservation

National concern about the widespread loss of native forest and its natural inhabitants gathered strength from the 1870s onwards. Local public recognition of the historic and scientific value of Riccarton Bush contributed to this growing concern. Both the value of the remaining bush and its vulnerability to the pressures of an expanding city had been reinforced by the almost complete disappearance of the other bush remnants on the plains within 10 years of the arrival of the Canterbury settlers. By the end of the 1860s, what little remained had all succumbed to accidental fires. Of Riccarton Bush itself, fewer than 10 hectares were now left of the original 22 present in the 1840s. That any was left was due solely to the efforts of the Deans family.

Prominent amongst the Christchurch advocates for public protection of Riccarton Bush were two founder members of the influential Christchurch Beautifying Association, established in 1897. Harry Ell, Member of Parliament, was instrumental in gaining reserve status for many bush remnants on the Port Hills, initiating the associated Summit Road walkway, and pushing through the Scenery Preservation Act 1903. Dr Leonard Cockayne later became one of New Zealand's most influential forest ecologists.

With the help of these two men and the equally eloquent Johannes Andersen, informative articles were published in *The Press* urging the preservation of the bush. They pushed for its possible purchase by the city as a public reserve, on the basis of its historical and scientific importance. Their efforts came to a head in 1906, perhaps influenced by the nationalistic zeal aroused by preparations for the International Exhibition that opened in Christchurch in November that year. Andersen penned an emotional ode that was published in a promotional and informative leaflet in July and later won a prize at the Exhibition. The crux of his poem was an overt appeal for public support in preserving the bush:

> *The forest springs eternal; gnarled, o'ergrown.*
> *... The trees of centuries stand mute and hoar*
> *... Silent the link 'twixt past and present stand;*
> *shall it be spared, or perish, at your hands?*

A Preservation Committee held many meetings throughout that year. The Government promised £1500 towards the £5000 needed to buy what was left of the bush from the Deans family. Fundraising efforts were launched and favourably reported in local newspapers.

Dr Leonard Cockayne and Harry Ell in 1904, early advocates for the preservation of the bush.

But the doubts and negativity expressed by various unmoved and ill-informed council officials — presumably not avid readers of learned articles published in *The Press* — eventually scuppered the proposed purchase a month before the Exhibition opened. Part of the problem seems to have been the perceived artificiality of the remaining bush since its ancient kahikatea trees were now well hidden behind the boundary plantings of oaks.

Efforts to purchase the bush as a public reserve faded away after this disappointment. Jane Deans was to die in 1911 knowing that its future was still dependent on the efforts of her family. Perhaps prompted by his awareness of how important the bush had been to his grandmother, three years later the third John Deans (Ian) arranged for the larger part of the bush (nearly 6.5 hectares) to be gifted to the people of Canterbury. The main condition attached to the family's gift was that the bush was 'to be kept for all time for the preservation and cultivation of trees and plants indigenous to New Zealand'. The family retained a small area of the bush (about 1.5 hectares) adjacent to the house as a buffer zone to protect their privacy.

Entrusted with a generous gift

Late in 1914, the bush and the conditions under which it was gifted by the Deans family achieved legal status with the passing of the Riccarton Bush Act. As well as various local authority representatives, the Board of Trustees incorporated by the Act included two representatives of the Deans family. At any one time, these were to be the oldest two descendants of the eight family members alive at the time the bush was gifted (children of John and Catherine Edith). Jane's grandson, the third John, was elected as the first chairman. He served for 54 years until 1968, when he stepped down aged 88. By 2014, the year of the Trust's centennial, three generations of Deans had served as trustees, with Charles Deans being the second family member to be elected as chairman, serving from 1999 to late 2014.

In recognition of the bush's scientific significance, the trustees also included a member of the Philosophical Society of Canterbury (this became the Canterbury branch of the New Zealand Royal Society after 1933). These have all been illustrious names in the field of botany, starting with Charles Chilton and ending at the time of the centennial with Brian Molloy, who by then had served for 41 years — half his life.

By the time Brian became a trustee in 1973, the founding Act had been amended several times, first to accommodate the City

Council's 1947 purchase from the Deans family of Riccarton House, the remaining section of bush, and most of the grounds, and then to raise the levy on local authorities required to manage the expanded reserve. The final triangle of land between the Kahu Street bridge and the drive — site of the original houses and farm buildings — was bought from the Deans family in 1975.

After the various local authorities were amalgamated into the one structure under the City Council in 1989, significant changes were made to how the bush was managed. With the impetus provided by the associated restructuring of the Trust, a first formal management plan was drawn up in 1991 to provide direction and purpose for the ongoing restoration of the bush. Added to the Trust's intended projects was an extended restoration programme for Riccarton House and Deans Cottage.

Further Amendments to the Act were passed, the last in 2012 to allow the Trust to accept bequests and legacies. Charles Deans was involved in the lengthy and rigorous process of seeing this latest amendment through Parliament. Initially, the Trust had considered seeking an entirely new Act, but eventually opted to retain the original 'quirky wording' because of its historical significance.

The Riccarton Bush Trust is 'an unusual beast', says Charles. It is the smallest of the half-dozen entities in New Zealand with their own Act. But its singularity lies in its preservation in an urban environment of a patch of ancient forest. A patch of forest that is not only the one surviving representative of its type but also one that combines both natural and cultural values spanning an uninterrupted sequence from pre-human to modern times. Both Brian Molloy and Charles Deans point out that one of the main issues throughout the life of the Trust has been ensuring that recognition of Riccarton Bush's significance is kept to the forefront to prevent the bush being treated as 'just another city park'. To that purpose, Charles points out that:

The entrance gate to Riccarton Bush and the newly built ranger's cottage in 1917, *Canterbury Times*.

The opening ceremony at Riccarton Bush, February 1917, *Canterbury Times*.

Having our own Act has been invaluable as it means the City Council can't override it at any stage.

This protection has helped the Trust negotiate its way through complex legal, financial and political management issues over the years, dealing with the expectations of councillors, locals and neighbours as pressure continues to mount from the increasing density of housing around the reserve. As a result, the present trustees, many of whom are long-serving, have built up a vast experience. One of the most important areas of their expertise has been becoming highly skilled at sourcing funding to supplement the major annual contribution from the City Council:

That's a political game — you need to understand the funders, how and when to approach them.

The third John Deans, Jane's oldest grandson, who initiated the gifting of Riccarton Bush to the people of Canterbury and served as chairman on the Riccarton Bush Trust Board for 54 years.

A daunting task

Before the bush was opened to the public in 1917 by no less than the Governor, Lord Liverpool, during a well-attended and widely reported ceremony, the newly established Trust removed some of the accumulated debris in the bush, fenced its boundary, built a cottage for a permanent ranger and cut a series of walking tracks.

Where the bush had been least disturbed, its interior was in good shape and required little attention. Overall, the distinctive profile of floodplain kahikatea forest was still intact. Kahikatea towered above a layer of smaller native trees, cabbage trees and shrubs. But it was a different story wherever there were gaps — the central gap already present in the 1840s (probably the result of a fire), those created by historic tree removals, and openings along the retreating boundaries exposed during the development of the farm at Riccarton and the settlement of Christchurch. These gaps had been invaded by elderberry, wild cherry, sycamore and other exotic trees. Debris from felled and naturally fallen trees was overrun by vigorous climbers, both natives that had always been a component of the bush and invaders like blackberry. These climbers had grown up into the surrounding trees where they formed smothering masses. Exotic herbaceous weeds and grasses had already been taking advantage of any disturbed ground by 1870, since they featured on John Armstrong's first plant list.

Once the surrounding farm land was sold off for suburban development, a process that began in 1925, pressure on the integrity

of the bush increased. Drainage issues developed, both from excess runoff from the encroaching built-up areas and from the compacted pathways within the bush. Gates and private tracks proliferated, leading into the bush from neighbouring residential properties. The margins of the bush became a dumping ground for garden rubbish, aggravating the already problematic increase of exotic invading plants being brought in by birds.

Leonard Cockayne expressed concern about the invasive exotic species in the bush as early as 1914, and more emphatically in 1924. He recommended that all 'foreign species' should be removed and any replacement plantings should be restricted to those native species already present. It was to be many years before his advice was heeded. Inevitably, two world wars and a major economic depression disrupted any attempts at consistent management. Many positive actions taken by the Trust were often negated by other well-intended but inappropriate practices.

Inconsistent weed control programmes put in place by successive rangers had varying results. Efforts to free young native trees and shrubs from the overwhelming masses of climbers were spasmodic and dependent on the initiative of individual rangers. A major snowstorm in 1945 caused the collapse of many trees already burdened with climbers, with the mammoth task of clearing the resulting debris not being completed until the late 1950s.

On the positive side, all the exotic trees planted in gaps by the well-meaning Jane Deans had been felled and the timber removed by the early 1950s. For the next 20 years, major efforts were made to plant the many gaps in the bush with native species, both donated and bought from commercial nurseries. The last section of the bush to come under the Trust's jurisdiction (bought from the Deans family in 1947) was in particularly bad shape. For many years, this section had been treated more as an extension to the house grounds than as an integral part of the bush. As a result, the

The open, sparse interior of the bush about 1915, photographed by J Bird.

tree canopy was open, which had encouraged dense grass and weed growth on the forest floor. Many species had been planted that were not natural components of Riccarton Bush. Among them were several beeches, rimu and hybrid lancewoods that were now well-established trees.

Few of the plants used to restock the bush during the 1950s and 1960s were raised from seedlings taken from the bush itself, which would later come to be seen as 'best practice' for restoration projects. Some plants were locally sourced from Banks Peninsula, but many came from elsewhere. Some species not native to Canterbury were also planted. Seedlings of kahikatea, matai and totara (obtained from the New Zealand Forest Service and sourced from outside Canterbury) were planted in the bush in an attempt to ensure a new generation of the dominant canopy trees. Kahikatea from this planting did well, being more suited to the conditions, but the matai and totara struggled.

Perhaps the most unfortunate management practice in this first era of the Trust was treating the bush as though it was English woodland. Fallen debris and forest floor litter were regularly raked into piles and burnt. Grassy clearings and even the forest floor were machine-mown. This practice maintained the clearings by encouraging a dense sward of grass that prevented the natural establishment of any native tree or shrub seedlings. Worse, it also damaged the extensive surface roots of some of the mature kahikatea. Root and butt rot was the result. The loss of two climbers once present in the bush, the white-flowering clematis (*Clematis paniculata*) and the white rata (*Metrosideros diffusa*), is also seen as a possible consequence of mowing.

The cumulative effect of all these issues and practices was dire. When Brian Molloy was first employed by Botany Division, DSIR (in 1969), he was invited to walk through the bush by Lance McCaskill, who had been a previous Royal Society representative on the Trust. On being asked for his honest opinion, Brian made no bones about replying:

This is the worst-managed bush in the whole country.

Years of managing the bush as though it were English woodland continued to deplete the forest floor and damage kahikatea roots until the 1970s.

Mowing maintained grassy clearings dominated by cocksfoot, such as this one photographed by Brian Molloy in 1977.

Two historic houses

As well as the already taxing responsibility of preserving and managing the bush, by the 1950s the Trust was further burdened by the acquisition of the two houses that encompassed the entire history of the Deans family at Riccarton. In 1947, the Christchurch City Council bought Riccarton House and its grounds (nearly 5.5 hectares, which included the remaining section of the bush) from the Deans family for £16,500. That same year, the 1843 cottage was plucked from its original site on the river bank near Kahu Road and transported by traction engine to a spot north of the house (where the Riccarton scout den is now).

Anne Mace, the last of the Deans babies born in Riccarton House (1942), remembers the occasion well. A child of five at the time, she and her older brother were by then living nearby with their mother. They had lived in the house for the first year of her life. Before the war, her father, the fourth John Deans, had an apartment upstairs in 'the back of the house', with a kitchen installed in what is now the office. After he was killed in an air training accident in 1943, the house was requisitioned for accommodation for officers from the Royal New Zealand Air Force. Anne and her brother often played in the 1843 cottage when visiting their grandparents, the third John and Ruth Deans, now retired from Kirkstyle and living in the converted stables (which became known as Riccarton Cottage, at 30 Kahu Road).

On the day the 1843 Deans Cottage was moved, a great crowd gathered to watch. When the traction engine slowly moved off with its load, Anne, who was more daring that her brother, leapt on to the back of the porch projecting from the side of the cottage. She intended jumping off its front edge, but tripped and fell headlong underneath:

> *I can still hear Grandmother shouting at me to lie still. 'Anne, don't move!' The traction engine and its load trundled on, leaving me unhurt in its wake, but Grandmother held on to me firmly after that.*

Once installed on its new site, the 1843 cottage was restored to its original condition by Rotary volunteers. Sometime in 1969–70 it was moved again, to its present site near Riccarton House, and further restored. The Riccarton Bush Trust, with expert help from the Canterbury Museum and using evidence provided by contemporary documents, including Jane Deans's letters to her grandchildren and Charlotte Godley's descriptions, then reconstructed its interior furnishings. These are all items on loan from the Canterbury Museum, not family pieces. But the papers on the desk in the living room are facsimile copies of genuine letters and accounts from the Deans family archives. The figure of the first John Deans, sitting at this desk, was based on his portraits and sculpted by the museum model-maker. The figure's hands have an even more direct family association. They were cast from those of great-great grandson Neil Deans, who happened to be working at the museum at the time.

Riccarton House had been lived in only intermittently since Edith's death in 1937. The fourth John Deans and his young family had been the last Deans descendants to occupy any part of the house. Once its wartime requisition by the air force was over, the house seems to have remained empty. The third John's retirement to Riccarton Cottage at 30 Kahu Road constituted the last years of the Deans family living on Riccarton land — a time that had covered over 130 years, from 1843 to 1975, when the family sold that remaining corner of land to the Council.

In the 1960s, the Council converted Riccarton House to serve as a social function and meeting centre. This conversion paid little heed to historic integrity. Downstairs, rooms available for public

The modelled interior of the living room in Deans Cottage, showing John Deans sitting at his desk.

use were lined with laminated plywood sheeting to dado height and fitted with cupboards and shelving. A false floor was installed in the 1856 morning room to bring it up to the height of the 1900 entrance hall, and it was equipped to serve as a bar. The 1900 kitchen and service rooms at the back of the house were converted into a flat for a resident caretaker. The scullery and a storeroom were modified to provide a commercial kitchen for catering purposes. Public toilets were installed both downstairs and upstairs, where some of the grand bedrooms were adapted for meeting rooms.

The upstairs bedroom wing on the south side of the house was closed off by a heavy curtain and abandoned. Charles Deans remembers pulling this curtain aside on one of his childhood visits:

> *The passageway was completely festooned with thick grey cobwebs — so thick, you couldn't see to the end. It probably hadn't been cleaned since the Council bought the house.*

Many Christchurch residents will remember attending dances, weddings and 21st birthday parties at Riccarton House. Among the social events held there from the 1960s through to the early 1990s were many Deans family occasions. Although the house had long been sold, the family still saw it as theirs; it was the repository of their family history and contained a multitude of memories. Charles Deans visited numerous times with members of the older generation and listened to their stories of playing in the house during their own childhood visits to Grandmother Edith. He himself was married at Riccarton House and celebrated his 50th birthday there:

Riccarton House in 1977, function centre and wedding venue.

> *The family retained emotional ownership of the house, and we still do so today.*

• 13 •
Ensuring
the Future

The Riccarton Bush Trust's efforts to restore the bush were to gather pace from the mid-1970s. Managed with a clearer direction and renewed enthusiasm, the bush was quick to respond. Over the next 40 years, it would recover from a depleted 'woodland' appearance to something close to a natural state. In the early to mid-1990s, the Trust would extend its attentions to Riccarton House, restoring the house to a condition that better reflected its significant status in the social history of Christchurch.

Turning the bush around

Brian Molloy was to become the longest-serving and most active Royal Society member of the Trust. Appointed in 1973, he promptly set out to 'turn the bush around' by introducing an ecologically based management regime aimed at restoring it to health. His earlier forthright opinion about the parlous condition of the bush (see Chapter 12) had been confirmed the previous year when Geoff Kelly surveyed the Canterbury scenic reserves.

Kelly concluded that two small central areas of mature kahikatea, pokaka and lemonwood were 'tolerably natural', although much of the associated understorey tree growth was secondary. Together, these two patches comprised only about 12 per cent of the total area of Riccarton Bush. Two even smaller, associated patches (just over 6 per cent) were dominated by mahoe. The bulk of the surrounding area (over 40 per cent) contained scattered kahikatea with open clumps of other trees, little or no undergrowth, and a forest floor of rank grass and weeds. Beyond this depleted area, an outer ring that was mostly open rank grass with few trees made up nearly 28 per cent of the total area. The balance comprised the oak-planted boundaries. Although Kelly gave the bush an overall scientific rating of only four out of 10, he considered it still had value as a 'relic'.

Over the next few decades, Brian Molloy's recommendations for improving the management of the bush built on his personal observations of how it responded to simple tactics:

I acted on the best scientific advice I ever got — from eminent botanist Lucy Moore. When I started at DSIR, she called me into

The nursery in 1980, where thousands of native plants were raised to fill gaps in the bush.

her office and said, 'Don't believe what you hear or read. Go into the field and talk to the plants.'

Although the problems initially seemed insurmountable, the bush was to prove remarkably resilient. Brian brought ex-Forest Service ranger Jack Wildermoth over from the West Coast as the new live-in ranger. Jack promptly dealt with 70 or so possums luxuriating in the bush, then set up a programme of ongoing control of all animal pests. Brian 'got rid' of City Council workers wanting to treat the bush like a city park. After the practices of burning debris and mowing the clearings and forest floor were stopped, the gradual build-up of forest litter provided ideal conditions for the almost instantaneous natural establishment of seedlings. A new nursery was set up behind the ranger's house to raise supplementary plants propagated only from seed sourced within the bush. Thousands of seedlings were raised for planting out in clearings and gaps. Most of these were quick-growing species like matipo, lemonwood, ribbonwood, mahoe and marbleleaf, all species Brian had observed were among the first to spring up naturally in the bush.

At the same time, the decision was made to remove the wide borders of oaks and other exotic trees originally planted in the 1860s to 1870s at Jane Deans's instigation in the mistaken belief that the remaining kahikatea groves needed protection from wind damage. As Brian Molloy points out, kahikatea, with its massive spreading root system, is one of the most wind-resistant native trees. Jane herself had noted in 1882 that these plantings were suppressing any young native trees (see Chapter 12). The problem had worsened now that the oaks were mature 100-year-old trees.

The last block of 120-year-old oaks on the north-western boundary of the bush were felled in 1984, *The Christchurch Star*.

The south-eastern boundary of the bush in 1978, photographed by Robert Lamberts after clearance of oaks in 1975 and subsequent planting of nursery-grown native seedlings.

Their presence constituted too large a proportion of the total area of the bush — over 10 per cent by Geoff Kelly's 1972 calculations — and their influence extended well beyond that.

The border trees were felled in three stages. With the reasons well publicised, the logging took place between 1975 and 1984, mostly with public support. But the final stage, the removal of the last 50 or so oaks, caused some neighbourhood controversy, an organised protest and the excitement of a tree sit-in. As each area was cleared of logs and debris, it was planted out sparsely with seedlings raised in the nursery to provide initial shelter for the naturally regenerating seedlings that soon followed. Brian Molloy says:

> *The recovery of local natives where the oaks had been, and in other gaps, was spectacular.*

Other areas where natural recovery was triggered were created by closing many of the tracks, both official and unofficial. Over time, these tracks have merged back into the forest floor. The main circuit was concreted to provide an all-weather surface, which in itself helped stop visitors from straying off the official path. A new boardwalk extended the main path through the least disturbed part of the bush, giving controlled access to a handsome grove of 300–600-year-old kahikatea.

More consistent weed-control programmes were put in place, targeting in turn individual problem species like male fern and blackberry. Local groups and volunteers helped with much of the time-consuming grubbing and hand-pulling. In addition, a new boundary fence eliminated the problem of private use of the bush along its margins and the dumping of garden rubbish.

Once natural recovery gathered pace, conditions became unsuitable for many weed species. By the 1990s, three-quarters of the exotic invaders present in the bush in the 1950s had disappeared. Different species continued to invade from the surrounding urban area or were brought in by birds, so weed control was an ongoing management requirement.

After 25 years of this new ecologically based regime, Brian Molloy was able to conclude in his 1997 Banks Lecture that:

> *Substantial parts of the bush are now difficult to distinguish from undisturbed forests elsewhere in the country.*

Vigorous growth of planted and naturally seeding native trees in an area where exotic trees had been removed.

A living laboratory

Some of the earliest scientific endeavours in Christchurch had been centred on Riccarton Bush. Collections of plants were made at various stages, including ferns, mosses and fungi. Studies of insects began early. The first known collection was from 1859: a moth now housed as part of the Fereday Collection at the Canterbury Museum. Richard Fereday collected and described many insects from the bush in the 1860s to the 1870s. He was followed by many other noted collectors. As a result, the bush became the 'type locality' (site of first archived specimen and its formal description) for about 100 insects — mostly butterflies and moths. For this reason alone, the bush is of international significance.

From its early days, the Riccarton Bush Trust encouraged the use of the bush for school visits and student study. For many years, Canterbury University had contributed financially to the upkeep of the bush in return for access for student experiments and graduate research. Once the university was sited nearby in Ilam (the move from the city centre began in the 1960s), the use of the bush for this purpose continued.

In keeping with the scientific importance of the bush, the Trust set up photographic monitoring points to record any changes associated with the major planting and restoration programme initiated in the mid-1970s. Photographs were taken at regular intervals from these points. By 1990, many of the original photo points installed in 1976 were becoming overgrown — a measure of success in itself. No one would have predicted the speed with which the bush responded to the new ecological management regime. Brian Molloy says:

The bush has been a tremendous place of learning. It's a living organism. Just observing its response to the changes we made has taught me a lot about dynamics, ecology and reproductive behaviour.

About 1990, David Norton, School of Forestry, University of Canterbury, surveyed the bush in detail, using standard measurements recorded on vegetation plots located on a regular grid. He identified five vegetation sub-types based mainly on the density of kahikatea present. These types bore a rough resemblance to the categories described by Geoff Kelly nearly 20 years earlier, but their condition differed considerably. Beneath the old emergent kahikatea and pokaka trees, the main canopy of the bush now ranged from six

Cabbage trees are scattered throughout Riccarton Bush, but dominate on the southern border.

to 10 metres high where it was dominated by lemonwood and ribbonwood, and from four to five metres high where it was dominated by shorter-growing species like kohuhu, karamu and mahoe. Cabbage trees were scattered throughout, but co-dominated with kahikatea in the southern part of the bush. Although canopy gaps were still obvious, overall understorey cover had improved and the forest floor was fully covered, mostly with litter, but with ferns and mosses in many places. In some places, natural seedlings of kahikatea were establishing under broadleaved trees like pokaka.

David Norton concluded that the structure and composition of the bush reflected both its natural history as an isolated relic on the plains and the impact — both negative and positive — of human intervention over the last few hundred years. Inevitably, because of the location of this small remnant of floodplain kahikatea forest stranded in the middle of a city, he considered its survival would to some extent continue to depend on human intervention.

In the early 1990s, as part of the Trust's review of how best to proceed with the management of the bush, Brian Molloy led an initiative to pull together all that was known about its natural history, both published and unpublished. The resulting book, *Riccarton Bush: Putaringamotu* (published in 1995) encompasses everything that was known at the time. Written by experts in their fields, with Brian as overall editor (as well as a major contributor), this excellent and authoritative book is still in print and can be purchased from the Trust.

In summer 2012, new permanent plots were set out in the bush to cover all the identified habitats and vegetation sub-types, with photo points marked at the four corners of each plot. These photo points will be used to provide ongoing monitoring of the bush and continue the accumulation of knowledge about its ecology, dynamics and management.

Recovery of the forest floor after mowing ceased, with ferns establishing in many areas by the 1990s.

A gentle touch

Since the mid-1990s, the Trust has built on its earlier success. In 2014, Brian Molloy was able to claim that the bush now needed only 'gentle management' as much of its ongoing recovery would be self-regulating. The second cohort of kahikatea, now 50 or so years old, although planted and not sourced locally, does ensure the continuance of kahikatea as a major element in the forest for generations to come. Its seedlings are now establishing naturally. Comparisons with old photographs show that the condition of even the emergent kahikatea canopy has improved. That the bush had reached this satisfying stage has been helped by three major initiatives put in place in the last 20 years: removal of the aggressive North Island lacebark, installation of irrigation, and the erection of a predator-proof fence.

Although most of the exotic woody weed species had been removed from the bush by 1990, one native introduction, the North Island lacebark (*Hoheria sexstylosa*), had become rampant. It was not only seeding vigorously throughout the bush, but it was also hybridising with the local, narrow-leaved lacebark (*H. angustifolia*). John Moore, who has been the ranger at Riccarton Bush since 1994, undertook the removal of this last invasive tree species as his first major project. With the help of volunteers, it took six years of hard effort:

> *I foolishly offered to do the work, not realising what would be involved. We felled hundreds of big trees, ring-barked thousands of smaller trees, and cut then poisoned tens of thousands of saplings too big to pull out. Pulled more than a million seedlings.*

By the end of the 1980s, biomass in the recovering bush had built up so much that the extra growth was placing too much demand on the available soil moisture. This situation was not helped by the ongoing changes in drainage caused by the surrounding suburban intensification. A pilot irrigation scheme was followed in 2006 by the installation of a fully reticulated system that runs as four individual sectors, with timed programmes pumping water from an on-site bore. Specially made brown tubing was used to blend in with the litter, with the result that the surface-laid piping is now close to invisible. John Moore notes that the coverage achieved is spotty as the nozzles spray in circles and tree trunks create rain shadows:

> *We probably cover only fifty per cent of the bush, so upgrading*

with extra pipes to double that coverage is something I've recommended to the Trust.

When privately endowed 'mainland islands' were being established at Karori in Wellington and Maungatautari in the early 2000s, the Trust sought a price for installing a predator-proof fence around the bush. On learning the cost would be $250,000, they shelved the idea. But word spread, and the Gama Foundation offered to cover most of this cost. Installed in 2004, the predator-proof fence and the four-metre wide mowing strip around its perimeter proved a total success for the first four years as no predators or vermin got into the bush.

As a result, from 2008 to 2011, Riccarton Bush was used as one of the Department of Conservation's kiwi crèches for Operation Nest Egg. Hatched chicks from Willowbank were kept in the bush for one year until they were large enough to resist predator attack. The bush sheltered three lots of six kiwi chicks, the last lot leaving in summer 2011. In preparation for the first lot of chicks, John Moore collected lengths of hollow logs to serve as burrows, placing them carefully in the bush and camouflaging them with litter and fern. The first six chicks were released into these burrows. They promptly abandoned them the next night:

They found their own burrows, like tunnels under piles of debris from vines. They preferred dirty natural holes to my clean dry logs.

Brian Molloy thinks bellbirds might now be nesting in the bush, but is sceptical about plans to introduce other species that had once been present. He is not sure the bush is the right environment for

A predator-proof fence was built on the boundaries of Riccarton Bush in 2004.

geckos and skinks sourced from Banks Peninsula, a current release project, and considers that the tui released at Hinewai and now spreading will eventually find their own way to Riccarton:

It would be better to let any native animals decide for themselves whether to stock the bush than to introduce them artificially.

Evidence is already appearing at Riccarton to support Brian's contention that interventions like the predator-proof fence are at best only a deterrent. For the past six years or so, sporadic invasions by rats have caused the occasional problem, requiring discrete poison baiting. In spring 2014, rats built up sufficiently for John Moore to notify the public that poison baits had been laid in the bush:

We don't know how they gain access. We do have the occasional owl nesting in the bush, and they could drop a live rat or two — that is known elsewhere.

An unanticipated aftermath of the Christchurch earthquakes was the displacement of feral pigeons from the demolished city centre. These pigeons have become a major problem in Riccarton Bush. More than 600 were shot between 2012 and 2014, using a high-powered air rifle in the early mornings while the grounds were closed to the public. That pigeons will continue to be a problem was confirmed by the build-up of numbers after a shooting hiatus of three months over the winter of 2014. Not all the corpses can be retrieved from the now-dense undergrowth in the bush, and John Moore suggests these corpses may be one of the reasons for the ongoing rat problem in the bush as they provide an attractive food source.

One of the most striking visual characteristics of the bush today is the climbers scrambling through areas of canopy below the emergent kahikatea. Lianes or climbers have always been a feature of Riccarton Bush, as recorded in the early plant lists. Pohuehue (*Muehlenbeckia australis*) is the most common climber present, and the most aggressive. New Zealand jasmine (*Parsonsia heterophylla*) is the next most common climber. Numerous seedlings with their characteristic twining stems and tiny, fiddle-shaped leaves spring up beside the paths as a result of their seeds being washed off the concrete surfaces. The third most conspicuous climber is the passionvine or kohia (*Passiflora tetrandra*), which reaches its southernmost natural limit at Riccarton.

From 2008 to 2011, Riccarton Bush served as one of the Department of Conservation's kiwi crèches for Operation Nest Egg.

With pohuehue, passionvine is the main component of the large masses that still smother trees in some parts of the bush. There is debate about whether these dense masses are natural or induced, and whether they should be curbed. The weight of snow accumulating in these masses in the winter storms of the last few years caused a lot of damage and some tree collapse. Brian Molloy concedes that the aggressive nature of these climbers can be a problem, and agrees that judicious manual clearing should be done around young pokaka and kahikatea, but he remains averse to any suggestion that the climbers should be poisoned:

This immensely valuable bush is thriving and now needs minimal interference. Its future is secure. I have no doubts about that — or about its continued national importance.

An emphasis on authenticity

With the successful restoration of the bush well under way, in 1992 the Riccarton Bush Trust embarked on restoring and redeveloping Riccarton House in a manner that was more in keeping with its historic significance. Not only did the house retain the three distinct stages of its construction — the modest colonial house of 1856, the consolidation and extension of 1874, and the late Victorian grandeur of the 1900 substantial addition — but the interior was also largely in its original condition behind the superficial conversion imposed in the 1960s. In particular, heritage experts and conservators were excited by the retention of the upstairs nursery wing and the service rooms at the back of the house as 'a rare intact group'. That Jane Deans had lived in all three stages of the house, covering a period of 55 years until her death in 1911, added an unusual element of continuous social history framed in the fortunes of one family.

By the beginning of the 1990s, although the weatherboard exterior of the house had been adequately maintained, with regular repainting and replacement of rotting boards, decades of use as a function centre and meeting place for local groups and clubs meant the interior was dilapidated. Water damage triggered by heavy rain in the mid-1980s had caused the southern corner of the ceiling in Granny's 1874 bedroom to collapse, and the southern nursery wing was 'in an interesting state of abandonment and decay' — heritage interior conservator Stephen Cashmore's perspective.

Finding original wallpapers, like this 1856 one in Jane's bedroom, was a highlight of the restoration of Riccarton House in the 1990s.

After commissioning several successive and detailed conservation plans, then raising the necessary funding (half the estimated $1.5 million, which included the projected cost of installing commercial catering facilities, would be provided by the Christchurch City Council over three years), the Trust began an intensive three-stage restoration of the house. In Stephen's words:

It was time the community became more aware of the historic value of the house. So we set out to restore the essence of the Deans family home.

The first stage was re-roofing the whole house in 1993–94 to arrest the leaks and associated interior decay. Imported cedar shingles were used to replace the original kahikatea shingles sourced from Riccarton Bush. While the roof space was exposed, the opportunity was taken to install a sprinkler system for fire protection. This stage alone cost $350,000, which included the services of Stephen Cashmore to produce an interior conservation plan.

Stephen's input focused on ensuring that the renovation of the ground floor entrance hall and adjacent rooms restored both their original structure and the early Edwardian interior style introduced in 1900, with an emphasis on providing opportunities for heritage and architectural interpretation. Much of the information came from the enormous volume of papers and photographs held in the Deans family archives, which had been recently sorted into numerous boxes and catalogued by Graham Hemming (manager at Riccarton House) to create an immensely valuable and accessible resource.

As part of the 1990s heritage interpretation scheme, the original brick nogging was left exposed in the 1856 morning room downstairs.

The original delicate tints of the 1900 ceiling roses were revealed once layers of paint were stripped.

Architectural historian Jenny May worked closely with Stephen Cashmore during the restoration of the ground floor in 1995–96:

> *Stephen's meticulous research and careful deconstruction revealed the decorative history of each room, particularly that represented by the layers of wallpaper.*

For both Jenny and Stephen, finding traces of the original wallpapers was the highlight of the restoration — a process helped by fragments left inside wardrobes and behind skirting boards. When the restorers stripped back the walls in the downstairs study, they found that the whole of its south wall was lined with newspapers, among them an 1856 copy of the *Ayrshire Times*, complete with its penny stamp. It is clear from William and John Deans's letters to Scotland that they were regularly sent copies of newspapers, so Jane Deans must have continued to receive papers from home.

Although the Deans family had few interior photographs, a series of images was found in a family friend's album, dating from 1906. This provided the basis for recreating many of the interior decorative features and furnishings of that era, including help in identifying the patterns and style of the wallpapers. A receipt still existed for the original 1856 grey lattice-pattern wallpaper in the morning room. As far as possible, these papers, Axminster carpets and curtains were replicated, some of them being purpose-manufactured for the Riccarton House project. Stephen was particularly delighted by the wallpaper for the drawing room, matched then reproduced using traditional techniques by a Lower Hutt firm:

> *A return to the historical design and colour scheme restores the original sense of volume and space to a room.*

Similarly, replicas were made of a roller blind found in the back of a cupboard and thought to date from 1874. These blinds were used in the windows of the study and the dining room. Bob McTavish, a painter and decorator trained in traditional techniques, worked his way through the house room by room, stripping and restoring timber, plastering, painting and wallpapering. In the grander rooms, the ceiling roses proved to be one of the many surprises and delights. Once the layers of paint obscuring their detail were carefully stripped back, their original delicate distemper tints were

reinstated. For Stephen Cashmore, it is this process of 'bringing decorative objects back to life' that keeps him in the industry.

In accordance with best practice for heritage interpretation, one room was chosen to reveal all the stages of the house's structural and social history. This was the morning room, part of the 1856 house, added to in 1874 and refurbished in 1900. Once the raised floor installed in the 1960s was removed to expose the foundations, a pier was built out into the room so visitors could see the original 1856 stone piles, the later concrete piles and footings, the foundation for the fireplace and the concrete beam supporting the bay window, added in 1874. Walls were stripped to reveal the 1856 brick nogging and internal lath-and-clay wall fillings. The successive layers of wallpaper from 1856 right through to the latest layer were retained on one wall to illustrate the changing fashions in decorative styles. Stephen was aware that not everyone would approve, preferring to see the room fully refurbished:

It's easier to restore, so this was a brave treatment, and one that was really successful for interpretation purposes.

In this room, as throughout the house, reconstruction used the skills of craftsmen trained in traditional methods wherever possible. Some compromises were made — in repairing the external walls of the morning room, traditional lime mortar and proper plaster, not available in 1856 Christchurch, were used to replace the clay filling and flimsy plaster much lamented by Jane Deans (see Chapter 8). A marble fireplace was not reinstalled at this stage as conflicting stories abounded about the fate of the original and whether it had been sold or retained by the family.

The requirement to enable a money-earning function for the house meant compromise was needed. The commercial kitchen installed in what had been the day nursery and adjacent service rooms at the back of the house was constructed as a 'formica box', so it could be removed at any stage. This left the original wall panelling and an Italian-style painted mural on one wall intact behind the fittings.

Upstairs, the cobweb-shrouded nursery wing was cleaned and the floors swept, then the original lath-and-plaster, paint finish and woodwork varnishes were left as they were, in keeping with Stephen's assessment of these rooms:

The back of the house upstairs was a fabulous decorative

The ornate late-Victorian timber fire surrounds characteristic of the 1900 house were stripped and restored.

survivor — the family had just removed the furniture then walked out of it.

In contrast, the main upstairs bedrooms were refurbished in Edwardian style. Although the Riccarton Bush Trust followed Stephen Cashmore's conservation plans for this part of the house, diminishing funding meant they had to do without his on-the-spot decision-making and supervision of the work, so they chose replacement wallpapers themselves, mostly Laura Ashley florals. Donations of Edwardian-style furniture, including some family pieces, were used to furnish the rooms.

Another major stage of the restoration project was the reinstatement of the 1900 kitchen and the service rooms at the back of the house. This work began in 2000. In the kitchen, the original William Morris wallpaper was discovered behind the dresser, and much of the tongue-and-groove woodwork throughout the service area was restorable. A double-oven Shacklock coal range (bigger than the original oven) was sourced and installed in the kitchen. Once the work was completed, many of the original elements had been restored, revealing the grand and up-to-date kitchen complex enjoyed by the domestic staff employed by John and Edith Deans.

Stephen Cashmore was thrilled with the overall result of this lengthy restoration project and the return of many of the rooms to their original decorative elements:

It's such a surprise for people to see reproduced historic decoration like this. I consider the community was richly rewarded by this restoration of Riccarton House.

A final flourish in 2001 was repainting the exterior of the house in its original colour scheme. This scheme was reconstructed from analysis of paint scrapings, and details of the design were painstakingly ascertained for each facade from contemporary photographs. Far from the pinkish beige of the paintwork used during regular maintenance up to the 1990s, the rich-cream background and decorative features picked out in deep burgundy were colour-matched as closely as possible to the original 1900 colours.

Although plans were proposed at various stages to make best use of the refurbished house by developing 'living history' displays and social history re-enactments as a revenue-spinning tourist venture, these plans have not yet come to fruition. They remain a desirable

goal for the future. In the meantime, since 2002 the Riccarton Bush Trust has run regular guided tours, using knowledgeable volunteers to tell visitors stories from the rich history of the house and the Deans family who lived here for so many years. Among these volunteers was Charles Deans's mother, Ruth, who continued in this role until 2010.

Just when the Riccarton Bush Trust considered it could justifiably rest on its laurels, with both the bush and the house in good repair after decades of concerted effort, catastrophe struck. In September 2010, Christchurch experienced the first of a series of damaging earthquakes that continued through 2011. Although timber-built Riccarton House remained standing, damage to its interior was considerable. Most of the meticulous restoration work completed by the early 2000s would have to be redone. In keeping with Jane Deans's own response to calamity — grit and perseverance — the Trust took on the burden of yet another major period of reconstruction and restoration.

Riccarton House in 2001 as the painters finish restoring its original colour scheme.

• 14 •
Shaken but Not Shattered

When the face of Christchurch was changed forever by a series of earthquakes in 2010 and 2011, followed by several years of continual aftershocks, Riccarton House was one of the city's heritage buildings to suffer considerable damage. Once the aftershocks diminished, the Riccarton Bush Trust embarked on an extensive restoration of the house that again brought it back to its former Edwardian glory. But these were not the first earthquakes experienced by the Deans family at Riccarton.

A shaky past

Many people were shocked and surprised by the powerful and destructive earthquakes that hit Christchurch in 2010 and 2011. Although the perception had been that the city was comparatively safe from seismic disturbance, collective memory is unreliable. Christchurch has a history of earthquakes — many in the mid to late 19th century and some with their epicentres in Canterbury. John and Jane Deans were among those who recorded their experiences.

The Deans brothers had not been long at Putaringamotu when John had his first encounter with an earthquake one night in 1844. William, who was used to earthquakes from his two years in Wellington, woke him a few minutes beforehand to warn him that one was coming. John's comments about buildings were to prove only too accurate in the earthquakes that would hit Christchurch more than 150 years later:

… it reminds me … of … when a heavy loaded cart is passing … The wooden houses yield to it, but the brick ones are thought to be rather unsafe. I should say stone ones would be still worse.

During the early 1850s, a few more tremors were felt in Christchurch, but severe shaking was not experienced until January 1855. This earthquake was centred on the Wairarapa fault. Badly affecting Wellington, this was the most severe earthquake felt since formal colonisation began in 1840. At Riccarton, Jane Deans was sitting reading. It was nine in the evening:

When all at once the house began to rattle, and my chair felt to be upsetting. The pictures swung on the walls, and the lamp on the table shook from side to side as if it would capsize … That was a 'shake'. In the middle of the night a very sharp 'upheaval' one came, shorter but more alarming.

Jane comments that the aftershocks continued 'for many weeks after', but noticed them only at night as they were not felt if moving about — an observation that would be endorsed by Christchurch residents today.

With this experience so fresh in Jane Deans's mind, the use of brick nogging between vertical wooden posts in the exterior walls of the house built for her the following year may well have been as an earthquake protection measure. Architectural historian Jenny May points out that the same construction was used for this purpose in

The top of the Cathedral spire, already slightly damaged in 1881, toppled in the 1888 earthquake centred near Hanmer.

Early settlers experienced quite frequent earthquakes, so were used to damage like that shown in these Robert Park sketches after an 1848 earthquake in Wellington.

the wooden part of the Provincial Chambers, built in 1858.

Closer to home, a shallow earthquake at eight in the morning on 5 June 1869, centred under the Addington/Spreydon area, caused widespread chimney collapse and minor damage to stonework in Christchurch. This was one of the most severe earthquakes experienced in the city up to then. Dr Barker's description in a letter to his brother refers to the noise being more of a roar than the 'distant deep mumbling usually accompanying a quake'. Jane Deans is even more graphic in her letters to her grandchildren:

> *It came, as they usually do, without warning. A loud report like a cannon ball hitting the house, then a long rumbling noise like a long, heavy train passing over a wooden bridge, shaking violently all the time ... it seemed interminable.*

Several more earthquakes were felt over the next few days, and the aftershocks continued for some months. Then on 31 August 1870, another 'very similar in character' rocked the city again. This one was centred on the southern edge of Banks Peninsula. It caused some damage in Christchurch. Stone buildings were the worst affected, with a coping, gable apex and arch being damaged at the new stone addition to the Provincial Chambers. At Riccarton House, after the first shaking subsided, the hams in the kitchen 'swayed backward and forward for a quarter of an hour'.

Other tremors were felt in Christchurch through the 1870s, then more damaging ones struck in December 1881 (centred near Castle Hill) and September 1888 (centred near Hanmer). The latter caused the top of the spire on the Cathedral, already slightly damaged in 1881, to topple. It was again damaged in November 1901 during a large earthquake centred at Cheviot. It was after this earthquake that the top of the spire was rebuilt in wood and sheathed with copper. Neither of the 1880s earthquakes is mentioned by Jane Deans in her letters, perhaps inured to the experience by then.

Over the next century, many earthquakes centred in Canterbury and others centred further afield in the South Island were felt in Christchurch. Some caused minor damage: chimneys toppling, crockery smashing, windows cracking and masonry falling. Many of these were reported widely in the newspapers of the day — including in Australia. But it was not until 2010 that the city and Riccarton House itself would suffer the devastating impact of a series of major earthquakes.

The 1901 Cheviot earthquake caused slips and severe local damage to roads.

A series of shocks

After the first earthquake woke Christchurch before dawn on 4 September 2010, Rob Dally, manager at Riccarton House at the time, initially thought the house had suffered little harm. But once the maître d' for the catering company noticed that one of the ceiling roses in the dining room had pulled away, Rob made a closer inspection of every room. None of the lath-and-plaster was damaged, but a brick had come through the ceiling in Jane's bedroom upstairs in the 1856 part of the house. When he climbed into the roof space, he found that a third of the brick chimney had collapsed. Further inspection revealed that six of the seven chimneys were badly damaged:

> *They had snapped like carrots and slightly swivelled on their axes.*

As a sensible precaution, the chimneys were dismantled down to the level of the first floor ceilings. Fortunately, this had been completed before the 22 February earthquake in 2011, preventing the major damage that would have been caused by falling brick chimneys. As it was, the fireplace in 'Granny's room' in the 1874 part of the house collapsed outwards, spewing bricks across the floor.

Rob, sitting in the office upstairs, experienced the movement and noise of this earthquake as extreme. When the shaking subsided, he ventured downstairs to find the few lunch guests traumatised and white-faced. Returning to the house the next day, Rob says it was like walking into a scene on the *Marie Celeste*; half-eaten lunches were still sitting on tables that had not been cleared and everything was shrouded in plaster dust. A remarkable indication of the severity of the movement of the house during this earthquake has

The chandelier in Kirkstyle, where the glass shades on the north-south axis broke in the February earthquake.

Rob Dally investigating the lateral cracks that extended under the house, causing the bay window in the morning room to pull away.

been retained by the Trust. The central chandelier in the bedroom on the north-western corner of the house ('Kirkstyle') had swung on an arc high enough for the two glass shades on its north-south axis to hit the ceiling and break. The two shades on the opposing axis were undamaged. Later that year, during the double whammy of the 13 June earthquakes, Charles Deans was talking to the gardener on the river bank. He was quite sure he was witnessing the inevitable end of the grand old house. When the shaking at last stopped, he was amazed that, far from collapsing, the house was still intact.

Being a timber-framed building, Riccarton House had stood up to the movement well. Despite the severity of the shaking, the house had not suffered any critical structural damage. Its old-style construction was effective, and some earthquake strengthening had been done during the restoration completed in 1996. The concrete foundations experienced minor cracking in places. Where the different wings of the house joined, some of the weatherboards had separated slightly. Lateral spreading towards the river caused some ground cracking, including under the bay window in the morning room, which pulled away from the main structure.

Unlike many modern buildings in Christchurch where windows shattered or cracked, there was little or no damage to window glass. Only one door jammed to the extent that it needed to be planed to fit. Very little damage was done to contents (only $10,000 worth). Nevertheless, the internal destruction was extensive and typical of that expected for a house of its age and type. As well as the collapsed chimney breast in Granny's room, others were cracked, as were most of the fireplaces. The lath-and-plaster ceilings and internal wall linings throughout the house suffered everything on the scale from minor to severe cracking through to complete separation from their framing. Even apparently intact walls revealed softening or crushing of the plaster on their lower edges and corners.

The ground floor rooms were the most affected because they bore the extra loading of the upstairs structure. Of the two 1856 rooms, the study was the worst damaged. The structural bracing in the adjacent morning room may have been weakened when lath-and-plaster linings on the exterior wall had been removed in the 1996 restoration to reveal the brick nogging. The floor had also been removed, with just a 'pier' from which visitors could see the original piles and concrete footings (see Chapter 13). Both actions may have

overloaded the adjacent study. Substantial amounts of the original timber framing in both rooms were also affected by borer and rot, which contributed to the damage. Charles Deans says:

Seeing so much damage throughout the house was upsetting — fifteen years of the Trust's hard work restoring it down the drain.

A complicated process

Overall, the engineering assessments showed that Riccarton House had below 34 per cent of the seismic strength required by the post-earthquake new-building regulations. Some parts were estimated to be as low as 10 per cent. The new, more stringent Christchurch City Council requirements for 'earthquake-prone buildings' meant that restoration would probably need to strengthen the house up to 67 per cent of the new building code. To achieve this, major and invasive strengthening work would be involved.

Although heritage architect Tony Ussher says there was room to negotiate a lower strengthening percentage for a heritage building that would involve less invasive work on the historic structure, the Riccarton Bush Trust opted to comply with the 67 per cent requirement. Understandably, it may have wanted to avoid any risk of having to repeat such major restoration in the future.

Gritting its collective teeth, the Trust took the opportunity to do more than bring the house up to 67 per cent and again restore the house to its 1900 Edwardian glory. It would renew all the wiring and install a sophisticated switchboard, insulation, an underfloor heat pump, automatic fire doors and a modern alarm system. The improvements would not stop there. A modern, top-of-the-line commercial kitchen would replace the 1990s version installed in what had once been the children's day nursery. This new kitchen would enhance the continued and financially necessary use of Riccarton House as a restaurant and function centre. This ambitious restoration and upgrade programme would be completed at a final, eye-watering cost of $2.3 million. Charles Deans says it was worth doing:

I'm proud of what we've achieved. There's always major maintenance work needed with an old house, and now that's all been done for the next twenty years.

Damage to lath-and-plaster and wall linings in the 1856 study.

Inevitably, insurance would cover only the earthquake damage, not the improvements. Finding sponsorship for the uninsured parts of the restoration effort was a challenge, so Rob Dally took on the work of collating information and preparing reports that were a vital part of this process. In September the previous year — before the first earthquake — he had been on the point of retiring from his position as manager. After the February earthquake, he decided to stay on, feeling the Trust needed his engineering expertise and administrative skills to see the house through the lengthy restoration ahead:

> *Besides, my own house out at Halswell had suffered huge damage in September. Living in the garage at home and retirement didn't seem a good combination.*

With a grant of more than $128,000 from the Christchurch Earthquake Appeal Trust added to the insurance pay-out, work on the extended restoration was ready to begin in February 2013. Charles Deans says that, apart from the emotional distress of the damage to a place he was passionate about, confronting the huge and ongoing costs of the restoration was the worst issue for him:

> *Even in February 2014, only five months before the work was to be completed, there was still so much to be done.*

The management team for the earthquake repairs at Riccarton House. Left to right, at the back: Tony Ussher, Josh Simon and Justin Roberts; in the front: John Radburn, Euving Au, Alan Brown, Darryl McIntosh, Jenny May and Rob Dally.

Fortunately, in March 2014, a further injection of over $33,000 in the form of a Heritage Incentive Grant was approved by the City Council to fund much of the structural strengthening and maintenance work not covered by insurance.

One of the vital decisions made by the Trust was to take advantage of John Radburn's appointment as project director for the City Council heritage repairs, initially for any needed after the first earthquake in September 2010. John's long-established project management company, Insight Unlimited, is based in Gisborne. His many years of experience in major construction work on heritage buildings, both here and in Australia, meant he was first port of call for the City Council insurers' loss adjusters, Cunningham & Lindsay. What was identified that September as 'one or two assets' grew to a list of 65 buildings as successive earthquakes wreaked increasing levels of damage throughout the city:

The rest is history, but I love the work and I'm here for the duration.

This workload meant John would be commuting to Christchurch from Gisborne on a weekly basis throughout the rebuild. At the time of writing this book, he had already been doing so for more than four years — with the support of his understanding wife. Echoing Jane Deans's own attitude, John's philosophy is that if a job is worth doing, it is worth doing well.

Riccarton House was one of the first heritage projects off the blocks. John Radburn became the 'go-between' between the insurers and the Trust. Immediately aware of the enormity of the task ahead, he had the necessary skills and experience to pull together the best team for the entire process, from initial stabilisation of the house through funding, design, customer approval, consents and construction to the final handover.

One of the first major challenges John faced was 'driving' Riccarton House through the early design, consent and approval phases at the same time he was managing the Council's 65 heritage assets through each of the four earthquakes considered to be separate events by the Earthquake Commission. Each time another substantial earthquake caused more damage, the costs of the new damage had to be calculated separately for insurance purposes. This meant constantly reworking the damage scoping and repair budgets — the first phases of the process:

Charles Deans, chairman of the Riccarton Bush Trust and one of the fifth generation of the Deans family in Canterbury.

While these events were continually occurring, we often thought, 'Are we fighting a losing battle?' But we knew we had to push on.

At Riccarton House, the open and rewarding relationship that developed between John Radburn, Charles Deans and Rob Dally (on behalf of the Trust) and loss adjuster Tim Stephenson was what made the process put in place by John successful. John worked closely with Tim, reviewing the substantial changes in the budgets involved every time another issue was discovered during the deconstruction phase. The transparency imposed by John and the resulting trust that developed between the two men meant that the loss adjuster was usually happy to approve additions to the budget, sometimes amounting to as much as $130,000. Charles Deans says the relief felt by the Trust when John Radburn took over control of the whole complex process was enormous:

> *We didn't know where to start. Insight has been fantastic. John Radburn himself is the unsung hero of heritage Christchurch.*

Deconstruction and design

Already on board after the September 2010 earthquake was heritage architect Tony Ussher. For Riccarton House, he was busy drawing up plans for reinstatement of the damaged chimneys when the impact of the February earthquake on the city meant the rules changed. Tony then had to work with engineers to redesign the chimneys and fireplaces in a way that preserved as much of the original fabric and structure as possible, as well as incorporating the strengthening now required.

Tony says ruefully that the process of working on Christchurch's earthquake-damaged heritage stock is very different from conserving undamaged buildings. The compromise needed between conservation and compliance with the new regulations results in the inevitable loss of authenticity, a hard lump for any heritage architect to swallow. Because the regulations require the installation of bracing and other structural strengthening, original framing and linings often have to be sacrificed:

> *Many of the engineers working with damaged heritage buildings in Christchurch need some re-education. It's not enough to settle for the final look — the traditional way of doing things needs to be respected and followed.*

Tony's choice of wording like 'loss of authenticity' and 'sacrifice' is

deliberate. A heritage conservator aims to achieve the retention of as much as possible of the traditional linings, such as the brick nogging and lath-and-plaster characteristic of the 1856 and 1874 parts of Riccarton House. Although many builders would be satisfied with replacing such linings with modern plasterboard, this would be inappropriate during restoration or conservation of a heritage house.

Often it is at the corners of rooms that sacrifices have to be made because the original timber framing differs from more modern structures in having only a single post in the corner. This leaves no structural surface for the attachment of linings for the adjacent right-angled wall. At Riccarton House, for example, this meant the brick nogging had to be removed from the corners of the exterior east and south walls of the 1874 dining room so studs could be installed to support the new linings.

Despite the many heart-wrenching compromises needed in restoring and strengthening earthquake-damaged heritage buildings, Tony Ussher will work on many of the projects John Radburn is managing in Christchurch. His role is to provide the essential conservation advice needed to ensure as much as possible of the original fabric is preserved and traditional construction techniques are used wherever possible.

At Riccarton House, apart from new designs for the chimneys, Tony was not required to prepare the detailed working drawings normally needed for tendering purposes because the restoration team was already on board. Instead, the process set up by John Radburn involved him in series of sketches and reports that were used as the basis for gaining heritage and resource consents for the ongoing — and constantly changing — scope of work.

Stripped back to the bones, the 1874 dining room at its worst stage.

Although one of John's biggest challenges was coming up with a reinstatement scope and design that was sympathetic to the heritage fabric of the house while at the same time meeting the building code requirements for strengthening of walls and fireplaces, he had all the necessary contacts for specialist craftsmen. On his advice, Simon Construction had been appointed to do the overall construction work, while he put together a team of dedicated and skilled craftsmen:

It all boiled down to people — matching appropriate people to tasks. And having a 'can-do' attitude. Some people look for problems.

Riccarton House manager Rob Dally says being part of the resulting team was a privilege and the highlight of his working career, despite the stress and long hours the restoration entailed:

An amazing synergy built amongst all those involved. Everyone had the same commitment, energy and vision about what was needed, and that soon grew into a passion for the house itself.

Throughout the 18 months needed for the physical phase of deconstruction and restoration, Rob's day-to-day contact with the tradesmen as 'the man on site' meant he needed to draw on all he had learnt about developing relationships during his long career of dealing with people. That he succeeded is borne out by Darryl McIntosh, Simon Construction's site manager for Riccarton House, who says that pressure usually builds from clients or as deadlines loom, so everyone is just pleased to get a job finished and move on. The Riccarton House project, despite its size and complexity, was different:

Doug Hohepa, the Simon Construction carpenter who was on site for the entire restoration process, at work on deconstructing the 1856 morning room.

Rob was a big factor in that. There was never a cross word between us. At first, the guys wondered who this old man was, pottering around taking photographs and asking heaps of questions, but they soon learnt. Within hours of anyone new coming on site, Rob knew their name and what their role was.

Deconstruction of much of the interior of the house in preparation for the necessary strengthening work was the hardest part of the project for everyone involved. Each time another wall was stripped, new problems emerged. Every time this happened, new solutions, drawings, reports and budgets were required. These all had to go through the complex heritage consent process yet again — although Jenny May's assistance in her role with the City Council was invaluable in streamlining this wherever possible. And then it had to be determined whether the work would be insurance-funded or not.

Each time a new problem emerged, that part of the job came to a halt. As a result, Darryl felt that whenever members of the Trust visited to look at that element, no visible progress was evident — even though lots would be going on elsewhere in the house. This stage was at its worst in the three-month period leading up to June 2013. With the house stripped back to its bones and littered with piles of lining debris, timber fragments, torn wallpaper and dust, Rob Dally says it looked like a total wreck. He was living in his garage at home and coping with the cramped space of a cold Portacom on the lawn at work:

It was a bad time.

The careful restoration of the 1900 drawing room in ruins after being stripped away for strengthening work.

• 15 •
Restoration to Former Glory

The intricate and skilled process of strengthening and restoring Riccarton House followed the initial deconstruction that had caused those who loved the old house so much heartache. Once the strengthening work was completed, different areas and rooms would, one at a time, receive the attention of a sequence of craftsmen. During the following year, each craftsman contributed to the final goal of a restoration that would preserve much of the original fabric of the house and incorporate many traditional techniques in its refurbishment.

Structure and strengthening

Vital and extensive strengthening work was the essential first step in the restoration of Riccarton House. For several months, Simon Construction's builders and carpenters Doug Hohepa and Robbie Lange worked tirelessly in difficult, confined spaces with limited access. Most of their painstaking work would become hidden behind new wall linings, under floors and in the roof spaces — especially around the chimneys. In addition, borer damage and rot were exposed in many places when the walls were opened up, requiring replacement of the affected timbers. The interiors of all damaged bracing walls were lined with structural plywood, and in some areas diagonal steel rods were inserted.

Even though the new regulations required extra strengthening to be put in place, site manager Darryl McIntosh and the builders were impressed by the old-style construction techniques they encountered. Cast-iron columns and big beams had been installed in the 1874 dining room, and its eastern wall contained floor-to-ceiling diagonal bracing with the studs cut around them. These, like the use of brick nogging, were presumably in response to existing earthquake knowledge (see Chapter 13). Rob Dally comments:

> The house was built like a tank. One of the engineers evaluating the damage reckoned it wouldn't fall down, even in another 6.2 earthquake.

While some of the brick nogging had to be removed for structural reasons (mostly from the corners, see Chapter 14), large sections were retained behind the new interior plastering. Throughout the house, in keeping with Tony Ussher's directive, the aim was to ensure the maximum amount of any traditional structure was retained behind the new linings and strengthening work in the interests of preserving as much of the architectural heritage as possible.

In the 1856 morning room, new concrete foundations had been laid during the 1900 extension of the house, but these were too fragile to support the added strengthening work required after 2011. So the Simon Construction builders put in new concrete footings, then laid a new floor, using kahikatea planks to match the original flooring in the study next door. In keeping with the earlier restoration in 1996, the completed room still serves as a display of exposed historic building techniques. The original 1856 concrete footing around the fireplace and one of the original piles are still

Diagonal bracing in the dining room walls installed in 1874 during the house extension.

visible, a section of repaired brick nogging has been left open on the outer wall, and lath packed with clay is exposed on an inner wall. Although not as much of the early construction has been left exposed in this latest restoration — the concrete beam supporting the 1874 addition of the eastern bay window is now hidden, for example — everything is *in situ* behind the new walls. Jenny May says this retains the option to re-expose more of the original at a later date if the house's potential as an interpreted colonial house museum was to become more prominent.

Next door, the badly damaged 1856 study also acquired new concrete foundations to support the structural plywood put into the walls. New bearers were placed beneath the floor, but only a few of the original kahikatea planks needed replacing. The southern wall was originally lined with old newspapers, discovered during the earlier restoration (see Chapter 13). During the earthquake repairs, this wall and its other side (forming the northern interior wall of the 1874 dining room) were disturbed as little as possible. A section of its historic newspaper lining is being prepared by conservator Lynn Campbell so it can be framed and eventually be put on display in the room.

The southern wall of the study had been an exterior wall of the original 1856 house. When the builders opened up the necessary sections for repair work and strengthening, they discovered the 1856 weatherboards were still there, hidden between the linings of the study and adjacent dining room walls. Jane Deans perhaps would have considered this to be further evidence of the poor workmanship displayed by the 1874 builders (see Chapter 8). Whatever their reason for not removing the weatherboards, this unexpected section of the exterior of the oldest part of the house has been carefully retained between the newly restored interior walls.

Doug Hohepa working on the extensive structural strengthening needed in the badly damaged 1856 study.

Challenge and compromise

Most of the constructive restoration work had started by September 2013. It would continue until June 2014. Different rooms were worked on concurrently, with each being at different stages. As far into the project as February 2014, Charles Deans says much of the house still looked shambolic:

> *It was hard to see an end to it. There was still so much to be done, but the team brought the house back again.*

For John Radburn, the Trust's enthusiastic and grateful reaction on seeing the completion of each phase 'was always a buzz', even though he knew himself each time what the end result would look like.

Amid all the various challenges the work posed, Simon Construction's site manager, Darryl McIntosh, says the biggest one during this restoration stage was managing the complex rebuild of the four functional fireplaces as well as all seven chimneys:

> *Inserting modern structures into heritage fireplaces involved so many different trade skills and processes, from architecture and engineering to brickwork and waterproofing. Even making a replica chimney pot to replace the one that broke.*

Heritage architect Tony Ussher picks up the story. He worked closely with the engineers to decide how to strengthen chimneys that were only one brick thick and extremely narrow where they penetrated the roof. The resulting aperture left little room for any new strengthening. The solution reached was to insert steel pylons bolted in place at each floor level to take the load, with additional structural plywood bracing in the roof space. Modern steel flues were installed in the chimneys for the four fireplaces that needed to be functional. Rebuilding the chimneys above the roofline was done by Nick Fletcher of Make Lelei Bricklaying, whose brickwork proved visually indistinguishable from the original.

Although the final result is far from meeting Tony Ussher's exacting conservation standards of authenticity — all that hidden steel and structural plywood — at least proper bricks were used, not lightweight imitation veneers. He acknowledges that a good job done means no one can tell how much damage there had been or what reconstruction techniques were imposed: 'Look, Mum, no hands!'

Installing one of the steel chimney pylons.

This intricate and elegant drawing of the solution reached for the restoration and strengthening of the functional chimneys is typical of Tony Ussher's meticulous design process.

TONY USSHER Registered Architect (B.Arch. ANZIA)
ARCHITECT & CONSERVATION CONSULTANT

33 Sandy Beach Road
Governors Bay, RD1
Lyttelton 8971

PO Box 4452
Christchurch 8140
New Zealand

t: (03) 3299 591
m: 0292 439 814

f: (03) 3299 597
e: tonyussher@xtra.co.nz

PROJECT: RICCARTON HOUSE CHIMNEYS
FILE REF: TYPICAL DETAILS DATE: 10·09·13

℄ weepholes

CHIMNEY 2.

Drain/breathe hole in each corner.

ss flue (one pot only)

·Existing chimney pots

·chimney shaft vent

·chimney pots 360mm diameter at base.

·800 × 428 × 200 m.s. plate fabricated tray.

PLAN 1:10
(Brickwork not shown)

weepholes in chimney pots

·5mm m.s plate capping tray

·Mapei Primer MF to haunching inside pots
·2 weepholes each pot

·Mapei Primer MF over Blackseal Plus.

·Plaster haunching

·Primer/A D Gabo Industrial coating concrete with waterproofing additive. eg Aquron 300

·Brick slips on LATICRETE Adhesive

·Copper pipe vent to top of chimney shaft!

·weepholes

·Avdex on Eterpan

·Approx 15mm cavity.

·chimney steel structure.

s.s. Flue

chimney pot weephole 2 each pot on opposing sides

anchoring spigot cast in

weepholes in steel casing

Stainless steel Transition

Weepholes.

Insulated Flue (rectangular)

SECTION 1:10.

℄

Only the one fireplace that collapsed completely, in Granny's room, had to be reconstructed from scratch. An old photograph existed for this fireplace so was used to recreate its design. Reluctant to deconstruct the other 15 fireplaces, Tony and the engineers worked out how to dismantle the brick fronts then slide the fireboxes out. Once the necessary strengthening steelwork was put in place in the cavity, the fireboxes were encased in concrete, then slid back into position. On the ground floor, the concrete was poured around the back and over the top of each firebox once they had been replaced because of the tight spaces involved. The brickwork fronts were then rebuilt and repointed by heritage stonemason Simon Taylor of Stonelay Stonemasons. Despite the success of this approach, Tony points out that only the four functional fireplaces succeed in appearing truly authentic:

Unless fires can be lit, fireboxes will always look new and unused.

Art and craft

Only once the strengthening work was complete and all the fireplaces reinstated could the other specialist craftsmen get to work on the other visible features. This work continued from September 2013 until June 2014. Granny's room upstairs, part of the surviving section of the 1874 addition, was the first room to be relined and plastered. Rob Dally says this first sign of restoration was uplifting after all the mess of the deconstruction and strengthening work. Overall, Darryl McIntosh estimates 30 per cent of the house needed full re-plastering, and the rest was at least skimmed before painting or papering. The success of the rest of the finishing work would depend on the quality of the plastering, which was done to a professional and exacting standard by John McVicor, Paul Smith and Mick Brady of Interior Solid Plasterers. In the nursery wing upstairs, Jenny May would run a discerning hand over one of their finished surfaces and come close to drooling with delight.

Riccarton House features large expanses of timber panelling and ornate woodwork, most of it decorative elements from the 1900 expansion (see Chapter 10). As much as possible of the original woodwork, built-in cupboards and wardrobes was salvaged and repaired, mostly by Simon Construction's own builders. All the dadoes, skirtings and decorative finishing beads were photographed and sketched before being deconstructed. Each section was

A pylon in place in the roof space.

One of the insulated rectangular steel flues in place.

Nick Fletcher's traditional exterior brickwork on a set of chimneys hides the modern strengthening work.

Internal tubular steel flues link the functional fireboxes with the new chimneys.

The drawing room fireplace with its reinstalled firebox encased in concrete and its reinstated brick facade.

John Moore lights the fire in the fully restored drawing room fireplace.

numbered so it could be put back in place. Restoration of the timber work involved a mix of reinstatement, matching, or totally new work.

Upstairs, stripping the walls in the 1856 section of the house uncovered a small, timber-lined wall niche in both bedrooms, which may have served as bookcases (James Johnston's original specifications referred to built-in bookcases). No attempt was made to level the floor in Jane's bedroom, which remains in its original, pre-earthquake condition. It slopes from the door and from the window opposite towards the centre of the room. Charles Deans has fond memories of rolling marbles across this floor when he was a child visiting Riccarton House.

Interior finishing, both painting and varnishing, was the province of Andrew McTavish (McTavish & McTavish). Jenny May, Charles Deans and Rob Dally all agree that he did 'a brilliant job'. The rimu dadoes lining the upstairs landing and the hallways in the children's wing were stripped back, sanded and restored to a glowing patina. Downstairs, the oak panelling in the entrance hall, inner hall and drawing room (now set up as the restaurant) received similar treatment. The ornate main staircase and all the decorative timber fireplace surrounds and mantelpieces were stripped back and painstakingly refinished. Although the woodwork is probably several shades paler than the finish favoured in 1900, the natural beauty of the timber has been revealed.

The final stage in the restoration was the paperhanging, which could only be done room by room as the carpenters, plasterers and painter finished. Downstairs, as far as possible, an attempt was made to find wallpapers that were a reasonable match to the originals, as was done in the 1990s restoration (see Chapter 13). During that earlier restoration, the Edwardian paper in the drawing room and the study had been replicated from a photograph by a Lower

The three expert plasterers at work in Jane's 1856 bedroom. From left to right: Paul Smith, John McVicor and Mick Brady.

Mick Brady at work on the dining room ceiling.

Hutt company, technically drawn and produced in the traditional way. This company was able to reproduce this paper for the 2014 restoration. In an ideal world, Tony Ussher would like to have seen replicate papers made for all the rooms, but he accepts that the cost would have been exorbitant. The drawing room alone cost $10,000. At some time in the future, small sections of the original papers, currently being stabilised and preserved by conservator Lynn Campbell, will be put on display in the relevant rooms.

In the grand upstairs bedrooms, a 'somewhat contentious' decision was made to follow the last decorating scheme used in the house while the Deans family still lived there, rather than attempt to match the original, early Edwardian papers of 1900. Thus the strips of 1930s wallpapers surviving in the wardrobes — 'Art Deco stripes meet florals', in Tony Ussher's words — were used as the basis for selecting papers.

Both Charles Deans and Rob Dally were on the 'wallpaper committee' and say choosing these papers was great fun and a welcome break from the more serious business of managing the administrative load for the restoration. Particularly successful from Tony Ussher and Jenny May's heritage viewpoint were the choices that matched the scale and delicacy of the historic patterns, as well as their themes and colours. Other than the replicated drawing room paper produced in Lower Hutt and the one in Jane's bedroom, which was best matched in style and scale by a paper from the United States, all the papers chosen were available from Sanderson, which now also owns William Morris.

Paperhanger Lawrence Ford was a find. John Radburn had seen his work in a private house, and on his recommendation Lawrence replaced the original paperhanger employed by Simon Construction. Lawrence runs a small interior design firm in Christchurch, but his passion has always been heritage wallpapers.

Skilled plastering work under way in the 1900 kitchen.

Painter and timber finisher Andrew McTavish installing lining paper before painting a wall.

Brought up in Devon, he says he 'fell into paperhanging by chance', having learnt how to do it as a child from watching his mother, who was equally enthusiastic about wallpapers:

> *What I love is the artistic side and the history — all those old, hand-painted papers and patterns; William Morris and the French wallpapers you can still see in chateaux.*

At Riccarton House, Lawrence's favourite paper would be the William Morris example in the kitchen — he even loves its smell. At the time the earthquakes rocked the city in 2010–11, he was the main caregiver for his young family and only doing odd jobs here and there. So when he was approached by Simon Construction, he jumped at the opportunity to be involved in such a unique project:

> *It was the historical value of the house, being able to make a contribution to its heritage and knowing that would be there for a long time.*

The gleam of restored oak panelling lightens the finished entrance hall.

The paperhanging was spread over the nine months from October 2013 to the completion of the restoration in June 2014, working

Paperhanger Lawrence Ford at work in 'Homebush', one of the three grand 1900 bedrooms upstairs.

An American paper was the best match for style and form to the original 1856 wallpaper in Jane's bedroom.

Fragments of the original William Morris wallpaper used in the 1900 kitchen, uncovered behind the dresser during restoration in the late 1990s.

The new kitchen wallpaper closely matches the original William Morris paper.

Lawrence Ford's final effort in Granny's room, after dealing with its many angles and non-straight walls.

American replacement paper in Jane's room.

on one room at a time after the other craftsmen had finished. Paperhanging techniques have not changed much, apart from a pasting machine that applies the paste evenly, a more modern glue than flour-and-water paste, and the use of a laser to align the strips. But Lawrence found he had to revert to plumb line and ruler because none of the walls was straight. Walls in old houses undulate as a result of the original hand-finished lath-and-plaster, and this is accentuated by the inevitable subsidence or settling of the building over time:

Riccarton House is a classic example. It's like wrapping an awkward Christmas present: difficult to match up the patterns when the walls aren't straight.

Lawrence points out that the papering quality can only be as good as the underlying plastering, and the plasterers were fantastic craftsmen: 'They did a superb job.'

His main challenge was stretching and massaging each strip of paper as much as possible to get the pattern matching at least at eye level where mismatches would be the most conspicuous. Getting the work right was not always easy. Lawrence had to redo several rooms before Simon Construction was satisfied. Granny's room proved both the toughest to get right and his favourite room:

This was the one I cocked up. I made some major errors and had to redo the papering about three times. Lots of angles, and none of the walls was straight. I had to use geometry in the end to get the pattern matching.

For Lawrence Ford, Riccarton House will remain the 'pinnacle' of his work with heritage papers. The opportunity was a one-off, and he is not expecting to tackle further similar projects. He is proud of what he achieved and says it was a wonderful experience.

But there were some disconcerting moments. Lawrence occasionally worked on his own through the night in the creaky old house, with the room he was in the only one lit. He swears he heard the rustling taffeta of Jane Deans's ghost (see Chapter 11). All he could think of doing was to turn up his music and turn off his imagination.

Finishing touches

At the same time that work was continuing inside, other tradesmen were working outside. On the roof, Jim Herdman (Jim Herdman Roofing) replaced shingles around the new chimneys and fitted new lead flashings. Nick Fletcher completed his own work on the chimneys by refitting the chimney pots. Charles Deans had salvaged the one damaged chimney pot, installing it as a feature at his front door, with its inscribed reference to its manufacture at the Homebush Brickworks prominently displayed.

One of the final crowning touches was the installation of the replacement for that chimney pot. One metre high and 55 kg in weight, this replacement was made by local ceramic artist Cheryl Lucas to match the other six, which had survived the September earthquake. Crafting replica chimney pots has become part of Cheryl's repertoire since the earthquakes. Such work is time-consuming, involving testing several glazes before she is satisfied with the colour match, and the thick-walled pots themselves need several months of air-drying before they can be kiln-fired.

Not least was the major transformation achieved by the team of Filipino cleaners, who came through the house three times during the last month or so, getting rid of the ubiquitous plaster dust and

Jim Herdman and his offsider cutting and fitting lead flashing around the base of a new chimney.

the other detritus associated with interior decorating. Once the work was completed in each room, it was Simon Construction's builders who moved all the furniture back into the rooms, not only placing it but adding personal touches, such as a kimono spread on the bed in 'Kirkstyle', and a black chiffon scarf on the bed in Jane's bedroom — gestures that summed up the proprietary feeling all the tradesmen had developed for the house.

In June 2014, the restoration was celebrated with functions firstly for all the tradesmen involved in the project, and then for a gathering of Deans family members to 'warm the house' in the traditional Scottish manner. Although the interior and all the structural work was now complete, ending John Radburn and Simon Construction's involvement at Riccarton House, the Trust's usual contracted maintenance crew worked on a complete repaint of the exterior woodwork for several months after the celebrations. They replicated the intricate cream and burgundy design characteristic of the house, which had first been restored in 2001 (see Chapter 13). John would return in 2015 to manage the earthquake repairs to Deans Cottage, which centred around replacing the damaged chimney with one made of bricks. This was to replicate the original chimney built with bricks brought from Wellington in 1843 (see Chapter 1). These were the bricks William Deans initially off-loaded on the banks of the

Ceramicist Cheryl Lucas at work on the replacement chimney pot.

Avon (near the corner of Oxford Terrace and Barbadoes Street). Some were still there when the Canterbury settlers arrived, resulting in the site being given the name 'The Bricks', which it still retains today.

Along with many of the craftsmen who worked on Riccarton House, Lawrence Ford will have some lasting memories. Like Rob Dally and Darryl McIntosh, what comes high on his list was the great camaraderie and the uplifting experience of working with a team of like-minded, dedicated craftsmen. All three speak of being proud of what they achieved and say it was a wonderful experience. John Radburn, who had made it all possible, says simply:

> *Working with Charles Deans, Rob Dally and the Trust — it was fun.*

And what of the end result? Both Charles and Rob talk wryly of the somewhat muted reaction to the completed restoration. Deans family members walked through at various times towards the end of the work, and all commented that it 'looked just the same'. As the architectural historian and heritage consultant whose enthusiasm for Riccarton House matches her expertise, Jenny May's interpretation explains and expands on the family's reaction:

> *It's a delight to see the house looking like it did in the 1990s, and that's because of the care taken by Simon Construction's team to respect Stephen Cashmore's earlier meticulous restoration.*

Charles says there could be no better acknowledgement of the magnificent job done by the restoration team. Riccarton House has indeed been restored to its former glory, with the added bonus of knowing that beneath its fine feathers lie not only the retained architectural record of its construction history but also modern strengthening and updated safety systems that should ensure the grand old house remains standing for generations to come.

The completed morning room, with structural features left exposed for interpretation purposes.

The completed study. The window blind, and its companion in the dining room, is a replica of one found in the back of a cupboard during the 1990s restoration and thought to be from 1874. The wallpaper used in the study and the drawing room is the one replica early-Edwardian paper specially made for Riccarton House.

Conclusion

In December 2014, the Riccarton Bush Trust celebrated 100 years since its inauguration. The Trust can look back on those years with considerable pride in what it has achieved. Although the first 40 years or so lacked coherent purpose, since then the bush has been returned to something approximating a natural state and the future of the two significant historic houses that came more recently under the Trust's jurisdiction — Deans Cottage and Riccarton House — has been assured.

For the past year, the Trust has been debating the way ahead, developing a new management plan as part of that process. The previous management plan, written in 1991, focused on maintenance and upkeep projects for Riccarton House as well as ongoing restoration of the bush. The amount of extra work achieved during the restoration of the house after the earthquakes brought forward all the planned major maintenance projects likely to be tackled in the next decade or so. This has left the Trust free to establish a fresh direction. Potential projects are not in short supply; it has come up with a wish list of 15 or more. These range from practical schemes to enhance the health of the bush to cultural and historical interpretation initiatives.

As well as streamlining existing maintenance and restoration processes in the bush, the Trust is assessing the prospects of doubling the irrigation coverage, installing a fire protection system, re-establishing a totara/matai element on dry ground beyond the present north border, and encouraging ecological research to inform any management initiatives. These are some of the highlights among other, smaller projects. The list of potential social history projects includes cooperative interpretation of Ngai Tahu's association with the bush, both historical and cultural, replicated landscape plantings that illustrate the historical sequence of the Deans family gardens, a visitors' centre that includes interpretation exhibitions and retail items, and the eventual return of Deans Cottage to its original site as part of redeveloping that area to reflect the first farm, including recreating some of the early farm buildings.

Any such projects would be enhanced by the use of interactive interpretative technology to provide visitors and school groups with the best possible experience. Jon Ward, new manager at Riccarton House since Rob Dally's retirement in June 2014, waxes lyrical about the need to engage with visitors of all ages, interests and nationalities in this way. In particular, he talks about the potential to liaise with educational authorities and local schools to develop a youth-oriented interactive programme that takes advantage of the ecological and cultural history represented at Riccarton, a programme that could be used by other visitors as well as students:

The time frame for achieving any of this is the problem — the technology is changing too fast and is still too expensive. But I see the use of virtual reality accessed through smartphone apps as a definite probability in the future.

Both Jon and Charles Deans acknowledge the difficulty of funding such ambitious projects. Since the earthquakes, most of the funding sources established over the years by the Trust have dried up, including the City Council's, whose previous support for projects at Riccarton had been generous. Not only is lack of funding an issue. Any plans adopted for Riccarton have to take account of what is happening in the wider area of Christchurch. Since the earthquakes, visitor numbers and bed spaces have dropped dramatically. This alone affects the likely viability of any project that needs to earn its keep.

It is vital that the Trust's wish list of potential projects is ranked and rationalised. Those likely to be embarked on first need to be properly costed before any funding is sought. This will constitute the final and most difficult phase of developing a feasible new management plan. Although Charles Deans is enthusiastic about the scope for 'big picture' projects, he points out that realising them will not be easy:

That conundrum caused by the conflict between heritage and commercial needs hasn't changed in my twenty years on the Trust. Yet, although it's not a requirement of our Act, we do need to find revenue-raising ways of making the best use of Riccarton House and justifying our major investment.

By the time this book goes to print, the new management plan will have been finalised. Once that is signed off, two long-standing trustees will probably stand down from the Riccarton Bush Trust, retiring chairman Charles Deans and Royal Society representative Brian Molloy. Over the last 20 and 40 years, respectively, both men have contributed substantially to bringing the house and the bush into good shape and ensuring a clear direction has been established for the future. It will be time for new blood to carry on the work of preserving and enhancing the significant ecological and cultural legacy left to Christchurch by the Deans family.

References

Five published sources provided much of the information for this book:

Ogilvie, G., 1996: *Pioneers of the Plains: The Deans of Canterbury*, Shoal Bay Press, Christchurch.
This book provided substantial background information and sources of reference material for the 10 chapters on the Deans family history.

Deans, J. (Ed.), 1937: *Pioneers of Canterbury: Deans Letters 1840–54*, A. H. & A. W. Reed, Dunedin.
The numerous letters written by William and John Deans, transcribed and collated by the third John Deans, informed chapters 1–6.

Deans, J., 1964: *Pioneers on Port Cooper Plains: The Deans Family of Riccarton*, Simpson & Williams, Christchurch.
This volume provided essential information for chapters 7–9 on the history of the farms at Riccarton and Homebush during the 20 years of Jane's management (1854–74), then during her son John's reign (1874–1902).

Deans, J., 1923: *Letters to My Grandchildren*, Canterbury Publishing Company, Christchurch.
This book offered many insights into Jane Deans's life at Riccarton and the social history of early Canterbury, providing a good source of quotes, mainly for chapters 5–11.

Molloy, B. (Ed.), 1995: *Riccarton Bush: Putaringamotu*, Caxton Press, Christchurch.
This book consists of expert essays on all aspects of the natural and human history of the bush and its management, covering Chapter 2, and the work of the Riccarton Bush Trust presented in chapters 12–13.

SUPPLEMENTARY REFERENCES

Other source material is listed by chapter, including, in order: published books, electronic sources, journal and newspaper articles, published and unpublished reports, Deans family papers, and personal interviews.

CHAPTER 1

Bagnall, A. G., 1976: *Wairarapa: An Historical Excursion*, Hedley's, Masterton
Ballara, A., 1990: Te Puni-kokopu, Honiana ?–1870, *The Dictionary of New Zealand Biography* Vol. 1, Allen & Unwin, Wellington
Broad, L., 1892: *The Jubilee History of Nelson: From 1842 to 1892*, Bond, Finney, and Co., *Nelson*
Byrnes, G., 2001: *Boundary Markers: Land Surveying and the Colonisation of New Zealand*, Bridget Williams Books, Wellington
Easdale, N., 2009: *Mungo Park's Trunk: A Journey — Scotland to New Zealand*, Te Waihora Press, Christchurch
Fairburn, M., 1990: Wakefield, Edward Gibbon 1796–1862, *The Dictionary of New Zealand Biography* Vol. 1, Allen & Unwin, Wellington
McClymont, W. G., 1940: *The Exploration of New Zealand*, Chapter IV, Department of Internal Affairs, Wellington
Pascoe, J., 1983: *Explorers and Travellers: Early Expeditions in New Zealand*, A. H. and A. W. Reed, Wellington
Wakefield, E. J., 1845: *Adventure in New Zealand*, John Murray, London

Phillips, J., updated 2013: History of immigration — British immigration and the New Zealand Company, Te Ara — the Encyclopedia of New Zealand: http:/Te Ara.govt.nz/en/history-of-immigration/page-3
Schrader, B., updated 2013: Wairarapa region — European settlement, Te Ara — the Encyclopedia of New Zealand: http:/Te Ara.govt.nz/en/wairarapa-region/page-6
The Port Nicholson purchase, http://www.nzhistory.net.nz

1840 first European settlers arrive in Wellington, http://www.nzhistory.net.nz

Goldsmith, P., 1996: *Wairarapa*, Working Paper: first Release, Waitangi Tribunal Rangahaua Whanui Series

NZ Gazette and Wellington Spectator (various articles between 1840 and 1843)
Ryan, P., 1900: An interesting career: Reminiscences of an old settler, *The Canterbury Times* 24 January 1900
Stokes, R., 1840: Report of the expedition, *NZ Gazette and Wellington Spectator* 7, 14, 20 November 1840

CHAPTER 2

Anderson, A., 2008: Maori land and livelihood AD 1250–1850, Chapter 3 *in* Winterbourn, M. *et al.* (eds),
  The Natural History of Canterbury, Third edition, Canterbury University Press, Christchurch
Cyclopedia Co. Ltd, 1903: *The Cyclopedia of New Zealand [Canterbury Provincial District]*, Cyclopedia Co. Ltd,
  Christchurch
Evison, H. C., 1993: *Te Wai Pounamu: The Greenstone Island*, Aoraki Press, Christchurch
Godley, C., 1951: *Letters from Early New Zealand 1850–1853*, Whitcombe & Tombs, Christchurch
Hocken, T. M., 1898: Tuckett diary, Appendix A *in Contributions to the Early History of New Zealand*, Sampson Low,
  Marston and Co, London
Moar, N., 2008: Late Quaternary vegetation, Chapter 7 *in* Winterbourn, M. *et al.* (eds) *The Natural History of
  Canterbury*, Third edition, Canterbury University Press, Christchurch
Molloy B., 1969: Recent history of the vegetation, Chapter 17 *in* Knox G. A. (Ed.) *The Natural History of Canterbury*,
  Second edition, A. H. and A. W. Reed, Wellington
Pawson, E. & Holland, P., 2008: People, environment and landscape since the 1840s, Chapter 2 *in* Winterbourn, M.
  et al. (eds) *The Natural History of Canterbury*, Third edition, Canterbury University Press, Christchurch
Shortland, E., 1851: *The Southern Districts of New Zealand: A Journal, with Passing Notices of the Customs of the
  Aborigines*, Longman, Brown, Green, and Longmans, London
Soons, J. M. & Selby M. J., 1982: *Landforms of New Zealand*, Longman Paul, Auckland
Tau, R. T-M., 2003: *Nga Pikituroa o Ngai Tahu*, University of Otago Press, Dunedin
Weaver, S. *et al.*, 1985: *Extinct Volcanoes*, Geological Society of New Zealand, Lower Hutt

Tau, R., (undated): Ngai Tuahuriri *in* Ti Kouka Whenua, http://christchurchcitylibraries.com/TiKoukaWhenua
Waitangi Tribunal, 1991: Ngai Tahu Land Report Wai 27, Legislation Direct, Wellington

Farr, S. C., 1907: Old time memories: New Zealand in the Forties. Nos I and II — Mary Tod's reminiscences,
  The Press 6 & 20 July 1907

Tau R. T-M., 2005: Cultural report on the southwest area plan for the Christchurch City Council, Christchurch City Council

CHAPTER 3

Godley, C., 1951: *Letters from Early New Zealand 1850–1853*, Whitcombe & Tombs, Christchurch
Hay, J., 1915: *Reminiscences of Earliest Canterbury and Its Settlers*, Press Company, Christchurch
Hight, J. & Straubel, C. R., 1957: *A History of Canterbury* Vol. 1. Whitcombe & Tombs, Christchurch
Hocken, T. M., 1898: Tuckett diary, Appendix A *in Contributions to the Early History of New Zealand*, Sampson Low,
  Marston and Co, London
Maling, P. B. (Ed), 1958: *The Torlesse Papers 1848–51*, Pegasus Press, Christchurch
Robb, J. A., 1968: *Tod the Pioneer: A Biography of William and Mary Tod, Pre-settlement Pioneers of Canterbury*,
  J. A. Robb, Christchurch

Ward, E., 1851: *The Journal of Edward Ward 1850–51*, Facsimile printed by Pegasus Press 1951

Ballara, A., updated 2012: Love, Ripeka Wharawhara, The Dictionary of New Zealand Biography. http://www.TeAra. govt.nz/en/biographies/3l14/love-ripeka-wharawhara

Deans, J., 1882: Canterbury past and present, first published *NZ Country Journal* VI, No. 6, then reprinted as The first farmers on the plains: The Deans family and their early experiences, *The Press* 15 December 1900
Farr, S. C., 1907: Old time memories: New Zealand in the Forties. Nos I and II — Mary Tod's reminiscences, *The Press* 6 & 20 July 1907
Mein Smith, W., 1842: Report to Colonel Wakefield, November 1842, quoted in *NZ Journal* 19 August 1843

CHAPTER 4
Evison, H. C., 1993: *Te Wai Pounamu: The Greenstone Island*, Aoraki Press, Christchurch
Hocken, T. M., 1898: Tuckett diary, Appendix A *in Contributions to the Early History of New Zealand*, Sampson Low, Marston and Co, London
Innes, C. L., 1879: *Canterbury Sketches: a Life from the Early Days*, Facsimile printed by Kiwi Publishers, 1995, Christchurch
Maling, P. B. (Ed), 1958: *The Torlesse Papers 1848–51*, Pegasus Press, Christchurch
Ward, E., 1851: *The Journal of Edward Ward 1850–51*, Facsimile printed by Pegasus Press 1951

Farr, S. C., 1907: Old time memories: New Zealand in the Forties. Nos I and II — Mary Tod's reminiscences, *The Press* 6 & 20 July 1907

Waitangi Tribunal, 1991: Ngai Tahu Land Report Wai 27, Section 2.4, Legislation Direct, Wellington

CHAPTER 5
Godley, C., 1951: *Letters from Early New Zealand 1850–1853*, Whitcombe & Tombs, Christchurch
Innes, C. L., 1879: *Canterbury Sketches: a Life from the Early Days*, Facsimile printed by Kiwi Publishers, 1995, Christchurch
Maling, P. B. (Ed), 1958: *The Torlesse Papers 1848–51*, Pegasus Press, Christchurch

Lyttelton Times 30 August 1851

Deans, J., 1878: Scraps of family history, quoted *in* Ogilvie 1996: *Pioneers of the Plains: The Deans of Canterbury*, Shoal Bay Press, Christchurch
Deans, J., 1895: Letter to grandchildren *in* Deans family papers, Riccarton Bush Trust, Christchurch

CHAPTER 6
Godley, C., 1951: *Letters from early New Zealand 1850–1853*, Whitcombe & Tombs, Christchurch

CHAPTER 7
Deans, J., 1856: Letter to brothers *in* Deans family papers, Riccarton Bush Trust, Christchurch

CHAPTER 8
Godley, C., 1951: *Letters from Early New Zealand 1850–1853*, Whitcombe & Tombs, Christchurch
Hight, J. & Straubel, C. R., 1957: *A History of Canterbury* Vol. 1, App. V, Whitcombe & Tombs, Christchurch

Maling, P. B. (Ed), 1958: *The Torlesse Papers 1848–51*, Pegasus Press, Christchurch

Britten, R., 1979: The lost island of Riccarton, *The Press* 27 October & 8 November 1979
Deans, J., 1882: Canterbury past and present, first published *NZ Country Journal* VI, No. 6, then reprinted as
    The first farmers on the plains: The Deans family and their early experiences, *The Press* 15 December 1900
Strongman, T., 1995: The garden at Riccarton, *Historic Places*, March 1995
Visit to the Deans estate, *The Press* 21 January 1878

Beaumont, L., 2009: Riccarton House Landscape Conservation Report, Riccarton Bush Trust, Christchurch
Morris, M., 2004/05: History of gardening in Christchurch. PhD thesis, University of Canterbury, Christchurch
Strongman, T., 1994: The gardens of Riccarton House, Riccarton Bush Trust, Christchurch

Johnston, J., 1855: Letter with 1856 house specifications, 1 March, *in* Deans family papers, Riccarton Bush Trust,
    Christchurch
CHAPTER 9

Easdale, N., 2009: *Mungo Park's Trunk: A Journey — Scotland to New Zealand*, Te Waihora Press, Christchurch

Robert Hart to Douglas Maclean, January 1881 & February 1881, quoted *in* Easdale, N. 2009: *Mungo Park's Trunk:
    A Journey — Scotland to New Zealand*, Te Waihora Press, Christchurch

Visit to the Deans estate, *The Press* 21 January 1878
A visit to the Deans' estate, *The Press* 2 February 1882
Attempt on Mr Deans' life, *The Press* 16 May 1882
Attempt on Mr Deans' life at Riccarton, *Lyttelton Times* 16 May 1882
An historic estate, *The Press* 31 July 1896
The return of Mr John Deans: Farming in the old country and the new: An interesting interview, *The Press*
    29 October 1900

Deans, J., undated: McIlraith recollections, Ruth Deans's private collection, Christchurch
CHAPTER 10

Acland, L. G. D., 1930: *The Early Canterbury Runs: First Series*, Whitcombe & Tombs, Christchurch

Visit to the Deans estate, *The Press* 21 January 1878
A visit to the Deans' estate, *The Press* 2 February 1882
A ramble round Riccarton, *The Press* 7 October 1884
Obituary: John Deans, *Lyttelton Times* 20 June 1902
Victoria League garden party: a notable gathering, *The Press* 1 December 1927

Espie, J. A. G., 1992: Conservation plan for Riccarton House, Riccarton Bush Trust, Christchurch
Strongman, T., 1994: The gardens of Riccarton House, Riccarton Bush Trust, Christchurch
Warne, M., 2008: An examination of Riccarton House in the context of 1900. Unpubl. BA Hons Art History research
paper, University of Canterbury, Christchurch

Deans, J., (undated): McIlraith recollections *in* Ruth Deans's private collection, Christchurch

References • 261

Deans, J., 1895: Letter to grandchildren *in* Deans family papers, Riccarton Bush Trust, Christchurch
Deans, J., 1899: Letter to James Deans 24 November *in* Deans family papers, Riccarton Bush Trust, Christchurch

CHAPTER 11

Easdale, N. 2009: *Mungo Park's Trunk: A Journey — Scotland to New Zealand*, Te Waihora Press, Christchurch
NZ Official Yearbook 1911: Wages & prices

Deans, J., 1882: Canterbury past and present, first published *NZ Country Journal* VI, No. 6, then reprinted as The first farmers on the plains: The Deans family and their early experiences, *The Press* 15 December 1900
Anderson, J., Recollections of early boyhood, *The Press* 15 December 1900
Death of Mrs John Deans, *The Press* 20 January 1911
Early settlers: Garden party at Riccarton, *The Press* 13 December 1926
Victoria League garden party: a notable gathering, *The Press* 1 December 1927
Twelve years' service: Mrs Deans resigns: Work for the Victoria League, *The Press* 1935, undated, *in* Deans family papers, Riccarton Bush Trust, Christchurch
Mrs John Deans: obituary, *The Press* 1937, undated, *in* Deans family papers, Riccarton Bush Trust, Christchurch

Deans, J., (undated): McIlraith recollections *in* Ruth Deans's private collection, Christchurch
Jane Deans's Will 1909

Alister Deans pers. comm.
Neil Deans pers. comm.
Ruth Deans pers. comm.
Sarah Deans pers. comm.

CHAPTER 12

Deans, J., 1882: Canterbury past and present, first published *NZ Country Journal* VI, No. 6, then reprinted as The first farmers on the plains: The Deans family and their early experiences, *The Press* 15 December 1900

Mr Torlesse's report upon the Canterbury block, *Lyttelton Times* 28 June 1851
Notice, *Lyttelton Times* 2 July 1853
Visit to the Deans estate, *The Press* 21 January 1878

Espie, J. A. G., 1992: Conservation plan for Riccarton House, Riccarton Bush Trust, Christchurch
Riccarton Bush Reserve Management Plan 1991, Riccarton Bush Trust, Christchurch

Anne Mace pers. comm.
Brian Molloy pers. comm.
Charles Deans pers. comm.
Neil Deans pers. comm.

CHAPTER 13

Cashmore, S., 1995: New life for an old house. *Historic Places* No. 52, March 1995
Molloy, B., 2000: History and management of Riccarton Bush: The 1997 Banks Memorial Lecture, *Journal of the Royal New Zealand Institute of Horticulture* 3, 1, October 2000

Cashmore, S., *et al. in* report annexed to Davis Ogilvie 1993: Phase II report on the Riccarton estate, Christchurch City Council
Cashmore, S., *et al.* 1994: Riccarton House; interior conservation policy, Christchurch City Council
Kelly, G., 1972: Scenic Reserves of Canterbury. Biological survey of Reserves. Report 2. Lands & Survey
Riccarton Bush Reserve Management Plan October 1991, Riccarton Bush Trust, Christchurch

Brian Molloy pers. comm.
Charles Deans pers. comm.
Jenny May pers. comm.
John Moore pers. comm.
Stephen Cashmore pers. comm.
Tony Ussher pers comm.

CHAPTER 14

Barker 1869: *in* http://ecan.govt.nz/advice/emergencies-and-hazard/earthquakes/pages/historic-earthquakes
Riley, W., 2011: Quakes haunt Christchurch since settlement began, 4 October 2011, http://lostchristchurch.org.nz

Structex 2012: Riccarton House: Detailed engineering evaluation report, Christchurch City Council

Charles Deans pers. comm.
Darryl McIntosh pers. comm.
Jenny May pers. comm.
John Radburn pers. comm.
Rob Dally pers. comm.
Tony Ussher pers. comm.

CHAPTER 15

Charles Deans pers. comm.
Darryl McIntosh pers. comm.
Jenny May pers. comm.
John Radburn pers. comm.
Lawrence Ford pers. comm.
Rob Dally pers. comm.
Tony Ussher pers. comm.

Index

at Putaringamotu 27
farming in Port Cooper 56, 57, 58
relationship with Deans family 17, 56–8, 92
Gebbie, John 17, 22, 26, 53, 54, 56, 57, 58, 59, 87
Gebbie, Mary 53, 56, 58, 92, 101, 111, 116, 117, 118
ghost, Jane Deans 188, 252
Godley, Charlotte (*see also* visitors at Riccarton) 33–4, 75, 77–8, 79, 86, 87, 88, 92, 99, 103–4, 134, 137, 208
Godley, John Robert (*see also* Canterbury Association) 45, 74, 75–6, 77, 86, 91, 93, 103
Graham, Douglas 94, 106, 108, 111, 115, 116, 117–18, 123, 126, 127, 151, 154
Graham, Helen 117, 123, 126, 151
Grey, Sir George (Governor) 67, 76, 91, 134, 136, 141–42, 171

Hart, Marion (*see* Park, Marion)
Hart, Robert 152, 154–55
Haulashore Island (*see also* Deans, John 1820–54, Nelson land orders) 24–5
Hay family 51, 57, 62, 116, 119–20
Heaphy, Charles 14, 16, 19, 25, 37
Hemming, Graham 188, 221
Heretaunga 16, 17–9
heritage (*see also* Deans Cottage; landscape gardening; Riccarton Bush; restoration, Riccarton House)
conservation 221–24, 236–37, 241, 242–44, 255
interpretation 221, 223, 224–25, 232, 242–43, 254, 256–57
trees 11, 129, 134–35, 138, 171
wallpapers 132, 171, 222, 223, 224, 248–52
Herriot, James 50–1
Hislop, William 116, 137, 138
Holly Lea 166
Homebush (*see* bricks; Canterbury Association; dwellings; farming; McIlraith brothers; sheep stations)
Hutt Valley (*see* Heretaunga)

Innes, CL 68, 88, 116

Jackson, Thomas (bishop-designate) 84, 136
Johnston, James 105, 109, 124, 126, 130–32, 143, 248

kahikatea (*see also* Canterbury plains; Riccarton Bush)
ecology 31, 198, 204, 206, 212, 213, 214, 215–16, 217, 219
floodplain forest 10, 11, 31, 33, 198, 204, 212, 216
timber use 54, 101, 130–31, 199, 221, 242–43
Kaiapoi 26, 34, 36, 37, 38, 39, 46, 67
Kapiti Island 21, 38, 39
Kelly, Geoff 212, 214, 215
Kemp's Purchase (*see also* Ngai Tahu) 44, 67
Knockdolian 82, 170

Lake Ellesmere (*see* Te Waihora)
landscape gardening (*see also* garden fashions; plantings) 11, 129, 134, 138, 139–41, 256
lifestyles
Edwardian 173, 174, 175, 185, 188, 192, 194–95
Ngai Tahu 10, 31–6, 44, 67
pioneer 53, 54, 55–8, 59–61, 68, 71–2, 79, 98–9, 101–2, 103, 108, 110, 119
Victorian 146–47, 156–57, 166, 169–70, 171–72, 182, 184–85, 190–92
Lyon family 117, 118–19, 125
Lyon, William 88, 103, 104, 110, 115, 116, 118, 146
Lyttelton (*see also* Port Cooper) 72–3, 77, 78, 79, 93, 98, 119, 136

Mace, Anne 207
Malvern Hills (*see also* farming, Homebush; sheep stations) 74, 75, 76, 78, 79, 85–6, 90, 118
Manson family 23, 25–6, 27, 56, 57–8
at Putaringamotu 27
farming in Port Cooper 56, 57–8
relationship with Deans family 56–7, 92

trees, ornamental (*see* Deans, Jane, tree planting; garden fashions; heritage; landscape gardening; oaks; plantings)

Tuckett, Frederick 33, 53–4, 66–7

Ussher, Tony 9 233, 234, 236–37, 242, 244–247, 249

Victoria League 192

visitors at Riccarton (*see also* Riccarton, social events)
    Godleys 77–8, 79, 92, 93, 99–100, 103–4
    Governor Grey 76, 134, 141–42
    Lyon family 110, 116–117, 146, 188
    Park family 91, 111, 149, 150–51, 152, 182, 184, 193, 194
    royalty 125, 140, 141, 185, 190, 208–9
    settlers 78–9, 86, 100–1, 102, 111, 137, 165, 191
    surveyors 65, 66–7, 68, 71–2, 77, 78

Waimakariri River (*see also* Canterbury plains; Canterbury Association, surveying) 30, 32, 34, 37, 68, 71, 72, 76, 78, 131

Waimarama 160, 161, 166, 176, 188, 193

Wairarapa 19, 21–2, 62, 69, 229

Wakefield, Arthur 25

Wakefield, Edward Gibbon 14, 16, 19, 25, 94

Wakefield, Edward Jerningham 14, 19, 78, 91

Wakefield, William 15, 16

wallpapers, heritage (*see also* Riccarton House, decorative features) 132, 171, 220, 222, 224, 248–52

Ward, Edward 57, 72, 77, 79

Watts Russell, John 76, 86, 98, 131

Weld, Frederick 73, 78

Weller, George 50, 51

Wellington (*see also* Port Nicholson) 15, 21, 23, 25, 26, 27, 29, 40, 41–2, 57, 59, 62, 87, 91, 103, 107, 119, 125, 149, 150, 152, 167, 182, 187, 229

Whanganui 19, 20

White, Tom 120, 121

Wildermoth, Jack 213

Williams, David Theodore 93, 102

Williams, Mary (*see also* farming, Riccarton) 100–1, 102–4, 116

Winchmore 152, 182

Wood, William 125, 131, 142

Wraight, Mrs (housekeeper) 101, 109, 110

Wright, William 105

PICTURE CREDITS